PATTERNS AND PLACES

PATTERNS AND PLACES

by
EDWARD DAVIS

WINCHESTER PRESS
NEW WIN PUBLISHING, INC.

Printing Code
12, 13, 14, 15

Library of Congress Cataloging in Publication Data

Davis, Edward, 1927-
Patterns and places / by Edward Davis.
p. cm.
Includes bibliographical references (p. 236).
ISBN 0-8329-0461-9 (hardcover) : $24.95
1. Fly fishing. 2. Fly tying. 3. Flies, Artificial. I. Title.
SH456.D27 1991
799.1—dc20 91-10429
CIP

Contents

THE LATE SEASON

Acknowledgements

Permission to reprint material written by the author and published elsewhere is appreciated. And the generosity of the following publishers and editors of periodicals is acknowledged. An abbreviated version of *Presenting the Midge Pupa* was published in the Flyfisher, Vol. XV/Number 1, 1982. *The Secret* was printed in Flyfishing Magazine during June of 1982. It contains material that first appreared in The Secret Stream. *The Bluntnose Minnow* appeared in Volume Five, Issue Two, of Fly Tyer, August, 1982. *The Condor and Grizzly* was featured in the May/June, 1984 issue of Flyfishing Magazine. It was subsequently reprinted by request, under the title *The Condor and Grizzly Inheritance. The Red Trout: Profile of a Rare Gamfish During the 1930s in Québec* was published in The American Fly Fisher, Volume 12, Number 1, Winter, 1985. *The Dry Fly and Salt Water* is the same version that was featured under the title *Davis Bonefish Dry* in the Spring, 1986 issue of American Fly Tyer. *Some Thoughts and Observations about Mayfly Impressionism* was published in the Summer, 1987 America Fly Tyer issue. *Shrimp On The Sawgrass* was included in the Winter, 1986 issue of American Angler and Fly Tyer under the title Visible Shrimp. *Green Waters* appeared in the March, 1988 publication of the Atlantic Salmon Journal. Anax junius, an extract from the story *A Creelful of Rain*, appeared in the Autumn (November), 1987 issue of Flyfishing Magazine. *The Past in Retrospect* was featured in Edition 185 of United Fly Tyer's Roundtable. *Sailfish Among The Eskers* was a featured article in the Spring, 1989 issue of American Angler and Fly Tyer. *Gathering Of The Family Chironomidae* was published in the Fall, 1989 issue of American Angler and Fly Tyer.

The author expresses profound appreciation to Breda Rooney who managed to cope with my handwriting,

and to

Mr. Henry Yee, of Henry Yee Studio Laboratories, for the developing and printing of some of the black and white photography in this book.

PATTERNS AND PLACES

Introduction

My purpose in compiling this book is to acquaint the reader with the techniques, procedures, and fly patterns which I have found to be productive on lake, stream, and salt water flat. The catch and release of selective game fish is rarely the result of hit and chance methods. The exception to this general statement is sometimes experienced in an area far off the beaten track where man has rarely trod, and where the quarry has seldom, if ever, seen an artificial fly. I have fished in such places, noting the lack of abundance of available food, and not been surprised when the trout eagerly attacked anything that appeared to be food and moved.

At the other end of the spectrum we, as fly anglers, experience the frustration (some persons feel anger) of continually casting to trout during a prolific hatch of mayfly without one take. The fly we present, of course, is one of many flies available to the trout. And the presentation may not be the best in delicacy, or the fly may be dragging, or in the wrong line of drift. Or the leader tippet may be too heavy and illuminated by bright sunlight. Some fly dressings have very little "natural motion". But it may also be the wrong fly imitation of the hour. I am reminded of an occasion may years ago of just such a circumstance. During the early days of my stream fishing, while a resident of Montreal, I frequently fished the West Branch of the Ausable River in Northern New York State. Early one evening during late May trout were feeding greedily on a prolific hatch of mayflies. I remember fishing the dry fly right up on the surface film for hours, changing the dressing periodically, and becoming increasingly frustrated at the lack of results. My efforts included the addition of a fly floatant with each fresh fly I presented to these aggravating creatures. I watched the fly floating over areas of water that contained fine brown trout. The fish continued to bulge but I did not catch one trout. Now, of course, I know that these fish were taking emergers, that is, right in or just under the surface film. They were not interested in the "high-riding" dry fly. Now, forty years later, I immediately recognize the distinct pattern of riseform created by trout feeding just under the film. It emphasizes the need for diagnosis before tying on a fly. In fact the most skilled fly fishers I know will observe the conditions at streamside, and often take samples, before opening a fly box. Not all trout are rigidly selective but there are times, during a specific hatch, when they are feeding on one particular stage of a mayfly hatch. I strongly recommend a study of the various food forms available on the streams you fish, and then the preparation of appropriate imitations at the fly tying vise. My experience supports the credibility of working from preserved specimens from the trout waters I fish. If the dressing is going to be fished underwater, I pay particular attention to color, size, and profile (shape). There is some detail about this particular approach in the chapters which address the ''Bluntnose Minnow'' baitfish imitation, and the ''Hackle Fibre Spinner''.

Every time I remind myself not to get too carried away by the precise-imitation syndrome for ''educated trout'', an interesting story comes to mind. A young lady who I gave fly fishing instruction to at age nine, and later fly tying lessons, who is now in her twenties, recounted this experience to me. She was fly fishing a river in Southern Ontario at the peak of a Black Quill hatch. The trout were taking the emerging pattern, and she had tyed emergers on size 10 and 12 hooks. It was late May and the light was good until about 8:30 p.m. on daylight saving time. Trout were bulging continuously to what, she emphasized, was a prolific hatch. ''The Quills were everywhere'', Sarah recounted, ''including my hat and sweater''. Ninety minutes of casting proved to be fruitless. ''I was so disappointed that I reeled-in and put the rod aside''. And then, while continuing to observe this hatch, she noticed that some of these flies were Green Drakes. ''Not many'', she recounted, ''but certainly some flies''. She changed the dressing to a Green Drake emerger and, almost immediately took a fat eighteen inch brown. She caught three more browns and a rainbow while fishing into twilight. The lesson, of course, points to the value of pre-observation prior to knotting on a fly.

Somewhere, probably in the middle of all this, we are able to catch trout on some rivers without resorting to exact fly imitation. We do not require the kind of hatch matching I describe in the story about the ''Clinger-Emerger'' and ''The Gathering of the Family Chironomidae''. We may make a shrewd guess and be wrong about the diet of the moment; but catch fish regardless. I well recall, for example, fishing the green Damselfly Nymph with success during the days I lived on the Pacific Coast. I was fishing in Montana and decided to keep one trout. While cleaning the fish I discovered that it was full of dark olive Damselfly Nymphs, and not the bright green Damselfly Nymph I had been fishing. The Calopteryx yakima served me well regardless of the different color fly I was presenting underwater.

Salmon fishing is a different kettle of fish (no pun intended). Why is it that salmon inhabiting a pool, and occasionally porpoising, will ignore a size 12 Blue Charm. And then, ten minutes later, when the same pattern is presented in a size 4, the fly will be taken so deliberately? Why is it that silver, black, and green appeal so frequently to salmon? I believe that Ernest Schwiebert was correct when he stated that there are no expert salmon fishers, but many good observers of salmon. The pursuit of salmon with the fly rod is one of the pinnacles of the sport. I have tried to convey to the reader the intense lure of salmon fishing in the piece "Green Waters" and to describe a rewarding pattern for salmon fishing.

The quest for fulfilling adventure with the fly rod can be enhanced by seeking the steelhead and the bonefish. I believe that I have highlighted the fundamentals of successful bonefishing in the chapters entitled "The Dry Fly and Salt Water", and "Shrimp On the Sawgrass". There is small doubt that salt water fly fishing will continue to attract more fly fishers in the future. The opportunities here are virtually limitless for the fly pattern.

I well recall asking a close friend, a director of a West coast paper company, the major reason for his executive success. "Timing," my friend replied. "By good luck or premeditation I always seemed to be in the right place at the time of opportunity."

That modest answer seems analogous to my career in fly fishing. I am not implying that I have always caught trout, bass, or other game fish on each occasion I have fished. But by good luck my fly fishing career has included an era during which good fishing was available close to home. Many of my experiences resulted in a unique kind of pleasure. The red trout (Salvelinus marstoni), for example, were a highlight of my early experiences with the fly rod. The marstoni is now a vanishing sub-species in most areas of the Southern Québec watershed. I recount my experiences with this incredibly beautiful game fish in this book.

But capturing and releasing game fish is just one aspect of fly fishing. The fly fishing experience for many of us is composed of several parts. I believe that considerable of the pleasure that we experience is because of the "setting" or surround. There is a restorative aspect about nature. For whether we are alone, or with good companions, we are very often immersed in beauty. The beauty, I am convinced, is the foundation upon which this sport is founded. We may not always be consciously aware of the beauty, but once in a while we pause and look around, and we see the image. And it is during these peak moments of awareness that the importance of preservation occurs to many fly fishers. We realize, at least during these fleeting moments, the worthy objectives of those persons, and organizations, who seek to preserve and restore our environment. Organizations such as the Federation of Fly Fishermen (F.F.F.) and Trout Unlimited (T.U.) deserve maximum support.

Those of us who love rivers and see the beauty that is part of them are also subject to change. We, as fly fishers, are susceptible to the process of maturation. As we grow older, hopefully, we grow in wisdom and understanding. If this be so, our dispositions and attitudes will be reflected in how we treat the surround. Rivers—and their conditions—are a reflection of the attitudes of men and women. Too often in our time, and in the past, a river has become a product of apathy. Most of us can reason with those persons who care. But who can rationalize with those who are steeped in the veiling mists of apathy. It is the latter kind of person we must reach—the indifferent. We must ignite their interest, relieve their pathos, and, somehow, breach their impassiveness.

There are some persons who are of the opinion that, considering the wealth of literature about fly fishing, there is no need for another book. I do not share that opinion. Good experiences deserve to be shared. Fly patterns which have proved to be productive for one fly fisher, or a group of fly fishers, are likely to be effective for many fly fishers. My preliminary instinct was to separate the fly tying chapters from the other experiences. But further analysis has convinced me that virtually all of our experiences as fly fishers consist of "Patterns and Places". Very often the condition of pattern is dictated by the place we choose to fish. The experiences described in this book result, of necessity, in a certain randomness. But none of the experiences were planned. They all occurred like chapters during my life as a fly fisher. The adventures took place sporadically, without intent, and few of the experiences were anticipated.

The content of this book was lived and researched over a period of almost half a century. It developed from a box of old photographs, some published articles, notes collected over the years, and fly dressings that progressed through trial and error. But most of all from recollections about people. There are many people responsible for this book. And to these I owe the benefits of wonderful experiences. To my parents, acquaintances, and friends, especially Brian Gulline and his father, Ed Delforge, the inimitable Wilson, Forsythe, Austin Amos, Dr. George Hale, John Palmer, Frank Charles, and a host of others. Without them this book could not have been written. Without them I would never have participated in the enjoyment of forest, stream, lake, and ocean.

None of the chapters in this book contain magic formulas for catching trout. I make no pretense as a seer. There is no discussion about infallible flies, solunar tables, or tinted leaders. All this time at the game has yielded one truth—game fish continue to fool me! But I would not have it otherwise; would you? For when the charm and mystery have disappeared much of the pleasure dies. And most of us tend to thrive upon challenge.

The Algonquin Streamer

Green Drake Spinner (Coffin Fly)

Anax junius

Visible Shrimp

Davis Bonefish Dry

Mobile Crayfish

(L) Pteronarcys dorsata (R) Isonychia bicolor

High Floating Duns

Three-Quarter Spent-Wing Coffin Fly

Gray Fox

Midge Pupa

Green Waters Hair-Wing Salmon Fly

Chironomidae

Hendrickson Subimago

Green Caddis Larva

The Golden Shiner

The Saugeen Streamer

The Bluntnose Minnow

Caenis (Female) Spinner

Soft Hackled Wet Fly

Snelled Flies for Red Trout

Fantailed Shrimp

Condor and Grizzly Dry

Litobrancha recurvata (Labrador)

The Early Years

Bruchesi, a typical stream for brook trout, could become almost impenetrable.

CHAPTER 1

The Past in Retrospect

The soft light of a gray sky illuminates the lustre of the straw-colored hackle neck on the fly-tying bench. Winter for the flyfisher is a time for reflection about the precious fishing hours of past seasons. It is the time to clean fly lines, examine rods, check the contents of fishing vests, and plan new strategies which will delude difficult to capture game fish. I was reflecting, this late February afternoon, upon the Small Mouth Black Bass which inhabit so many Laurentian lakes—with nostalgic yearning.

During the early nineteen forties my father would move the family to the house at Lake Lachigan for the summer vacation. The Lake was North of Montreal and nestled in the Laurentian hills near Shawbridge and St. Hippolyte. As a teenager during those days I was introduced to the Small Mouthed Black Bass of Lake Lachigan, and the following year Lake MacDonald. My father and I would drift quietly in the flat bottom boat. There were three likely places to cast the bass bug, although my favorite lure was an imitation of a small green frog. We worked the edges of weed beds and the rocky shallows off the peninsulas which abounded in Lake Lachigan.

The third almost certain location was our next door neighbor's raft. There were few rafts during those days because there were long stretches of shoreline without houses. But that raft was sitting there half water-logged, innocent appearing, and a menace to the occasional motor boat at night—unless you knew where to look. The underside of this diving raft, a relic of the days prior to using empty oil drums for floats, was a mecca for the predator Bass. Our friend, that magnificent game fish, possessed a passion for the underside of that floating monstrosity. You could be reasonably certain that during the evening there would be a one to three pound Bass under the raft. It was great sport to drift about thirty-five to forty feet from the anchored raft and cast a small bass bug to the edge of the nearest side. That feathered lure would settle for perhaps one second, be very lightly twitched, and then a veritable explosion occurred. At times there was no explosive splash. On those occasions the Bass would leap clear of the water with the bass bug in its mouth. The ferocity of attack would freeze you into immobility. I retain, to this day, the picture of the violent shaking action of the Bass throwing an imperfectly set hook, the game fish moving in a direction opposite to the bass bug. Then my father would quietly advise: "Keep the line and leader straight for these fish. The instant you feel the pull, you will know that the Bass has the fly in its mouth. It is at that precise moment you must set the hook". When I could discipline myself to arrange events that way I almost always caught the fish. Looking back, however, I know that I missed as many Bass as I caught.

The situation was different on the sand-bar at Lake MacDonald. Austin Amos and I made a special effort to fly fish the sand-bar by full moon. On cloudless nights you could see the surface commotion an incredible distance from the boat. When the Bass were chasing minnows we would fish a streamer fly. We always seemed to have more takes at night with a darker pattern. I was fourteen at the time and beginning to dress flies on hook sizes I now use for large bonefish. But these were the beginnings of pleasure for me with the cane rod. And the HDH and HGH tapered lines with their attendant gut leaders.

My association with the wild Brook Trout occurred the following year. Back of the house at Lake Lachigan, and at the foot of the mountain was a vast patch of wild mint. On days when my grandmother roasted a leg of lamb in the wood stove it was a ritual to pick mint. The mint was subsequently ground or chopped into small pieces and prepared, with malt vinegar, as mint sauce. But the interesting aspect about the geographical expanse of mint was its proximity to the stream. I had looked at the stream bubbling and flowing during earlier years. The pre-teenage years when, as you looked upstream through the forested growth, you conjured up visions of what you would find in the darkness up there. You were requested "not to go up there alone." But, as with most aspects of living, the process of maturation imposes change. And I had reached the age where, once more, I must "strike out" and explore this new mystery.

I remember the first day of exploration. It was preceded by cutting a seven foot slightly tapered stick. I would not take my nine foot S. Allcock Tonkin Cane rod. To the more delicate end of the stick (I think that it was Ash) I attached a nine foot gut leader, part of which leader was wound around the tip of the rod. The end of the leader boasted a Dark Montreal wet fly.

I moved stealthily through the trees along the edge of the river. Soon the bush became impregnable. The option was to move from stone to stone, boulder to boulder, upstream. I remember following that course for some time and then, abruptly, I ran out of boulders. Back to bush travel I went—with some misgivings. And not without reason for several times the rod, leader, and fly snagged on a variety of impediments. It was during one of the rituals of disentanglement that I heard the splash. Peering through the trees I caught sight of the ever-widening ring. That pool was a fair sized expanse of water. No wonder I had run out of boulders and rocks to traverse. But what had been the cause of that splash? I looked for a small animal. Nothing. Not a sign of disturbance now. No trace of the ring. Nothing floating on the surface of the pool. I must get to a casting position. But how was I to cope with this cedar lined creek and its brushy jungle-like shore.

Back to the boulders and my ungraceful ballet. Crouching at the edge of the pool I surveyed the water. Beyond the pool the creek flowed through dense forest. Not milky this current, but sparkling like spring well-water. I experimented by reaching for a pebble on the stream bottom. The water felt like melting ice cubes. I worked carefully into a position for casting. The cast; and then the drift of the slow-sinking Dark Montreal. Now the fly was near the place where the ring of the rise had appeared. Through the crystalline water I saw a submerged rock. And, suddenly, a flash and a long sustained vibrating pull.

I creeled the trout and covered it with ferns. It had seemed innocent and its sides reflected a myriad of colored spots. I brought three of them home that first day, their heads small and bodies fat.

During that first summer of experience with the wild Brook Trout I explored the creek to its source. This was high adventure for a fourteen year old boy. I discovered, above the headwater riffles and pools, a large marshy area. These were the springs; virtually impossible to penetrate. Impossible because of large windfalls covered with slippery moss. The upright and fallen trees had the appearance of an eerie lake; some relic of a pre-historic era.

This brook was typical of many to be explored in the Laurentians. The trout averaged seven to eight inches but, occasionally, one captured a ten or eleven inch lunker. One this size was considered a prize.

But the real prize, now clearly defined with the ease of hindsight, was the kindling of a flame. A flame that has never extinguished, one by-product of which flame has proved to be constant refreshment of the spirit. Odell Shepard described this prize as succinctly as possible, in my view, when he wrote the following words in 'Thy Rod and Thy Creel'.

"What can a man desire more when standing knee-deep in a mountain river, rod in hand, with trout on the rise? Here he has earth and air and sky before him, strangely interfused and woven into an element. The brook runs over the bones of the planet and carries the sky on its back, so that it is a complete world, and one who gazes into this crystal long and steadily will find there not food and drink but work and play, patience and excitement, knowledge and wisdom, fact and dream. Here indeed is one of the forms of nature that pass into our moods with tranquil restoration".

It is significant that Odell Shepard utilizes the word 'patience'. This habit, or capacity, is a by-product or integral part of stalking. And therefore an important ingredient for success on most streams. I believe, in fact bear witness, that the majority of skilled flyfishers I know received their baptism on the small stream or creek. For here stalking is vital for success. And it seems to me that if the small stream is inhabited by the wily Brown Trout, in lieu of the Brook Trout, patience is more vital to success. And so the challenge of the trout, with the supplanting of the brookie by the Brown Trout very likely constitutes an increased challenge.

But most of us who experienced those beautiful relics, the colorful and extraordinary fontinalis, will always associate that unique trout with our introductory years, and remembrances about the ceaseless flow of waters past.

Early Wheatley Fly Box circa 1945, Snelled Flies in leather case,
and Allcocks Reel now in the William Cushner Collection

Chapter 2

The Red Trout

(Salvelinus marstoni)

Profile of a rare gamefish during the 1930's and 1940's in Québec

The view is mid-winter through the small leaded panes of glass in the library. Patches of snow contrast with the dark somber tones of landscape.

I reflect upon times of the calendar more appropriate for fly fishing. Other days, some vintage years; each detail is clearly recalled. These reflections and some recent experiences have many pleasurable highlights however, like many memories, they are occasionally tinted with nostalgia.

There was a time when I was not certain about fly fishing. Not certain, that is, until I inherited the cane rod. The occasion constituted a memorable thirteenth birthday. Five Hendricksons in a Wheatley fly box accompanied the fly rod. The Hendricksons had been dressed to the original pattern. I recognized the original dressing during later years. The pattern included tails from the crest of a golden pheasant, almost colorless transparent hackle, and wings fashioned from wood duck.

"The rod and silk line go with the Hendricksons." And then my father smiled, "Release all of the small ones unharmed, and retain enough trout for the one table."

Looking back after nearly fifty years with the fly rod I realize the wisdom of those words. For the subspecies of trout that inhabited the waters which provided for so much pleasure during the 1930's are rarely mentioned in current angling literature. I refer to the Red Trout (Salvelinus marstoni) of the Southern Québec watershed. These magnificent game fish, keen to accept the dry fly and the streamer fly, are now a rare game fish.

The process by which this relict trout received its name, i.e. Salvelinus marstoni, is an intriguing story. To understand the origin of the name we must refer to one of Professor S. Garman's papers which appeared in the 1893 issue of Science. I quote from that paper.

> Our specimens (of Red Trout) were taken in Lac de Marbre, Ottawa County, Province of Québec, Canada, whence they were sent by favor of the Honorable J.G.A. Creighton. They reached us at the insistence of Mr. A.N. Cheney, fishing editor of Shooting and Fishing, who, when asked to suggest a specific name, replied with the question, 'how would it do to name it for Mr. R.B. Marston, editor of Fishing Gazette, London, an Englishman overflowing with good feeling for everything pertaining to fish, fishing, and America, and who is doing much to enhance friendly interest between the people of the two countries?' In consequence of this suggestion, this handsome char, one of the handsomest of our species, is introduced under the name, Salmo (Salvelinus) marstoni.
> CAMBRIDGE, MASS. S. GARMAN

Anglers with a sense of adventure and curiosity about the history of the Red Trout may marvel that it is one of very few subspecies of char which have survived in isolation since the Pleisocene glaciation. Two other examples of relict char which have also survived are the Oquassa Trout now almost extinct in Northwestern Maine and the Aurora char,[1] seldom found in the Wilderness Lake Country of Ontario.

We may call the Salvelinus marstoni the red char of Québec. Since the glacial period the Red Trout has survived and evolved in isolation as a important glacial relict. This char is characterized by approximately twenty gill rakers, sixty-four vertebrae, and forty pyloric caeca.[2] It is possible that this subspecies of char represents a Salvelinus alpinus dispersal from Northern Europe via the Atlantic Ocean, (probably with the Atlantic Salmon (Salmo salar), and the Smelt (Osmerus eperlanus).[3]

Red Trout are distributed around Québec wherever suitable waters could be reached from the early post-glacial seas. The Red Trout is not found in Ontario. It does not exist South or West of the line of the Nipissing Great Lakes outlet via Lake Nipissing and the Ottawa river.

Adventure with the author into that region of lakes which are localized North of the St. Lawrence River, approximately one hundred miles North-West of Montreal. And into a sparsely populated region which—in

---

[1]In 1923, a party of Pittsburgh, Pennsylvania anglers caught a "trout-like" fish in White Pine Lake North-West of Temagami, Ontario. It proved to be an Aurora trout. Since that time management targets have been set and the Ministry of Natural Resources are seeking to preserve this fish. Angling opportunities are being provided for on a restricted basis.

[2]See Kendall 1914, Quadric 1974, and Vladykov, 1954.

[3]See Chars, A systematic review, R.J. Behnke, ed. by Eugene K. Balon.

the main—consists of small farm communities with names such as Brébeuf and Vendée. These tiny villages are just beyond the end of the Canadian National Railways (C.N.R.) line in that region of Québec—the village of St. Rémi. (The C.N.R. no longer services St. Rémi.) This region, the Papineau-Labelle county of Québec, is an area of rolling hills and mountains. The roads during the 1930's consisted of gravel over logs and, very often, were characterized by a severe effect of "washboarding" when traversed by car. Lac Cameron was at the end of the road in that area of the County.

By fortunate circumstance I was raised in a milieu of fly fishermen. One of our family's friends was a contractor who had built a house on Lac Cameron. Building a house was a considerable achievement at this location. A large lake with almost twenty-three miles of shoreline, and a road in poor condition made building difficult. The road circumnavigated less than three miles of the shoreline, and provided for access to about four farms and nine cottages on the lake. Lac Cameron was renowned in the County for small mouth black bass, northern pike, and pickerel. The attraction for us, as fly fishers, focused upon tree small lakes beyond the mountain ranges surrounding Lac Cameron. During the nineteen years of fly fishing for Salvelinus marstoni in these three lakes I met three fishermen unknown to me; two of whom were local game wardens.

LITTLE TROUT LAKE

Little Trout Lake was reached by travelling to the South-East corner of Lac Cameron by boat, and then a twenty minute hike over a mountain. Frank Charles and his son, in company with my father and myself, occasionally portaged a birch bark canoe over the mountain. This lake, almost elliptical in shape and very deep, contained a large quantity of marstoni. I often caught the two day legal limit by 10:30 a.m. And not infrequently took two, one and one half pound fish together; one on the tippit fly and one on the dropper fly. Without a canoe, raft, or inflatable boat, fly fishing was restricted to a long tree trunk. This arrangement accommodated use of the fly rod, but to a restricted area of water. When fly fishing from the tree trunk or platform, we generally used a more powerful fly rod. Today such a rod would be classed as a number seven or eight weight. During those days we utilized a silk like designated as HDH for the five and one half ounce, nine foot cane rod. Seventy to eighty foot casts were not uncommon with such equipment, however, such casts require less effort today because of improved equipment. The silk line was ideal for fishing wet flies including streamer flies, but did not float for very long. It was important to have a well-dressed spare line on an extra reel if dry fly fishing was anticipated. We dressed fly lines, almost without exception, with Mucilin (when we could open the tin container).

Gut leaders were used exclusively. During the 1930's Wheatley produced a fly box with a top compartment for leaders. I generally soaked gut leaders in a glass tumbler overnight on the mantle of the fireplace at the house on Lac Cameron. But for purposes of transporting the leaders to the trout lakes the gut was placed between two wet felt pads in the fly box. Leaders were usually tapered to .011 or .012 inches. The rods were often fitted with an Allcock "POPULAR" Trout Reel, usually a number C753 size three and one half inches.[4]

Little Trout Lake nestled in heavily treed mountains. The central area of the lake was sixty to one hundred feet deep. Second growth timber grew to the shoreline—except at the outlet. Many deer were observed drinking at the outlet during early morning arrivals at this lake. Fox, otter, and moose were not uncommon.

Small Stickleback minnows were occasionally observed in this lake along with the usual leeches, tiny green frogs, grasshoppers blown into the lake during August and, once, a caterpillar epidemic. The scourge of caterpillars is worth elaboration. One early morning arrival revealed trees covered by green caterpillars. They were in the process of eating the leaves on trees which surrounded the entire lake. All of the rises we observed were close to the shoreline of the lake. On that morning we had portaged a birch-bark canoe. And when Frank Charles Jr. and I explored the shoreline it was obvious that the trout were feeding voraciously on caterpillars which had dropped off the foliage overhanging the lake. We selected two streamer flies with green bodies from which we removed the hackle, wings, and tails. The two-day legal (possession) limit was quickly obtained. There were, needless to say, a large number of Red Trout released that day.

Our knowledge about entomology was not significant during the 1930's. But the plentiful supply of marstoni and, very often, their intensive proclivity to feed resulted in excellent sport fishing. Many years of fly fishing for this trout revealed its constant habit of surface feeding

---

[4]This reel is currently part of the collection of the Fly Fishing Museum in Florence, Oregon.

immediately following the melting of ice from the lakes. The feeding occurred just after the warming of the surface water by the sun.

LAKE MUNROE

The late 1930's were a very early and formative time in my life. Long enough ago that I am left with the impression that the trout season opened in the region I write about on April 15. There were some years when the ice was not out of Lac Cameron. When such conditions obtained, there was no access to Little Trout Lake. Prevailing winds from the North or North-West pushed and piled the ice at the South side of Lac Cameron. No flat-bottom Versherres type boat could negotiate such an obstacle.

The option was Munroe Lake. Picture a sparkling sunlit morning during early Spring. Walk with us through the hills along an unused logging trail, now barely recognizable as a foot-path. Patches of snow and violets abound in the sheltered places. Thirty-five minutes of hiking were required to Munroe Creek. This creek, an outlet of Munroe Lake, eventually flowed into Lac Cameron. Leaving the trail at the creek it was necessary to circumnavigate a swampy area in order to reach a length of shoreline characterized by large, flat, gently sloping deciduous rock. These shale-like sloping rocks provided excellent casting platforms because, like most Red Trout lakes in this region, the trees and brush flourished close to the shoreline. As you may expect this can cause problems for the fly fisher. But fly fishermen will generally find a solution to such challenges and my companions were no exception. The major diet for the trout in Lake Munroe were leeches, dragonflies, and damselflies. One of the interesting features of Lake Munroe was that during a period of many years of fly fishing, nearly every Red Trout weighed almost exactly three-quarters of a pound. These trout were characterized by orange tinted ventral fins and iridescent gun-blue dorsal surfaces. Their table quality was superb and, as one who has lived and fished on our beautiful West coast, I rank them equal to the taste qualities of fresh Sockeye Salmon.

BIG TROUT LAKE

Hindsight predisposes me to remember this lake as the most beautiful and productive lake for Red Trout during almost two decades of fish-

Frank Charles (L) and the author with a two-day legal catch of S. Marstoni, Circa 1949.

ing and exploration in the area. I have enjoyed many lakes and trout streams in the Southern Québec watershed, including those lakes situated in the Singer Reserve in the area of Montpéllier, Québec. The Singer Reserve contained at least nine lakes. It could be entered for the purpose of fishing by obtaining a permit from the Singer Sewing Machine Company. Singer, during the period the author writes about, used a wood base for their sewing machines. The Reserve was a source for the wood. But Big Trout Lake was the Ne Plus Ultra!

It is now many years since I have fished Big Trout Lake. It is normal to want to go back but I know that it would be far less attractive than my memories are of this lake. There are roads through what was wilderness, and cottages are being built. I know nothing about the current quality of the water. But during the late 1930's we had samples of the water tested in Montreal. The water at that time was safe to drink.

My last journey to Big Trout Lake was at dawn during the second week of June, 1956. I recall the mist-wreathed image of Munroe Lake on my left. And the patches of moss along the trail—softer than a Persian rug. The area is reminiscent of Scottish highlands. There is ash-colored lichen, and the forest is silver birch, cut-leaf maple, and pine. At times there is no trail. You made certain that you retained the South shoreline of Munroe Lake on your left until, once past the lake, the terrain sloped downwards. Abruptly you reached the floor of a small valley, the decline levelled off, and the marshland appeared. It was necessary to cross the marsh by balancing oneself while walking from log to moss-covered log in order to reach dry land. There was no allowance for error. One slip could, at the least, result in a sprained ankle. You moved slowly and carefully now, aware of the objective close at hand. One final small mountain remained and then you were in the valley which contained the lake.

There were places on the North shore which allowed sufficient space for the backcast, and there were two wadeable areas. We had spent two consecutive days the previous Spring and had floated a network of logs to build a casting platform. This arrangement had a lifespan of one year. The Winter ice extracted its toll of this ambitious undertaking. Fly fishing technique often commenced with three flies. A dark fly on the tippit, medium shade of fly at the first dropper, and a light (perhaps Yellow Sally) fly for the hand fly. The flies were positioned approximately four feet apart. If the marstoni showed a preference for one fly, that fly would be fished as a single. When trout were surface feeding they were taken by fishing a small (usually light colored) wet fly dressed to float in the surface film.[5] The small wet fly was often sparsely coated with Oil of Citronella. (This oil was also used as one of the ingredients in fly repellant). The gut leader was drawn through a felt pad which contained Mucilin except for the two feet of gut nearest the fly. During later years two streamer flies proved to be productive. These were the Harlequin and Trout Fin. The silk fly line of the day was fine for fishing the dry fly but not for extended periods. False casting failed to dry the line sufficiently after it became saturated with water. The best cock hackle we had access to was not the quality of the specially raised hackle of today. Very often elk hair was used for the tails of dry flies. When diagnosis of the riseform indicated that trout were feeding on the surface we fished a dry fly. Patterns of the day included the Black Gnat,

[5]Today this technique would be referred to as 'fishing the emerger'.

Pale Evening Dun, Jenny Spinner, and the Blue Upgright. We used leaders made from silkworm gut material which tested to approximately three and one half pounds strength. This material was referred to as Fina.

During the late 1930's I acquired a nine foot cane rod made by S. Allcock and Co., of Redditch, England. It was a model designated as "The Conway".[6] And this rod was characterized by stiffer middle and tip sections than rods I had previously used. It made for improved casting accuracy, and could drive the fly line into wind with less effort.

The magic of the marstoni during May and June was always accompanied by the music of the mosquito. Black flies and mosquitos were inevitable in the region and survival depended upon an effective repellant. I offer you the recipe of the day.

Oil of Citronella (Burgoynes) 1/2 oz.
Cedar Wood Oil 1/4 oz.
Spirits of Camphor 1/4 oz.
White Petrolatum 2 ozs.

Melt the Petrolatum and add other ingredients, and place in jar on ice or very cold water. Stir until thickened. May be used as brillantine for the hair.

I cannot, unfortunately, offer a recipe, or formula, for the restoration of the Red Trout. Looking back with all of the disarming simplicity of hindsight I am reminded of what can be lost. Preserving the treasures which we possess, and which we presently enjoy, cannot be overemphasized. Our links with the past, and these links include the Red Trout, can be tenuous. The future for the flyfisher, indeed the heritage of the flyfisher of the future, is inescapably linked to what we preserve today.

[6]This fly rod, manufactured during the 1930's and 1940's, is currently displayed as part of The William Cushner Collection at The Fly Fishing Museum in Florence, Oregon.

Chapter 3

Sailfish Among The Eskers

The float plane banked to port and began its smooth controlled descent. Our eyes were captured by the winding ribbon of the river, its surface a glistening sheen of brightness. The touch-down was so smooth that the only sensation was a gradual decrease in forward velocity. My first experience with grayling was the by-product of a journey to the Arctic for char.

Early in my fly fishing career I listened to stories of adventure about the quest for Arctic Char. These were the halcyon days of the teenager; the era of the marstoni and the trout of the West branch of the Ausable. My early experiences in Montreal included after-school browsing at Gulline's fly tackle shop and Fraser Brothers on Victoria Square. Considerable of that experience included he dressing of flies for Landlocked Salmon and trout. "You must go to the Arctic," prompted Mr. Gulline, "and try your hand with the char. If you find yourself in a situation for Grayling keep the Tups Indispensable in mind, and the size 10 streamer fly I will give you now."

The years passed and, using the small streamer fly as a model, I dressed several of the small darkish streamer flies on size 10 an 12 hooks.

In 1956 I fished for char in the Arctic, taking many of these beautiful fish so renowned for their ability as a gamefish. Several of the char readily accepted the little streamer fly. We flew North from Winnipeg via float plane and, on the return journey, detoured to the Wolverine River. It was there that I discovered the value of the tiny streamer for Grayling. It is a land of sand dunes (eskers), vast open treeless space, and an almost constant feeling of dampness. But the Thymallus signifer made it worthwhile. It is, after all, not difficult to dress in order to retain body warmth. Layers of clothing, many layers, is the answer. And the outside garment should be waterproof.

Equipment and the "right fly" are another matter. My observations about Grayling are such that unless there is a prolonged and heavy hatch of fly, one is more likely to achieve success with the nymph or small

The Grayling, with its distinctive large dorsal fin.

streamer fly. Grayling always seem to rise from the bottom unless they are concentrating upon the emerger or dun during a prolific hatch. Even then, unlike larger trout which frequently occupy a line of drift for the duration of their selective target, Grayling, after the rise, frequently return to mid-depth water or the stream bed. The Grayling, in my experience, is more disposed toward avoiding strong currents than the trout. The majority of the Grayling I hooked accepted the fly on the swing, or at the end of a line of controlled drift. We cast across and upstream, as close to the river bank as possible, retrieving the fly slightly faster than the current. Striking too hard generally resulted in lost fish. That experience came to me quickly when, casting across and upstream, a fine Grayling rose quickly from six or eight feet of water and missed the rapidly moving streamer fly a foot or so below the surface of the water. I continued to retrieve the fly slightly faster than the current and watched the fish follow the fly. The Grayling made no attempt to take the fly but followed it closely, its large spotted dorsal fin now recognizable. I let the fly swing with the current, retaining a modicum of control. At the end of the swing of the fly the Grayling took the tiny streamer. As quickly as I set the hook the fish broke water, leaping in a shower of sparkling spray. The fly fell from the Grayling's mouth, swirled in the current, and was immediately taken by another Grayling which, in the process of running downstream, promptly hooked itself. This fish fought with a tenacity which rivals the versatility of a large brown trout. Lighting fast runs were alternated by leaps and surface swirls. After what seemed an interminable amount of time I reached behind me for the net and, while removing the hook, discovered that this fish had been hooked by the very edge of the lip. It revealed the necessity to tighten-up with the correct amount of firmness, and at the precise moment required to set the hook. For this reason I am convinced that a quick action tip on the fly rod is an advantage when fishing for Grayling. The mouth of the Grayling is small and relatively soft. And this gamefish, like many trout, can take the fly and eject the fly in a split second.

One of the fly fishers in our party left his position up river and described to me the fly he was using successfully for these Grayling. "It is a Black Prince wet fly," explained Dr. Hale, "with a body of black floss ribbed with gold tinsel. The tail consists of red hackle barbs, and the throat is black."

"What is the wing material?" I asked.

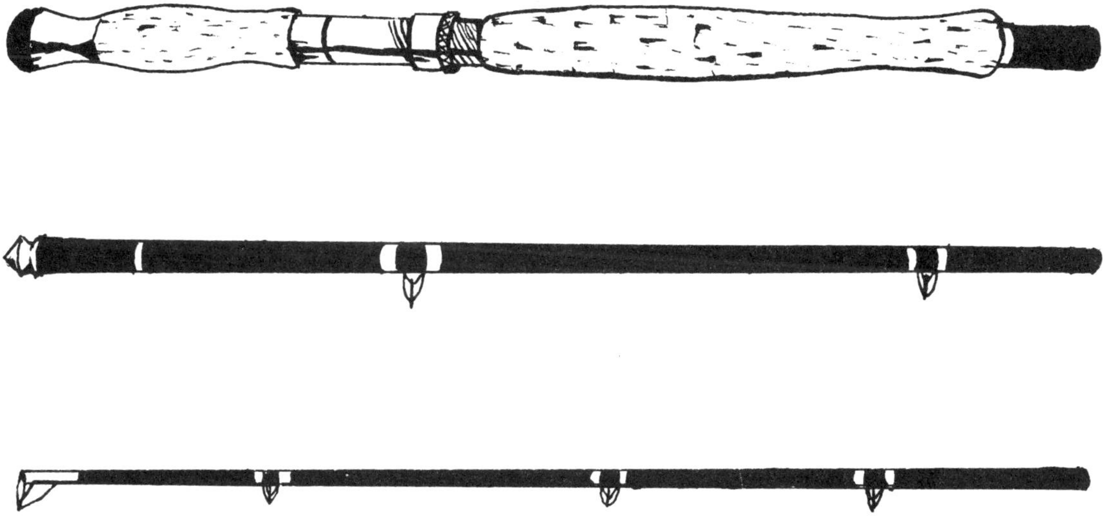

Fly rods exhibit a wide range of characteristics. The stiffer tip action that I recommend for Grayling (especially when using nymphs) depends upon how much deflection is in the rod. A fly rod's ability to absorb energy is characterized by its stiffness. A rod suitable for brook trout is not adequate for baby tuna.

A fly rod's frequency, on the other hand, is its ability to effect the act of casting. That means handling line load. Rods used for distance (tournament) casting have the property of a high frequency. Today's fly rods offer almost every combination of these charateristics. Rod frequency, however, has substantially increased since the era of Tonkin Cane.

"Black duck quill," he replied, "and the fly is finished with a black head." The fly was still damp and, except for the tail, closely resembled a small dark nymph. It had been dressed on a size fourteen or sixteen hook.

Cunningham, the pilot, arrived during this conversation and I asked him about the origin of the eskers as we headed back to the float plane for lunch. "The ridges of sandy drift," Cunningham explained, "were likely formed during the ice age and, later, further development occurred through the interaction of rivers with land surface materials."

We lunched on smoked salmon and cold fillets of arctic char with a dry crisp blanc de blancs.

It was beginning to get foggy and we had to leave. But not before I noted how closely the effective little streamer fly I had been using resembled the Black Prince wet fly. This small streamer for the signifers among the eskers which, for the purpose of identity, I call the Black Vulture, is dressed as follows:

BLACK VULTURE

STREAMER FOR GRAYLING

Hook:	size 10 or 12 MUSTAD No. 38941 or, VMC 9283
Thread:	black 6/0 nylon or black gossamer silk
Tail:	red hackle or red feather barbs
Body:	black floss
Ribbing:	gold wire
Wing:	chinchilla tail
Shoulder:	African vulture brown body feather barbs

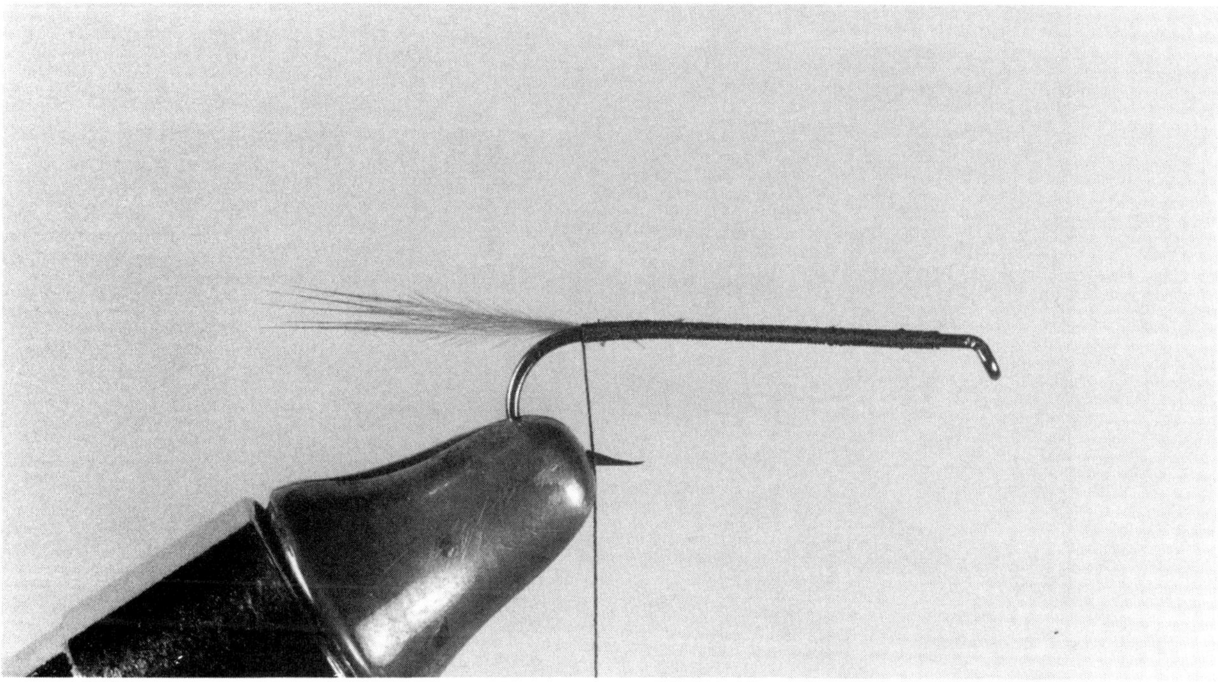

STEP 1 Place hook in vise and start black tying thread three-sixteenths inch from eye of hook. Cover shank of hook to a position two-thirds of shank length rearward of eye of hook. Select four or five short barbs from close to the base of a dyed red goose feather. These fine fibers are positioned on top of the hook shank far enough forward so that they will not pull out. I have removed most of the butts, leaving just a trace of butt material to illustrate the beginning of the tie-in position. You can see the furry characteristic at the base of these fibers which move so tantalizingly in water. The barbs extend about two-thirds the length of the hook shank—from the bend of hook.

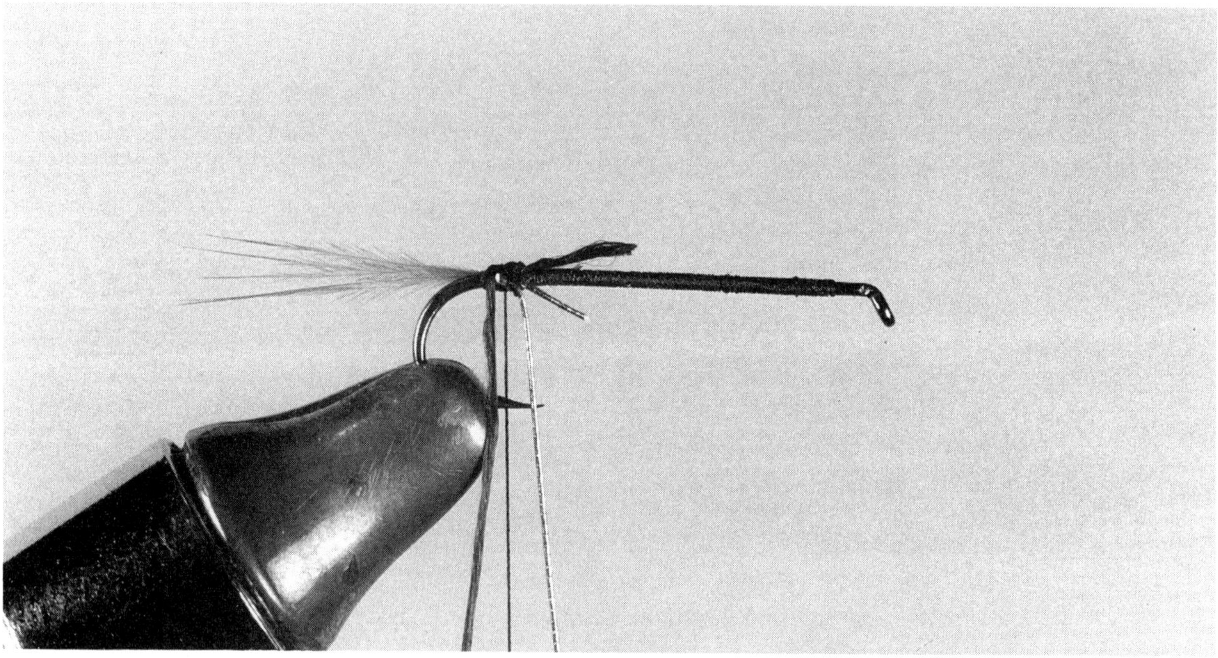

STEP 2 Advance the tying thread two or three turns and fasten the gold wire underneath the hook shank slightly forward of bend.

When the tying thread has been wound rearward two or three turns tie-in the fine black floss on top of the shank at beginning of hook bend as illustrated.

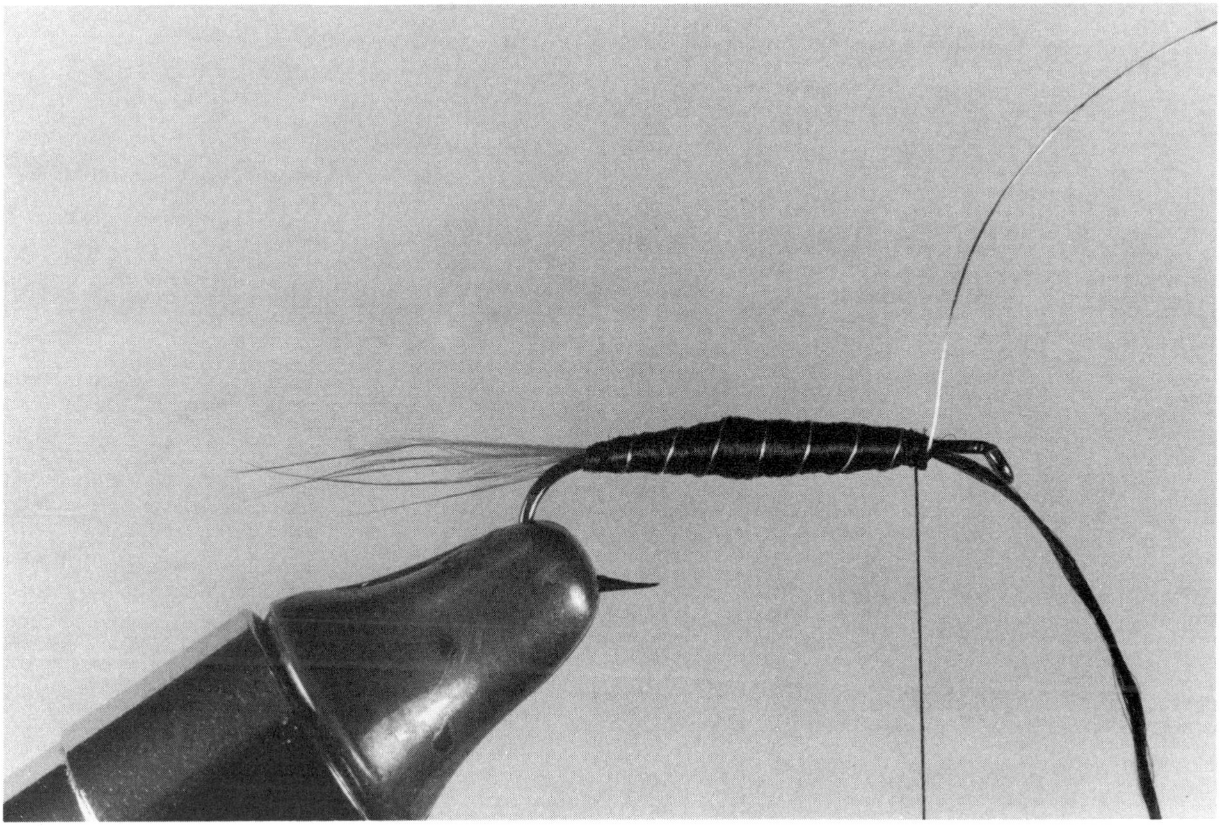

STEP 3 Shape the body as shown with the fine diameter black floss, and then rib the body with the gold wire. Tie both materials off three-sixteenths inch from eye of hook. If the black floss is fine in diameter, there is no need to split the end in order to achieve a neat tie-in on the hook shank.

STEP 4 Remove excess floss and wire.

Mount the chinchilla wing as illustrated. This hair wing extends slightly rearward of the end of the trail. The winging material should be sparse if good action is the objective. After cutting the section of hair near the roots, pull all the short hairs. The tip ends should be kept even. On this fly I do not wind the tying thread around the base of the hair while holding the wing material up. Experiments with these small streamers indicate that this procedure inhibits good wing action with a relatively stiff hair such as chinchilla. After the hair is secured cut off the excess at a tapered angle in front of the windings.

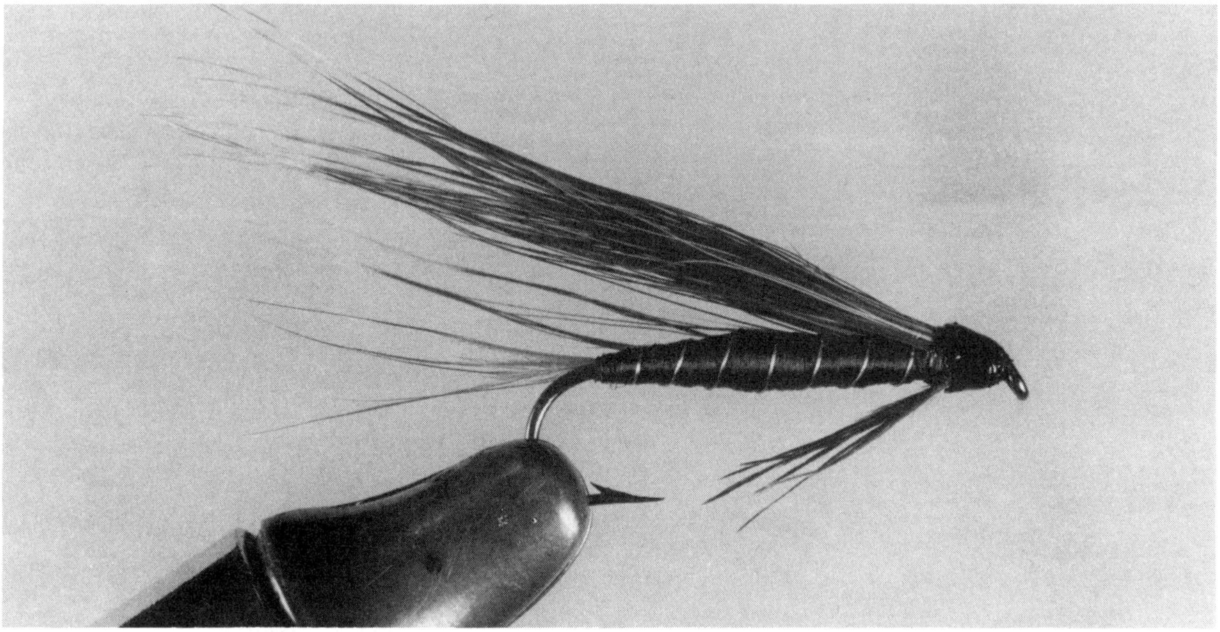

STEP 5 This tiny streamer fly which measures 37 mm (1.4 inches), is completed by securing seven or eight fibers at the throat from an African Vulture body feather (the medium brown barbs, not the white). Form a head and cement the head black. The Vulture body feather is a very soft material which has an excellent undulating movement in water. I varnish the head of this fly with No. 7 black "Cellire" varnish. It dries to exhibit a very good gloss. This completes the dressing for the Black Vulture mini-streamer.

Fly fishing for Grayling (or trout) with a small streamer fly or nymph, often includes a condition whereby the gamefish cannot be seen by the flyfisher. If the opening of the mouth is not observable, and the only strike indication is a sudden check of the leader, a quick action tip fly rod is a distinct advantage.

Subsequent experience with nymphing for trout and Grayling has served to emphasize the need for a fly rod with a relatively stiff (fast action) tip section.

The calm before the storm.

CHAPTER 4

Terror on Lake Louisa

Few action verbs can convey the fear I experienced that evening during the storm on Lake Louisa.

I have never believed in the survival of prehistoric monsters of the deep. I do, however, confess to moderate romanticism. Allow me, in due course, to paint the picture for you because the experience included another affirmation of the value of the soft-hackled wet fly.

I had paddled the small canoe up the lake and over to the place where an enormous flat rock projected from the shoreline. It was, traditionally, a place for trout. Lake Louisa is renowned for lake trout. But they inhabited the deeper water, surfacing to the fly for a brief time during the spring. At that period one could fish a streamer fly with a good chance for success.

But my intent that afternoon was to fish one of the two outlets of the lake; in this case the outlet near the big rock. Brook trout inhabited this outlet, however, it was impossible to fish the stream from the shoreline (like certain sections of the Battenkill in Vermont). The shoreline of the stream was heavily treed, and a thick growth of brush followed the stream shoreline on both sides. Wading was out of the question because of the depth of the water and the nature of the stream bottom. I used the small canoe because only this technique offered the freedom for a backcast under the canopy of trees. Of equal importance I used a surprisingly simple wet fly, a seven and one-half foot 5 weight cane fly rod, and a variety of fly lines.

The wet fly has probably caught more than its share of trout. Most insects during their underwater phase are agile enough to maintain movement against the stream current. Because of this mobility they breathe and pulsate. Their tails, legs, and gills are active. An old fly book containing many of Stewart's fly patterns such as the Grouse Spider, Starling Spider, Grouse and Green, and the Woodcock and Brown had, many years ago, aroused my curiosity. I began to reproduce these patterns and use them for upstream presentation. Watching the action of these flies in the water, with their soft pliant hackle and tail barbs, tyed on size 12 and 14 hooks, reveals the reasons for their effectiveness. And the sparser the dressing, the more effective they are. Partridge, mallard, and woodduck fibers offer the soft undulating movement created by a twitched retrieve. In the smaller sizes, 24 and 26, the fly may be taken for the pupa, an underwater food form which, like the caddis, is eagerly taken by trout. If the hackle is not tied sparse, the body effect is masked by the excess hackle.

The fly I used that day on Connaught Outlet is shown in one of the color plates in this book.

Many of these flies are tyed with long sparse grouse hackle on a fairly long hook shank, with slim body segmented with fine silver or gold wire. The weight of the hook and the amount of "quick-sink" material used on a soft and pliable leader determines the depth that the fly is fished. The depth of presentation may be increased by forming the slim body of fine single ply wool, or some other material which readily absorbs water.

The brook trout fed avidly that afternoon to a grouse and green, and a size 16 wet fly dressed on a Mustad No. 3906B hook. This hook is designated as 1X long, and is suited to this particular artificial with turned-down eye and a Sproat bend. It took a fat bodied 14 inch beautifully colored brook trout with small head. And about fifteen minutes later it captured a trout of almost 11 inches, which suddenly darted up from underneath a submerged log. It grasped the fly about two feet below the surface of the water, and immediately tried to dive under an overhanging bank, flashing and scintillating a reddish-orange hue in the ambient light which penetrated the smooth surface of the water.

One of my first trout on the wet fly came on the fabled Battenkill[1], but in New York State, not in Vermont. Wet fly tackle has changed considerably during the past few years. Relatively small rivers can best be fished with seven and-a-half-foot rods equipped with light-weight reels and a DT5 floating line with extra spools containing DT5ST and DT5S full-sinking design lines. These lines fall softly enough to avoid the easily spooked or skittish fish of small rivers. The full-sink line is ideal for working very fast currents or deep sections of a river, or a combination of these river features. Modern wet fly fishing has witnessed a decline of the bright feathered wet flies used before and during W.C. Stewart's time. There are, however, some ancient axioms about wet fly fishing

[1]The Battenkill eventually empties into the Hudson River in New York State.

which have survived because they are rudimentary and effective. These include keeping the fly in the water to ensure that the fly and leader remain wet; thereby enhancing sink-rate. The compulsion to cast, an obsession of our times, removes the fly from the only place to catch fish—the water. And if the cast includes a dropper fly, the slash of the frequent pickup will often alarm trout before they observe the fly.

THE SIMPLE FIXED LINE SWING allows the fly to move in a quarter circle. The swing is followed by pointing the tip of the rod at the fly and, simultaneously, the rod tip is raised and lowered with a rhythm that follows the speed of the current.

But it was THE CAST-and-STRIP method that accounted for a wily 13 inch brown that same afternoon. It had begun to drizzle, that rare combination of Scotch mist and tiny droplets of water. I had almost reached a wider part of the river, deeper than the water under the anchored canoe, and within fifty feet of casting distance. The cast/strip procedure involves making a longer cast and shaking out extra line with a side-to-side rod motion. This allows the fly to reach a greater depth of water, and the fly can be given action with the retrieve. It is a method for reaching deeper water. In this case I had allowed the fly to swing, while slowly stripping line with my left hand. The result obviously excited the brown trout, and he surfaced, jumping clear of the water, the fly in his mouth.

THE UPSTREAM DEAD-DRIFT method, or technique, is ideal for shallower water than the condition described above. It enables one to imitate the wriggling nymph, which hatches over some distance of drift just below the surface of the water. It can be a deadly method for wet-fly (or nymph) presentation, imitating the drowning terrestrial insect, by working the fly into currents. The technique is somewhat more difficult to master because of sensing the strike. Sometimes an almost imperceptible bulge is observed, a twitch of the leader, or the line and leader will pause during the drift. I do not wish to make a mystery of this kind of take by the trout, but the skill needs to be honed. I usually watch for a difference between current and line speed, and if this is detected I strike immediately to one side with the rod tip close to the surface of the water. A fly rod of nine to ten feet with a fast-action (stiffer) tip is ideal if conditions permit the use of such a rod. The floating line I use when employing this technique has a small fluorescent band where the line joins the leader. All this aside, it is important to study and understand the dynamics of the fly swing because nearly every situation on a river is unique.

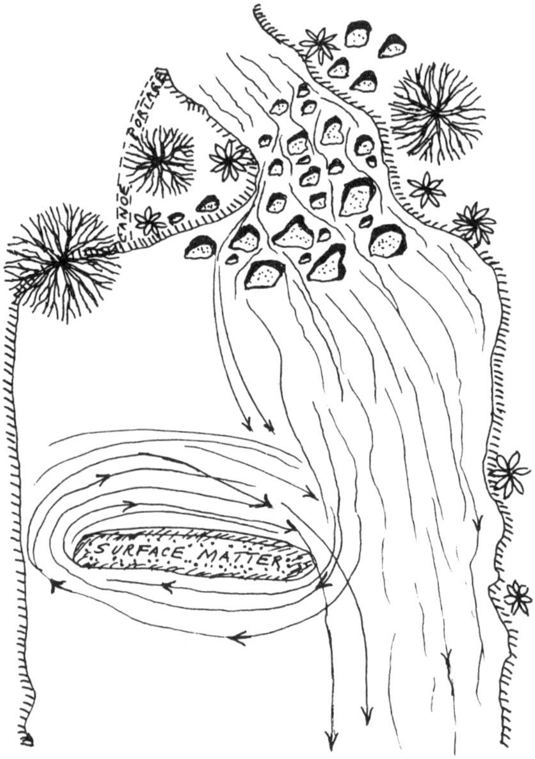

The surface matter is located at an eddy in Connaught Outlet. The same pattern obtains when well-aerated water flows into a pool under the illustrated conditions. The rocks have aerated the water. The rapids act as a food carrier. As the water spills into the pool a large patch of foam remains a constant feature on the surface of the water. It is a *residence* for trout. Here is an ideal location to fish the wet fly and the nymph. If the water is discolored (due to the tumbling action at the rapids) the casts under the floating debris should be spaced close to previous casts. This is because the brown water reduces the visibility of the trout under these conditions.

The pupal form of certain sedges often swim to the surface upon emergence. Their motion is characterized by pulsing movements, and these migrations can be imitated very closely with a HAND TWIST RETRIEVE. Some pupae are as long as three-fourths of an inch, and they were common in the faster shallower parts of Connaught Creek. This method includes a cast across and upstream, a long swing under the brushy bank, then a repeat series of casts with a slow retrieve back upstream, until the circular pattern is completed.

At the precise moment I began to reel-in to check the turle knot, it began to rain in torrents. Because of the fascination fly fishing holds for me I had also been oblivious to the failing light. I glanced up though the leafy tunnel of trees to a black forbidding sky. Now time was not on my side if I was to return to the cottage on Lake Louisa; some considerable distance away. First I had to paddle out of the stream, and I pulled up the light weight anchor where I was sitting amidship after reeling in, and placed the short fly rod in the aluminum case on the bottom of the canoe. I did not realize how fast the storm was building until I reached the mouth of the outlet. It was a squalid looking sky, no sun, torn clouds scudding before a northeast wind. There were heavy drops of rain, sporadic flashes of lightening, and the rumble of thunder in the distance like a barrage of artillery. I began to paddle against a stiff wind, staying close to shore. Twelve to fourteen inch waves tore at the canoe. I rounded a rocky point trying to keep the bow into the swell. By the time I had covered half of the distance to the house the waves were higher. It was now almost dark and the wind was howling like February on an English moor. I eased the canoe to a course eighty yards from shore.

The shoreline was a blur on my starboard side, and the wind drove me as though powered by a twelve horsepower motor. I speculated about how I could survive in a canoe when the time came to make a right turn towards shore. I ceased paddling and concentrated on steering, endeavoring to ease slightly cross-wind but not swamp the canoe. By this time the waves were two feet high, and the ease to starboard had to be carefully controlled. Finally I detected the lights from our cottage at water's edge, and I reasoned that if I could avoid the wharf it might be possible to beach the canoe on the sandy shoreline without damaging the canoe. I was now about eighty feet from shore.

Suddenly I saw an enormous ugly black creature, its head out of the water, approaching the boat. I cannot describe the fear that gripped me. They have come for me I reasoned. How could a creature of that size with such a large neck, have survived from prehistoric times. Terror gripped me and I turned the canoe abruptly, almost swamping the vessel in waves that splashed over he gunwales. The monster glided closer and I noted its glistening eyes in what, by now, was nightfall. Spray from the waves cascaded over the creature's head. Suddenly I leaned forward in the canoe. Imagine my relief when I recognized our next door neighbor's black Labrador Retriever.

The tranquillity of Otter Lake.

Chapter 5

Otter Lake

Mist shrouded the southern half of the lake in the cold, clear mountain air of Québec. The water was a pale azure blue. Maple trees, most with small leaves, crowded the shoreline. Looking south across the lake I could see a densely timbered island. The west shoreline of the lake approached the island closely. Access to the south part of the lake was complicated by protruding shoals of rock. One very large rock was located half way between the island and the shore of the lake. Two Black Mallard ducks flew with machine like precision toward some obscure destination.

"Can we pass through there with the canoe?" I asked Wilson, nodding toward the shoals of half submerged rock.

"It was touch and go last autumn," he replied "but the water level was lower during September than it is today."

The Wilsons were very skilled fly dressers and he and his wife were excellent casters. They enjoyed salmon and trout fishing. I admired his emerger patterns which imitated the march brown emerger and iron blue dun in particular. While I cannot be certain that Wilson was the first person to dress the fantailed shrimp tyed on the stainless steel hook in the color plate, it was a favorite producer for the Wilsons. I began to use this dressing many years ago for bonefish.

We were close friends for a quarter of a century until his recent death. So much so that because of his knowledge about fly fishing, I write about him and his family in *Battenkill Bounty*. And also, about Wilson the fly fisher in the story entitled *Otter Lake*; just two incidents during a long and rewarding association.

It was Wilson who introduced the author to experimentation with the glass slant-tank which featured a flow of water at the surface. Here one can simulate the view of a trout as different kinds of insects float into the trout's window or cone of vision. The tiny streaks created by the unique indentations of different insects produce a distinctive light pattern. This light pattern very likely prompts the beginning of the rise. Wilson maintained that a trout will feed selectively because it "locks-in" to a distinct pattern, or impression, during a particular span of time or period of feeding. The effects of refraction may also be observed with the slant-tank.

Wilson was a constant experimenter, and his quest for the truth about the fly and the fish was unceasing.

I pulled on a fishing jacket and stepped into the canoe.

"Keep your eyes open near the shallows," I advised. "You can instruct me about direction from the bow of the canoe. I will paddle slowly when we get to the narrows." Fifteen minutes later we were past the region of difficulty and over deep water. I stopped paddling the canoe to watch the rings of a heavy rise off-shore, about two hundred yards away.

"We may be fortunate today." I said.

"If these landlocked salmon accept a streamer fly today as they take a streamer during June and July evenings," answered Wilson, "we will have nothing to complain about."

I watched Wilson tie on a size 2 Light Edson Tiger streamer fly. We were not going to the south part of Otter Lake because, traditionally, further fields always appear greener. For some reason, or reasons, the landlocked salmon in this lake accepted the fly more frequently near

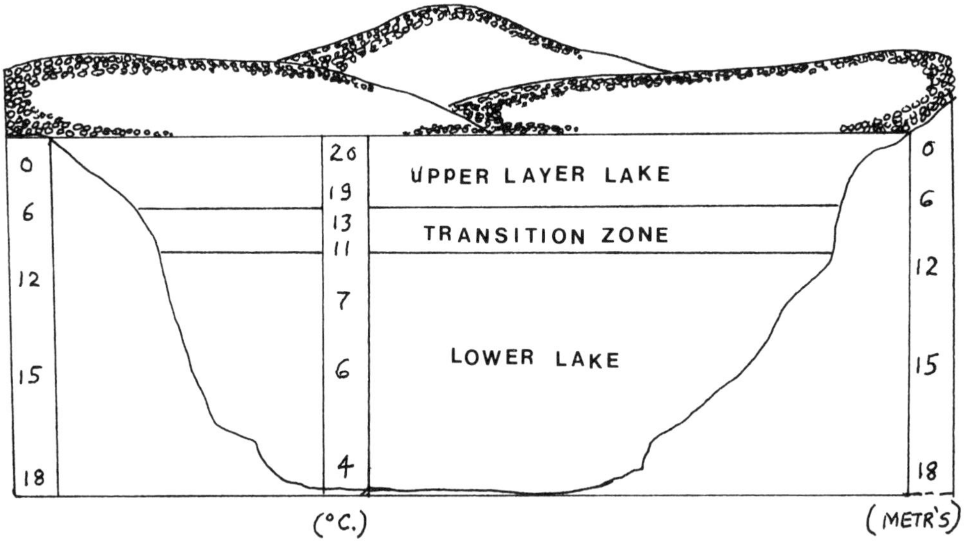

Layers of temperature in a lake are related to distinct temperature preferences of specific game fish. It is not likely that ouananiche (or trout) will be found at the surface of a lake during mid-summer. Lake trout, for example, require the cold temperatures of the "lower lake." Landlocked salmon in Otter Lake were frequently caught in the "transition zone" with a weighted streamer fly. The illustrated (summer) condition of water temperature and related depth depicts distinct layers of water. Note the warmer upper layer and a cold "lower lake." The layers are separated by a narrow "transition zone." The "two lakes" do not mix, and one consequence is a variation in the supply of oxygen from top to bottom.

the south end of the lake than they did at the north end near the access road. There were nine cottages on the lake during the mid nineteen-forties. All of the cottages were located near the road. Wilson frequently expressed the view that it was not a road but an unreasonable facsimile thereof. I could not disagree with his diagnosis.

"Why the Light Edson Tiger fly?" I enquired.

"The baitfish in this lake," Wilson replied, "have a yellowish-green hue. They are also about the size of a number 2 hook when the yellow bucktail wing is mounted to extend just slightly past the bend of the hook." Wilson paused to light a peculiar looking cigar, the odor of which could have tranquillized a Musk Ox. "Quite often," Wilson continued, "a wounded minnow is a special attraction to a large fish, and the red shoulder feather could be mistaken for an injured baitfish. Some of the classic patterns like the Gray Ghost owe considerable of their success because they are imitative of the smelt populations of many northeastern waters." I remarked about the reddish cast to the jungle cock eyes. "An injured baitfish shows its gill coloring towards the end of its life." Wilson replied. "And that also makes for an easy prey for the feeding fish."

I paddled slowly south towards the large area where we could begin to fly fish around the wooded shoreline. Wilson had the Edson Tiger streamer in the water to the end of seventy or eighty feet of fly line.

"Go slower if you will," requested Wilson, "we may as well indulge in some enticing on the way to the prime area for rises."

At that exact instant the reel on Wilson's rod screamed protestingly! I glanced eighty feet behind the canoe, still paddling slowly, to observe a heavy roll and splash. The reel continued its insistent throaty purr, and the line moved down at an increasing angle into deep water.

"This is a large fish," Wilson announced. "I can feel the weight of him."

"How do you know it is a 'him'?" I enquired.

"Paddle very slowly," answered Wilson, "this could take some time."

I controlled the canoe as carefully as possible in the moderate breeze. "What fly tying materials are, in your opinion, outstanding for streamers?"

"If you can obtain polar bear hair it has a wonderful translucent appearance in water," replied Wilson. "It can be mixed or color blended with dyed synthetics to achieve the color you wish to imitate. Fin and tail coloring can be achieved by marking the tips of a streamer wing with a waterproof felt-tip pen. Always try to imitate the natural baitfish in the water you are fishing. But that is only one aspect of fishing the streamer fly,'' Wilson continued. ''The impact of the streamer on the fish is dependant upon markings, profile and, above all, mobility or action. Action is not just created by a judicious blending of materials, but by the technique used to fish the fly. You should study the swimming action of the natural and imitate that action with the retrieve. Is the minnow, for example, a darter? Or does it swim with a smooth fluid-like motion, only pausing occasionally? Capture some minnows and make a sketch of their size, scale patterns, and body and fin colors. Do this as soon as possible after the minnow is removed from the water. Colors often change with prolonged exposure outside of water. Take a close look at all of your fly tying materials, and then select the most appropriate textures and colors. Do not hesitate to experiment. If you dress a hackle feather streamer make certain the feathers have no curvature in the horizontal plane. Marabou ''breathes'' like no other material. Experiment with imitating the gill structure of a baitfish by using a few turns of hackle in order to make the action of the gill area more life-like. The streamer is probably the most useful fly rod lure conceived. We are fishing here for landlocked salmon, but never underestimate it for bonefish. Try one on your favorite river at night for brown trout.''

''How about lake fishing procedure?'' I asked.

''My best results,'' replied Wilson, ''have resulted when fishing from an anchored boat far enough from shore to avoid hanging-up my back-cast in a tree. Baitfish will swim out from shore some distance, but they return to shallower water for reasons of safety. I have found it productive to cast out from shallower water, and retrieve the casts in a pattern which begins at the nine o'clock position, and work gradually to the three o'clock position. This technique can sometimes be achieved by wading.

I guided the canoe in a slow controlled drift, trying to keep Wilson's fly line angled away from the hull of the canoe. Occasionally the nine foot Hardy would bend more sharply. But, in the main, the rod remained static and appeared to be near its limit of stress.

''I have talked with fishermen who have trolled with monel metal line through here,'' said Wilson, as though reading my thoughts. ''There is small chance of snagging in this part of the lake,'' he continued.

The fight that this landlocked salmon offered seemed interminable. I glanced at my watch; eleven minutes had elapsed since Wilson had set the hook. The reel commenced yielding backing again with a slow throaty purr.

''This fish is enormous.'' Wilson said, in an awed and hushed voice.

"It is almost lunch time." I remarked.

Wilson laughed and made a comment about the inadequate size of the landing net. I watched him pump the fish lightly and then move the rod to one side while exerting a slow steady pull.

"Would you paddle at a right angle to the line," he requested, "so that I can see if I can move this fellow."

Three or four minutes elapsed while the canoe traversed its required course. I heard Wilson reeling, but I noted that the backing no longer angled away from the canoe. Its descent was perpendicular to the surface of the water. Wilson continued to slowly reel in backing. At least another four minutes elapsed before I saw this landlocked salmon. He was about twelve, or possible ten, feet below the water's surface and, suddenly, Wilson's reel began to yield line again at increasing speed.

"The fish is huge." I said.

"Yes." Wilson replied with a tremulous tone to his voice. "They have been taken up to twelve and thirteen pounds in this lake." "This one" he continued, "looks like it will go close to the record for the lake."

"If we take this fish," I suggested, "how would you feel about having it mounted? No one will believe the size of this salmon if we practice the usual catch-and-release."

"That is exactly what we will do," Wilson agreed, "and the mounting will include your name and mine. Because of this canoe, and that short-handle net, you will have to net this fish."

"We had better net him on the first pass." I emphasized.

Wilson was now managing slow retrieval of line. I placed the paddle on the floor of the canoe. The net had to be assembled. It was one of those nets that you formed into a triangular shaped opening. The sections snapped into place, and the handle was then screwed onto a short threaded bar. The bar protruded from one apex of the triangle. The net was not shaped like a tear-drop. And it did not have the depth for what looked like a thirty inch plus landlocked salmon. I ran the net through the water to check its assembly.

"Are you ready for this?" asked Wilson.

"I am as ready as I ever will be." I replied.

Wilson had turned the fish and was reeling in line. I positioned the net in the water and as far away from the side of the canoe as the short handle would accommodate. Having taught canoeing at a summer camp many years before, I made certain that I would use a reach that would ensure that I continue to sit in the middle of the canoe.

Wilson brought the fish into perfect alignment with the open end of the net. About two-thirds the length of this landlocked salmon entered the net, and I noted that his head had reached he bottom of the net. I turned the net and lifted the fish to place it in the canoe. The fish went right through the net! The net broke and then collapsed! Wilson grabbed for the leader. I let go of the net at Wilson's request. Wilson missed grasping the leader and asked me to take hold of the end of the fly line. Confusion reigned supreme. The fish splashed wildly throwing a spray of water into the canoe. This landlocked salmon was a giant. The fish ejected the fly on the second splash. We watched the huge salmon swim slowly away. There was a prolonged silence . . .

"My fault." said Wilson.

"The only fault," I said, "was simply not examining an old net. And either of us could have done that duty."

"Did you see the size of that fellow?" Wilson questioned in a hushed tone of voice.

"I will not swim in this lake again." I replied.

Rainbow trout feeding on midge pupae. You must cultivate an eye for shadows.

Chapter 6

Presenting the Midge Pupa

It is almost fifteen years since I have fished in Colorado and, later that Summer, the West Yellowstone area. There are memories of Hegben Lake, and Western Green Drakes on the Henry's Fork. Mayfly hatches abounded on the Big Horn, and small Western Olives on Henry's Fork during August and September. "Tricos" also appeared on Henry's Fork in August and September, and the Tricorythodes minutus provided for superb fishing with small flies. The Yellowstone country of Montana is a land of lakes and rivers. It is a place where the giant "Salmon stonefly" or Pteronarcys californica hatches on the Madison, usually during late June and the first half of July. The Gray Drake of the family Baetidae emerged in September. And the Pale Morning Dun made its appearance on the Firehole during the last half of June. There are size 16 Speckled Spinners during August and September on Hegben Lake, and one can fish the size 20 Iron Blue (Western) quill on the Yellowstone in the Park during late September.

Early that season, before proceeding to Yellowstone country, I commenced a long vacation of fly fishing in Colorado. It was to be a unique experience with the small fly. I started with the South Platte River and fished through part of the Waterloo Canyon, taking a few rainbow trout and one brown trout on nymphs.

But the thrill of fishing the small fly productively occurred on the Frying Pan River in Colorado. The water level here is controlled by a dam, however, the level of the water was normal during the early season. Two of the flies illustrated in the color plates, the green Caddis Larva dressed with green floss and green wire, and the Midge Pupa, were the stellar producers on the Frying Pan River during the last week of May before proceeding to the Yellowstone area.

The Midge Pupa has also been effective in the lakes of British Columbia. As a resident of the West I had the opportunity to refine the fly and the fishing technique I will describe for you now. The procedure for the process of presenting the fly requires a small amount of practice,

COLORADO

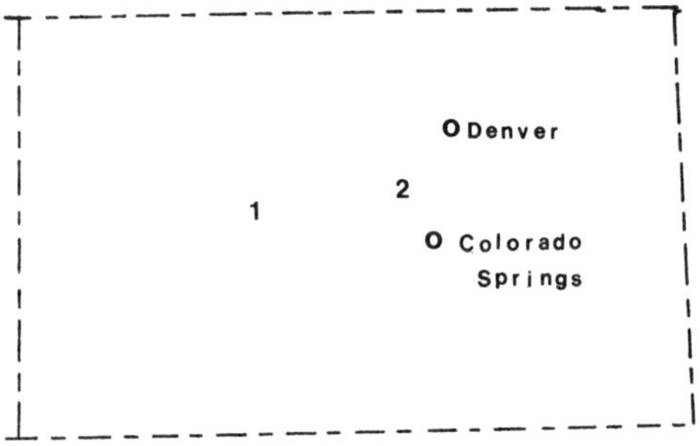

MONTANA

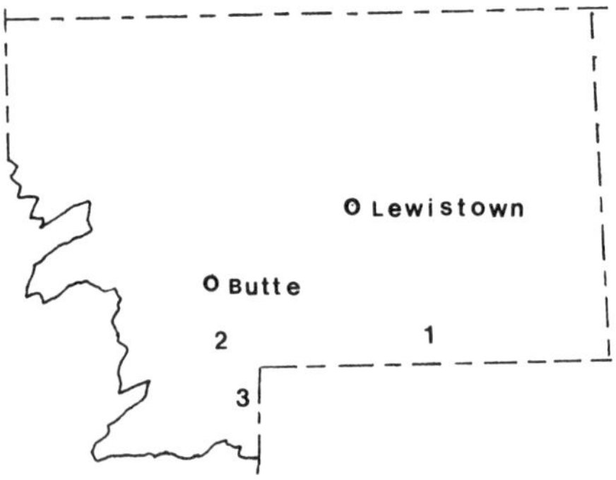

If you fish the South Platte River (2), in Colorado, be prepared to offer the brown and rainbow trout midges, pupae, and tiny caddis flies. Hooks sized 16 to 22 are appropriate. The fish are selective on the South Platte. February to April provide for good midge hatches on the Frying Pan River (1). The Green Drake is on in August and September.

There is good fishing in Montana on the Bighorn (1), the Madison River (2), and Hebgen Lake (3). The Bighorn can offer trophy sized trout. Rick Hafele's "Western Hatches" is a superb reference book. Summer and autumn is best for the dry fly on the Madison. Try the fishing downstream of Varney Bridge. The elk hair in a size 12 matches the July/August caddis hatches on certain sections of the Madison. Hebgen Lake is a mecca for Midge Pupae—especially in the shallow bays.

however, it will be worth the effort when trout are feeding selectively on Midge Pupa.

The pupal form of tiny Diptera frequently hang almost motionless under the surface film. One of their predominant features consists of minute gills which pulsate in the richer area of oxygen of the meniscus. Many anglers who have an obsession with the dry fly often make the wrong assumption that a visible surface rise must be a trout feeding on mayfly emergers or terrestrial insects. But fish frequently surface-swirl to pupae in, or under the surface film. These tiny insect forms are pupae struggling to shed their pupal skins, and they are often the target food for trout. Midge Pupae should be fished dead-drift and just under or in the surface film. The cast should be made ahead of a cruising fish.

The close-up color photograph in the front of the book illustrates the fly dressing that I have found effective when this kind of food form is the diet of the trout. Most of the hackle on this pattern has been trimmed away from the area surrounding the head of the fly. Three turns of hackle are sufficient. The short hackle fibres are intended to represent the pulsating movements of the gills just below the surface film. My dressings are made on size 24 hooks.

The important characteristic about the presentation is to ensure that the fly hangs perpendicular in or just below the surface film, and that the pattern is subject to natural drift. In order to accomplish this condition I have illustrated the technique in FIGURE 1. A leader of twelve feet is ideal. It should be rated about 6X, that is, with a butt diameter of about .023 inches, and a tip diameter of .005 inches. Such a leader will usually have a break-test of approximately three pounds. FIGURE 1 illustrates the Midge Pupa hanging vertically from the leader. A knot is formed in the leader on the tippet side of the leader, that is approximately three feet above the dry fly. The size of the knot is larger than the hook eye to prevent, when a fish is hooked, the midge imitation from sliding beyond the knot. This hook features a down-eye, however, its ability to make a positive connection is very satisfactory. My experience has confirmed that the design of the hook-eye, whether up, down, or ring-eye makes virtually no difference to hooking capacity. Quite often the trout hooks itself if the hook point is sharp.

The dry fly shown in FIGURE 1 at the end of the tippet assists with keeping the leader on or just under the meniscus, provided the leader is fully extended in a straight line on the water. It is important that this fly float high. In practice I have found that a size sixteen or eighteen 3X fine, dry fly hook is preferable for the tippet fly. In order to float

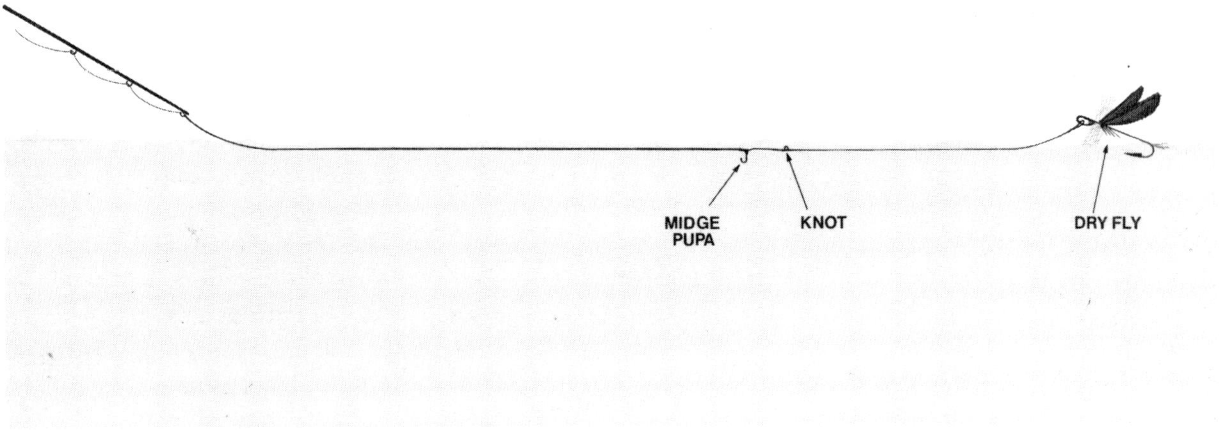

Presenting the Midge Pupa.

the fly high on the film I use first grade genetic-raised hackle, or deer hair construction for floatation. A small White Wulff or Gray Fox Variant is ideal for the tippet fly. The presentation technique which I have found successful, after spotting a cruising fish at the surface, is to cast seven or eight feet in front of the trout, and then give the line a small amount of slack to allow the Midge Pupa to dead-drift in the film. The amount of slack should be very small. I want to emphasize this aspect of the technique because, immediately the pupa is taken by the fish, one must usually tighten up quickly, ensuring line/leader retrieval to move the knot up to the hook eye so as to set the hook. With a small amount of practice you will find that this technique is not difficult.

A further word about the pupal imitation. This midge dressing is easily prepared by tying in the thin end of a well soaked, stripped quill at the location shown around the hook bend. (See color plate of Midge Pupa). I prepare these from black, brown, and gray five-inch stripped hackles. The quill is wound and tyed-off 1/8'' from hook eye. Then three turns of hackle are applied and tyed-off. The prewaxed 6/0 or 8/0 tying thread is run through the hackle to divide some of the barbs so that a few point above the hook eye. Many of the remaining barbs should extend in the horizontal plane. This articulation assists with "holding" the midge in, or just under, the surface film. The small head is whip finished and then varnished to complete the Midge Pupa imitation. The head is not pronounced and its relative size is almost an extension of the body dimension.

The color of the midge should be the same as the Midge Pupae found in the water being fished.

SUGGESTED HOOKS:

PARTGRIDGE K1A, size 24 VINCE MARINARO midge hook

PARTRIDGE CS21 sneck midge

TMC 501, ring eye, straight point, size 24

MUSTAD 94859, round bend, ring eye, size 24

Autumn in New England.

CHAPTER 7

Waters Of The Past

But should you lure
From his dark haunt, beneath the tangled roots
of pendant trees, the Monarch of the brook,
Behoves you then to ply your finest art.
THOMSON—The Seasons (Spring)

I remember all of them. The streams that were far from urban sprawl and abrasiveness. They were, for the most part, small and lively yet quiet and bright. I was guided to them or found them in New Hampshire and Québec, Wyoming, and British Columbia. I remember the one called West Creek in Maine. And there was the trouty-looking one that flowed through the golf course not far from Ticonderoga, New York. It became wilder and more challenging as you proceeded upstream. The trees seemed to close in about you and, of necessity, casts became shorter. You worked the fly in small pools and under tight banks. The pools became smaller but, amazingly, deeper and deeper. You wonder what monster might lurk there. Once I floated a hair-wing Coachman #18 and saw the flash of a heavy fish turn deep in the dark green of a pool. But

---

During the process of reviewing material for WATERS OF THE PAST the author's attention was arrested by the frequency with which the order Tricoptera constitutes a major role in fly fishing.

When not endeavoring to match the species which migrate to shallows and climb out of the water, one is imitating the swimming pupae en route to emerging from the film. And this condition usually provides for vulnerability to the trout. For the trout can feed on Caddis Pupae without expending too much energy.

Caddisflies of the genera Cheumatopsyche, Arctopsyche, and Hydropsyche are, among others, widely distributed in North American waters. They are found in streams, reservoirs, lakes, and beaver ponds. Their tolerance for pesticides, wide ranges of temperatures, and certain forms of pollution is greater than most mayflies.

there was no rise and, after that first cast, you knew the fish would have to be rested for a long time. The foliage closed-in eventually and you were faced with the prospect of dapping. Deadfalls criss-crossed the water and, not uncommonly, wild flowers grew from the dead trees above the watcr line. You were suspended from civilization, and the taste and tonic of wilderness was good. The trout you caught were carbon black on top, almost pure white of belly, and the speckles were a brilliant orange and bright red. It was the second year before I understood how to fish that stream. The pro at the Country Club advised me to work the water deep with a slow moving wet fly. "You sink a small wet fly deep if you want results", Tony advised. "Use a nymph pattern; try a Hendrickson dressing now that the water is fifty-eight degrees Farenheit."

The names of these small streams do not ring in my mind. Some have no name that I am aware of and may not be a thin dark line on maps. They are private places, still and steady, cold and clear, full of short white rushes and the mystery of silent glides. Sometimes they are discovered without intent and almost, it seems, by the sporadic nature of some mysterious design. It is certain that many such places exist.

Some years ago during a visit to the Keystone State I was reminded, once again, about the proliferation of the caddis. Although most caddis are captured by gamefish when they are in the pupal form, it is often possible to see trout and other gamefish feeding on caddis in or under the surface film. Trout also rise to egg-laying females. Such has been my experience on Green Spring Creek in Cumberland County, Pennsylvania, and also on Donegal Springs Creek in Lancaster County. Here the fly fishing water stretches for two miles, and most hatches adapt to a range of habitats. Caddis thrive in acid and alkaline environments.

Although gamefish are not always selective when feeding on caddis, there are occasions when selectivity is obvious. I have observed fish feeding exclusively on caddis in shallow water downstream of riffles where the current was smooth; feeding channels difficult to detect at first view. And where trout have the opportunity to examine a food specimen carefully. Matching the hatch, therefore, can be important when fishing an imitation of the caddis.

Flyfishers who have killed trout which have recently been feeding, and who can recognize the caddis stages of development will, upon examination of the stomach contents, appreciate the role of the caddis in the trout's diet. It constitutes a rich heritage for the person who is skilled with fly rod and fly.

The caddis, ignored by many anglers today, did not escape the notice of an obviously keen-eyed American angler of the past.

> Lately, there have been a good many small caddis flies on the water. These do not sail down gracefully after the manner of the May fly, but struggle and buzz upon the water. It is extremely difficult to imitate their movements, although a man who is an expert in manipulating his dropper fly may be successful. By moving this dropper fly four or five feet up the leader, one can command the water at fair range. If the flies are close together, one can only dap the dropper with a short line.
> —from *Little Talks About Fly Fishing* by Theodore Gordon (1854-1915)

Fly fishers such as Theodore Gordon, Skues, and Frederick Halford are must reading for the fly angler. Theodore Gordon prescribed an effective technique for imitating the erratic, darting, upstream fluttering motion of the adult caddis. I confess to fishing the adult caddisfly infrequently. But what sport it can be when there is a concentrated hatch and the trout are leaping for them. If you fish for the returning adult (female), there is no heresy in casting the dry fly across and downstream. Innovation can be the order of the day. There are occasions when one cannot fish across and upstream. I have a situation in mind where a large overhanging tree renders a section of brown and rainbow trout water inaccessible to any kind of upstream approach. But the water upstream of that tree which almost touches the surface of the water, is a prime feeding area. If you are there during surface feeding time you can hear trout sucking-in morsels of surface food. The only possible approach consists of kneeling mid-stream on a shallow gravel bar, and casting across and downstream to float the deceiver into this area of water. A rod of nine to ten feet assists with control. A tapered line, an eight-foot leader with 4X tippet, and the adult imitation illustrated, tied to a six-inch dropper, can be cast across and downstream. This procedure will facilitate fishing the adult up and across-stream. The fly, affixed at the dropper location five feet above the tippet fly, can be "danced" upstream by holding the long rod high. When the trout leaps at the caddis hooking is often automatic.

Not too many years ago I left the house at Craigville, Cape Cod, midway through the second week of my vacation. It would, I decided, be a change of pace to return to the city via New England by slow and easy stages. The second night en route I stayed at a small motel on a secondary road. The motel consisted of five units, and the owner admitted that the overnight accommodations were an afterthought. The predominant attraction was a dining room known by the locals for its cuisine. The only signs of activity occurred during evening dinner.

After dinner I walked along a path behind the motel. The magic sound of flowing water became quickly apparent. Now I could hear the soft whispering wash of water over stones. The aroma of vegetation surrounding the stream was discernible. Presently the stream banks revealed themselves, almost masked by forest and fern growth. I am caught up in this game again, I reflected, with thoughts which focused on the fly rod in my car. It was one of those streams which hold charm and surprise. The motel proprietor (I stayed an extra day and night) owned considerable of the acreage through which this water flowed. He offered detailed advice about technique, and described the lucrative stretches of water. But once on a stream and wading I am lost. I remember virtually nothing about sage advise. I think about nothing except my approach to the next pool, pocket water, or overhanging bank. This stream possessed all of the foregoing attributes. It contained several areas of riffles and glides, and offered one large pool of ink-black water below a small waterfall. If distance is measurable by walking time I travelled three quarters of a mile on land, in the downstream direction, in order to fish the water upstream. Most of the walk was through second growth timber. I reasoned that this procedure, give or take a few minutes, would bring me back to the large deep pool below the waterfall when dusk was approaching.

Entering the stream I could see a hatch of tiny white-winged caenis flies. Their erratic flight was similar to an adult caddis fly. I had a fairly close match for the caenis fly, and tied one on which had been dressed on a size twenty-two fine wire up-eye hook. Repeated casting to two trout, each at its own feeding station failed to interest either fish. The late June twilight promised to be extensive, and June is a prime month for late evening fishing—likely the best of the trout season. The twilight hours might give me enough time to identify the trout's food preference of the evening.

I continued wading upstream as quietly as possible, stopping occasionally to watch for a rise so that I could cast to a specific trout. Suddenly, not more than sixteen feet upstream, close to an undercut bank, a twelve to thirteen-inch speckled trout could be seen feeding just under the surface. It was the typical posture of a trout feeding in water which flows slowly. It was now visually apparent that the trout were sipping caddis emergers. Several adult caddis flies were hovering just above the water's surface. I remained motionless and watched "the little white wink" a few inches below the surface of the water.

Caddis pupa imitation.

About twenty-eight years before fishing this stream I had been given a size sixteen pupal imitation caddis pattern by the man who taught me fly-casting. The pattern has seldom failed to produce for me during a caddis fly hatch. The fly was specifically designed to deceive fish which hold just under the surface film in order to intercept food. It was now a question of remaining undetected by the trout, and a good presentation of the artificial. The first pitch with the tannish-brown pupa settled above the most recent riseform. The caddis drifted just under the film for approximately ten inches, and was quickly taken by a thirteen-inch stream-bred brook trout. This emerger, which I dress exactly as it was given to me, except for the Saran wrap wing cases, is shown above. The photograph illustrates this emerger (Brachycentrus fuliginosus) which is found so frequently in waters in Eastern North America. The wing cases on this American Grannom are five sixteenths inches long, and are fashioned from Saran wrap. The wing cases are secured at both ends of the side of the thorax. This material does not mask the radiance of the dark brown sparkle dubbing which has been blended with medium brown mink underfur. Because the Saran film has been dressed with moderate slack, the action of the water "working" on the film assists with the impression of a moving or partially loosened sheath. The Saran material is also durable, and yields a slate-like appearance when its surface becomes wet. The legs are mottled barbules from a partridge body feather.

While working upstream I met and talked with the one other angler I saw on the water. He remarked that he fished this small stream as often as possible. Over many years he had observed that the hatch occurred several hours before surface feeding became apparent. And he also assured me that he had experienced considerable success with emergers. "For some reason", he added, "the trout prefer caddis imitations to mayfly imitations even when flies of both types are in the process of emerging". When this fly fisherman realized that I was a visitor with fishing privileges he insisted that I accept a fifteen minute start upstream. I accepted his sporting invitation and moved on, continuing to fish the emerger pattern. But now the situation had changed. The trout were leaping for the adults on the surface and those caddis flies hovering above the water—particularly the smaller trout.

The adult imitation that I use so frequently is also simple to dress. It can be readily constructed by the neophyte tyer. Clamp an appropriate size hook in the vise and, using 6/0 black tying thread as a base, cover the shank from approximately one sixteenth inches behind the hook-eye to a point directly above the barb of the hook. (I remove all hook barbs and hone the point before dressing, but have not done so for the purpose of illustration.) The dubbing for the body is natural light colored mink underfur. You can color this material with a waterproof marking pen. Mink underfur, in my experience, is unexcelled as dubbing material for the dry fly. The body is slim, slightly tapered as shown, and not too dense. Position the two antennae as shown and, before starting to dub, tie in a dark blue dun genetic (cock) hackle at the start of the hook bend with black tying thread. After contouring the body as shown the hackle is closely palmered to one-eighth inch from the eye of hook and tyed-off. The hackle on top of the hook shank is trimmed at an angle, shorter at the front, to allow the wing to cock-up at the rear. (The wing will assume a position which is close to the horizontal plane when the hackle becomes damp.) The two simple remaining operations consist of mounting a sparse wing to match the natural, and formation of a black head. (The body color, hackle, and hair-wing color are easily modified to match a particular hatch.)

Hair-wing caddis adult imitation.

I use the superb Partridge K12ST Longshank Sedge/Caddis Hook for this imitation. It has a ring-eye and a (dull) black finish. The very light weight of this hook, slim fly body, and sparse wing result in a fly which is easy to float on the film.

The illustrated adult Caddis dry fly dressing often emerges in Southern Ontario rivers during late June. It also hatches (earlier in June) on rivers in New York State and Vermont. The hackle is dark blue dun. This adult boasts a dark gray body and wing—almost charcoal in color. The wing can be tinted with Pantone Marker 448M. In this case I have used a size fourteen hook, however, the same dressing, on a larger hook, has taken sea-trout on the river Aanon in Scotland, and Skeena Valley steelhead in British Columbia.

This dressing has often been fished, as described by Gordon, on a dropper and worked slowly in the upstream direction using his technique to simulate that dancing erratic flight motion that Gordon observed. When selecting the hackle I have, over the years, used the same hackle size as was on the fly given to me by Mr. Gulline, that is, one and one-half times the gap of the hook. Some fly fishers that I know often dress this fly with two turns of light color grizzly hackle close to the head of the fly. This procedure can provide for improved visibility during waning light. It has been my experience that hatches of caddis flies which occur about 7:00 p.m. often continue for some hours. It is helpful if you can see your fly on the water.

Whatever one's attitude may be about the ubiquitous caddis it remains a food form which demands, but does not always realize, equal time from the fly angler. Its predominant position in the diet of many of our gamefish is not likely to be de-emphasized in the foreseeable future.

I took several speckled trout that evening, returning all but two to the stream. What, you may ask, happened at that last deep pool upstream, just before dark? Well, quite frankly, a trout wound my leader around a deadfall and broke me off. Deadfalls and branches are very often one of the intriguing aspects of the small brushy trout stream. The small stream is the microcosm of the larger river. But in that microcosm dwells an intimacy, an intimacy revealed if you can "ply your finest art".

The Mid-Season

Chapter 8

Clinger-Emerger

I watched the elderly fellow as he waded sprightly around the bend of the river. There was nothing contemporary about him or his style. Old weather-worn Stetson, sunglasses, faded fly vest, cane rod, wide loop on the backcast, and a delicate presentation. It was all there and the total impact was a grace which, to say the least, was beguiling.

He did not see me at first. And I glanced away from this scene of rare and mobile tranquility to lodge a pint of ale between two submerged rocks in a backwater eddy. It was a hot spring day and I wanted it cold by the time I arrived back at that location. (Hot weather affcionados of the sport will understand.) Suddenly I was all attention because this fellow's reel was releasing line at a furious rate. Squinting through the sunlight across the water I perceived that wonderful image that we all dream about on cold winter nights. A trout was tail-walking across the current with gay abandon.

I watched this skilled past master play the fish and creel it and, then, suddenly conscious of an audience of one, wade quietly toward me with a hale and hearty smile. "You fish bamboo too I see," as he eyed my nine footer leaning against a tree.

"A gift," I acknowledged, "from back in the mists of antiquity."

This all happened many years ago on a mountain stream in the Adirondacks of New York State. We had, as I remember, some interest-

---

The author's first encounter with the illustrious Light Cahill or March Brown mayfy nymph was on the Frying Pan in Colorado. I am not certain the hatch was being matched, however, trout were eagerly taking the almost three-quarter inch jointed nymph with partly elevated darkish brown wing pads, and darkly barred wood duck tails.

The trout of the Luischine in Switzerland were also attracted to the dark brown distinctly ringed body one early evening.

With the exception of the Green Drake nymph and spinner, and the Large Mahogany Dun, I have not fished a pattern which has attracted large trout so consistently over the years as this Gray Fox of the shallows.

ing conversation. And I clearly recall one of his comments that "the ability to discern the meaning of river features, and the surround, often separates the successful flyfisher from the one, who at day's end goes fishless." I remember the lesson that I learned about the value of observation on the stream that long-ago day. The river was bordered by a boulder and rock-strewn steep hill on one side for some considerable distance. The elderly gentleman that I met near the stream discerned my hesitation about which side of the river I would choose to wade in the upstream direction. He was now resting quietly beside the water's edge—bamboo rod hanging, tip down, from a tree branch. "Look about you," he remarked, "and just think about the surrounding terrain for a minute. Some of those boulders and rocks have rolled down the mountain and into the water. The trout, for the most part, will be on the mountain side of the stream because the larger boulders offer protection and rest from faster currents. And, therefore, most feeding stations will be on the mountain side of the stream. Why don't you move quietly up the opposite side and fly fish across and upstream?" He was correct with his evaluation. And I observed the truth of his analysis as I proceeded upstream. It was a simple lesson about the value of observation at streamside.

The feeding habits of trout and observations about the habits and movements of trout food have been invaluable when imitating the emerger. Late spring river water often produces considerable hatches of a clinger-type nymph identified as Stenonema vicarium. This nymph, the March Brown (American), has a flattened body which assists its ability to cling. The interesting factor about this mayfly, for me, is the relatively small quantity of trout I have caught and released over the years using the dun dressing. Fishing the emerger has accounted for maximum success. The nymphs frequently flutter below the surface for some time. And sometimes their struggling takes place on the surface. Emergence can occur from mid-May until late July.

Some years ago I began to dress this emerger to imitate nymphs I caught and saved in a small bottle for reference at the fly-tying table. Observations of the natural reveal a life-like action. The fluttering motion of the natural is usually accompanied by considerable wing emergence before, and during penetration of the surface film. The specimens in my collection are almost three-quarters of an inch long excluding the tails.

The dressing I describe for your consideration has resulted in some very interesting days on stream for me during this hatch. It is a delight to tie and a joy to fish during those rises that are often mistaken for dry fly activity. The nymphs split their skin in the surface film prior to emerging, and this feature is reflected in the dressing.

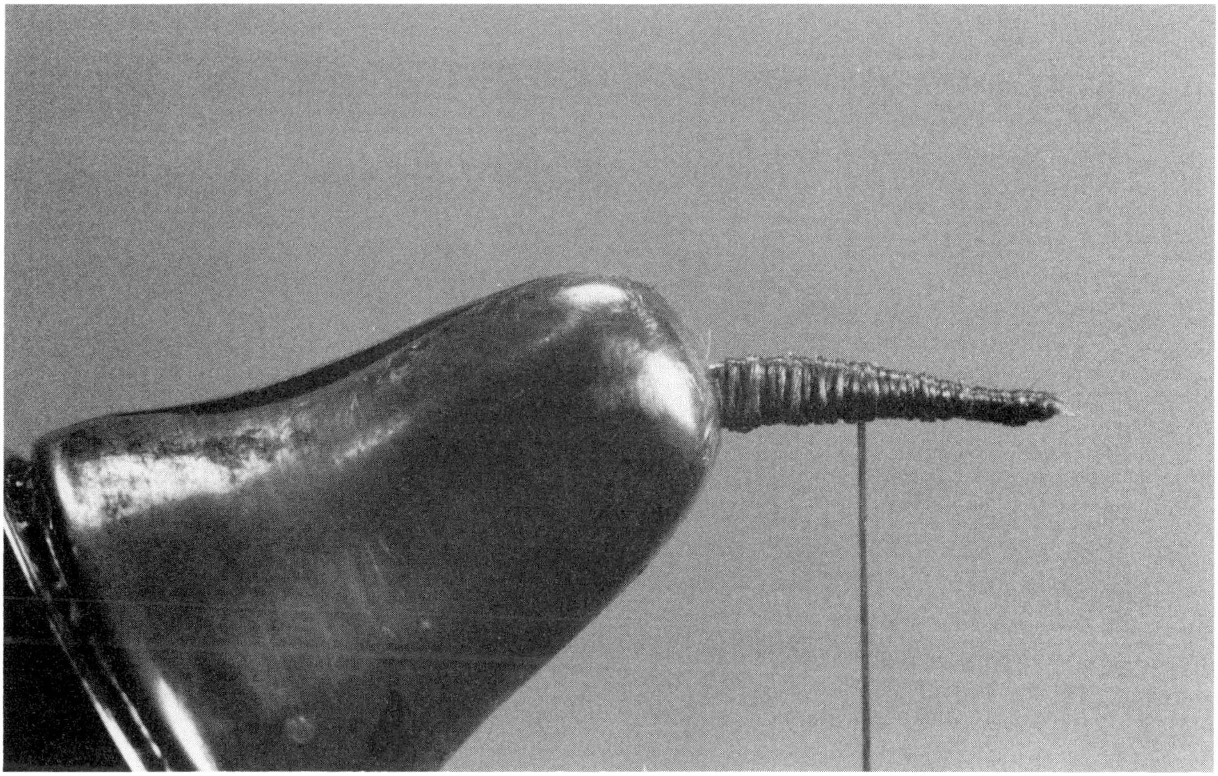

STEP 1 Cut a length of .012'' guitar or piano wire fifteen millimeters long. Make a loop approximately seven millimeters long. Clamp the loop in the vise. Attach brown pre-waxed 6/0 tying thread and, by varying the tension on the tying thread, cover the loop to the tapered configuration illustrated. Apply one coat of cement and allow to dry.

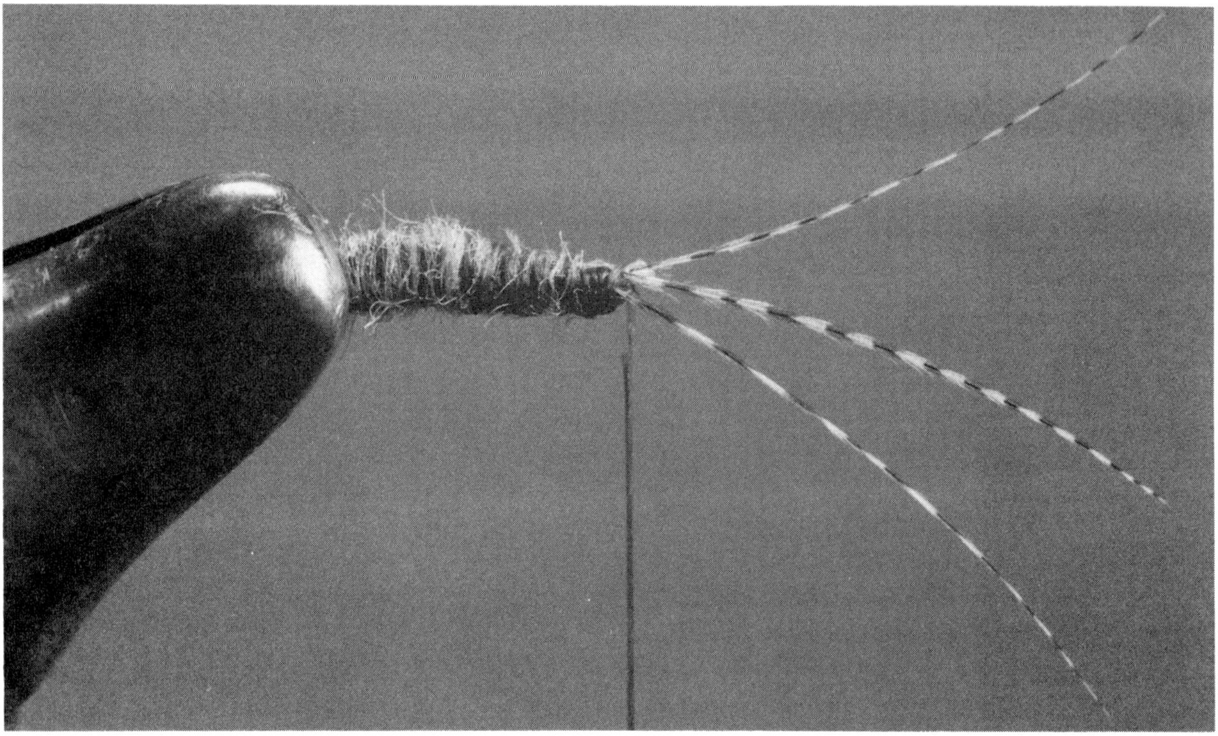

STEP 2 Select three barbs of dark barred wood duck. Each tail is positioned and secured separately so that, in the main, they are positioned in the vertical plane. The three barbs are dressed so that the tails extend sixteen millimeters beyond the tip of the wire loop. Place one small drop of cement where the five eights of an inch tails intersect at the end of body. Position the tying thread close to the jaws of the vise.

The body is dubbed with medium brown otter fur or a medium brown synthetic (polypropylene) material to a length of sixteen millimeters (5/8''). This will leave the ''eye'' of the wire loop barely exposed near the jaws of the vise. If you use white polypropylene material to dub the body, it can be tinted the correct color with a medium brown Pantone marking pen.

STEP 3 The body of the natural is ringed. Therefore use the tying thread to segment the body by winding toward jaws of vise. The thread will almost disappear in the dubbing, and it will serve to reinforce the dubbing material. The body is slightly longer than the thorax on the Stenonema vicarium. Whip finish thread at front of body, cement, and cut tying thread. Step 3 illustrates the completed body before removal from the vise. The body margins have been lightly touched with a dark brown marking pen.

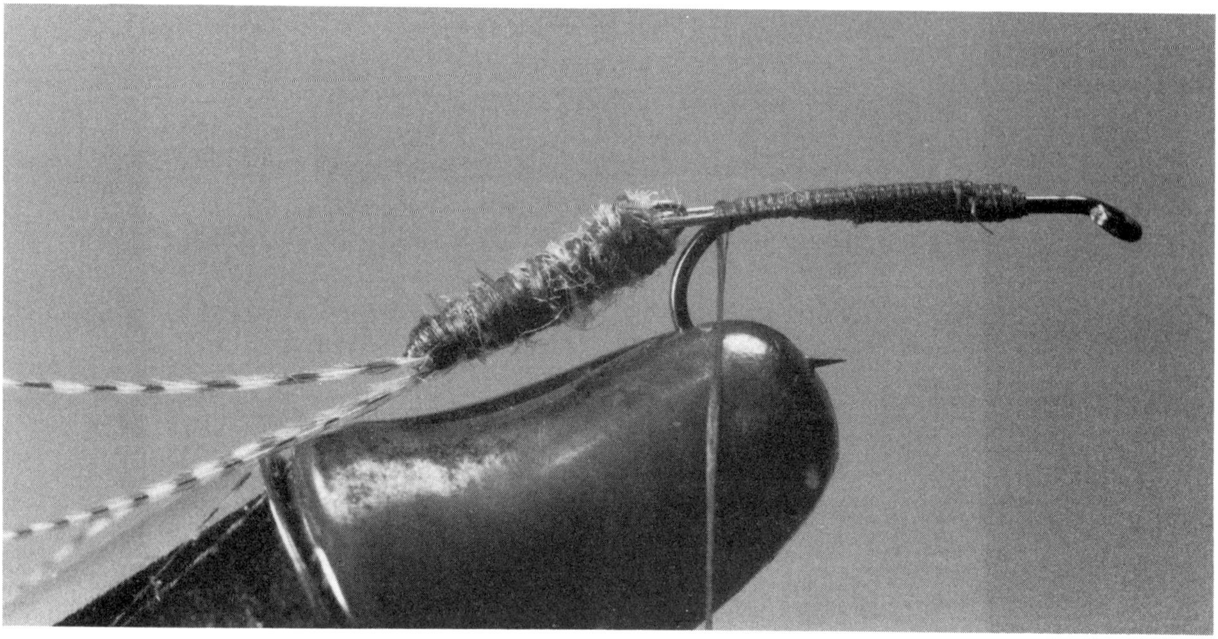

STEP 4 The thorax measurements that I have made approximate three sixteenths of an inch. I prefer to use a Partridge EIA hook. This hook allows for the three sixteenths of an inch body, the mounting of the legs and wing cases, and one eighth of an inch long head. The Hooper L/S 4X Fine dry fly down eye hook is barbless. This hook has characteristics which suit the dressing. It is very light in weight (important for this application) and very strong considering its dimensions.

Clamp the hook in the vise to position shown and, starting one eighth of an inch from eye of hook, cover the shank of hook to hook bend with the brown tying silk. Cut and form a second wire loop and insert it through the first loop (which holds the body). When this second loop is attached to the shank of the hook it extends three-quarters of the distance to the eye of the hook. I prefer to bind this second loop, which forms the second part of the hinge, so that each end of the wire is on opposite sides of the hook shank. This will result in a (shaped) flatter rear thorax—one feature of ''the clinger''. As I wind the tying thread forward, and reach the mid hook-shank position, I raise the two wire ends of the loop and thereby form the sight hump on top of the hook shank which assists the thorax contour. Step 4 illustrates this profile. When this hinge is secured apply two light brushcoats of waterproof cement. The first coat is allowed to dry before the second coat is applied to the shank of hook.

STEP 5 Dub the thorax sparingly to the profile illustrated with a material which is dark mottled brown. Such mottling is incorporated in a material known as SUPERLA NYMPH DRESSING[1] in extra fine texture.

Seal's fur is superb for this application. I use it—when available—by preference. It produces excellent results when formed into a chenile configuration with the tying thread doubled. Scissors are then used to shape the thorax.

I emphasize the correct color because there is considerable evidence that color is important to trout when an imitation is presented underwater.

Four darkly marked wood duck fibers are now fixed to the position shown to represent the well-marked legs of the natural. (Wood duck, darkly marked, more closely represent the legs of the natural than the effect realized with partridge material). The legs are one-half inch long. Remove the surplus (butt) ends of the wood duck fibers.

[1]This material is available in a range of colors from The Hackle House, P.O. Box 505, Oakville, Ontario, Canada, L6J 5A8.

STEP 6 After considerable experimentation with materials for wing cases, I prefer to dress this emerger with medium to dark brown Canadian grouse. There is a small feather, about a quarter of an inch long, at the secondary feather base, and this tiny feather boasts a white median stripe down the center. The two wing cases are shaped to three sixteenth inch length (shown in photo) and dressed on top of one other so that the white median (quill) stripe is on top of shank of hook. When performing this operation apply some pressure with the tying thread to ''flare'' the wing cases in the horizontal plane. This will achieve a silhouette, from below the fly, of splitting of the case, and will also assist the emerger

with flotation. This "emerging position" combined with the soft undulating movements of this feather material result in a life-like action. Some earlier season samples of this nymph that I have collected reveal a purplish cast to the wing cases. I can recommend Pantone marker No. 492 if you wish to duplicate the purplish-brown tint of the wing cases.

The formation of a head with brown thread, a whip finish, and clear cement completes the pattern. The head is one eighth of an inch long.

This clinger-emerger can be fished in the surface film or to a depth of one to four inches. The depth depends upon current speed, whether the emerger is silicone dressed[2] or untreated, the kind of leader tippet material used, and how far one casts above the trout observed to be feeding on the natural S. vicarium.

If you decide to fish this pattern in, or just beneath the surface film, I recommend a slight twitching or fluttering motion which can be imparted by the tip of the fly rod. This will make the fly perform more like the natural.

That too was the recommendation of the elderly gentleman I met with at streamside so many years ago, in a gorgeous valley in upstate New York.

---

[2]Recently I have applied Scotchgard (the fabric protector) to the body and thorax of this dressing, but not to the tails or wing cases.

The California angler, Dennis Amato, working with hands and feet.

CHAPTER 9

The Condor and Grizzly Inheritance

The Condor and Grizzly dressing proceeded from the fertile imagination of Finchley. It had likely been one of a number of winter projects.

Finchley knew the Pebble Grove water as I know the contents of my tie rack. He could ferret our large browns at high noon with predetermined accuracy. I have witnessed his ability to determine the holding positions which wild brown trout select. These sites were virtually always associated with some large deflector in the flow of water. Perhaps a rock, boulder, or deadfall. Finchley emphasized the need for ultra caution when approaching these sites. I have observed him motionless and with a low profile. He would discuss the qualities of the brown trout at the proverbial drop of a fishing hat, including his thesis about why strict nocturnal feeding is a myth without supporting evidence. Finchley insisted that wild brown trout indulge in a graded range of sequence, with the largest fish often located slightly upstream of the other brown trout in the grouping. This hypothesis often predisposed him to fish across and downstream with a deep sinking nymph. Finchley, like many of us, liked to catch the larger trout.

But today as he approached one of our club waters more productive pools and placed his rod aside, I detected the aura of another of Finchley's impending pronouncements.

''They come in high,'' he announced with the convincing air of understatement.

''What is meant by high?'' I asked.

Finchley proceeded to explain his current theory that trout will approach and obtain food according to the way their natural diet presents itself in the stream. "They get used to feeding a certain way," he remarked.

Why do trout frequently rise to and accept the esoteric pattern? Does hunger and the conditioned reflex often overcome caution? Or are there other phenomena about the attractor patterns which remain unanswered?

''How so?'' I enquired, noting that his creel looked weighty this ten o'clock morning.

''Elementary,'' answered Finchley, who had the reputation with our seven members as an innovator of esoteric patterns which could cause trout to blanch in terror. ''If the food forms float high the trout become conditioned to breaking the surface with typical dry fly action,'' he continued. ''This means that they do not bulge as when feeding on nymphs. It also means that you can miss setting the hook with a dry fly which sits well down in the surface film.''

''Are you saying that trout are creatures of habit'' I enquired, ''and that if the imitation sits too low in the film, and does not imitate the way in which the natural dun floats in a particular stream, the point of the hook—in this case—will pass below their lower jaw?''

''Exactly'' replied Finchley with the solemnity of a bishop presiding over a consecration. ''The trout become used to the food forms in their environment. They can also detect differences between hard and soft foods,'' he continued, eyeing me as one who is a novice to trout lore and freestone diet. ''I have designed the Condor and Grizzly,'' Finchley continued, ''to represent the same hardness as the majority of food forms in this water. If the material of which the natural is composed is significantly harder or softer than the deceiver, the wise trout will quickly eject the imitation.''

Pondering this hypothesis for a moment raised the question in my mind about the hardness of the steel hook, and why this condition would not be cause for rejection of the artificial by the fish. I was about to remark about this point when Finchley presented me with three of his exquisitely dressed creations. They were meticulously crafted, and the stiffness of the cock hackle was outstanding. I could not bring myself to attempt to refute his theories. Possibly the tranquility of the early June morning had disarmed me. Or perhaps I subconsciously detected the need to think about his claims more fully before rejecting Finchley's hypothesis.

The morning was bright but with small clouds billowing in genie shapes, and with just a hint of haze when viewing a distant scene. A blue jay scolded me for entering his territory. One small metallic-green dragonfly was developing an obsession with the tip of my fly rod.

The Condor and Grizzly Inheritance was originally published in Flyfishing under the title ''The Condor and Grizzly''. It is reprinted here by the kind permission of the publisher, Frank Amato Publications.

I sat on a fallen tree trunk near the upper reaches of our club water about 12:30 p.m. After consuming a sandwich and packing a pipe it seemed an appropriate time to examine Finchley's latest product from the vise. I must confess to confidence in the non-esoteric and established fish-producing artificials of the season. Not for me the unexplored—except in the realm of streamers. The old Quill Gordon, March Brown, and Hendrickson offer me sufficient challenge at the tying table. Perhaps as the Bard put it so neatly four or five centuries ago, the fault does not lie in the stars but in myself. Or words to that effect. At any rate because there was a small backwater near my feet, I casually dropped one of Finchley's unattached Condor and Grizzly patterns into the water. My curiosity was piqued about how this dry fly would float on the film. The fly landed on its feet or grizzly hackle, and then settled onto the forked Badger hair tails. I noted that the tails were longer than usual and tilted down slightly. The fly floated high enough to keep the bend of the hook out of the water.

Then my attention was diverted from observing the floating fly by movement downstream. And I saw Wilson moving quietly up-water at river's edge. Watching Wilson, and noting the absence of a petty contriving for technique, one instinctively knew that he had been doing this for a long time. It's a strange world I reflected, we are currently being invaded by the technique-oriented specialists. But here is a fly fisher whose casting is endowed with ease and grace. Nothing could have appeared more unrehearsed. Wilson projected the image of having been born to it all.

Returning my attention to the little backwater eddy I observed Finchley's fly escaping into the mainstream current of water where, slowly at first, the current began to exert its swift influence on the fly. It moved with increasing speed downstream paralleling the bank. Thinking that Wilson would be able to retrieve the Condor and Grizzly I was about to hail him when the fly disappeared in a swirl created downstream. I saw the farewell wave of the tail of a fish crest the surface of the water.

Wilson waded upstream and eased onto a log at water's edge. He had observed the rise to Finchley's fly but was not aware of the background and details. I extracted a second Condor and Grizzly from my fly box and gave it to Wilson while updating him about Finchley's latest claims.

Wilson looked closely at the fly. "The hackle is oversized," he commented, "and the twin tails longer than normal. And the Condor barbule makes for a very realistic mayfly body," Wilson added.

"And they come in high," I said.

"They what . . . oh yes; I see what you mean," Wilson laughed. "Were there any further claims for this style of dry fly dressing?"

I repeated Finchley's theory about the hardness or relative softness of food in the trout's diet.

There was the beginning of an afternoon rise now obvious upstream. Three trout were working at the surface of a pool about forty feet above our location at streamside. Two of the fish appeared to be ten or twelve inches long. But the trout that was feeding near the juncture of a small but steady-flowing spring entrance to the main river looked more substantial. The rise forms were of the suction variety with a residue of small bubbles. The water was deep and of quiet character at that location on the stream surface.

Wilson, at my suggestion, tyed a Condor and Grizzly to his tippet. I watched him wade quietly to a position mid-stream where his backcast would clear the trees. Wilson studied the large trout rising upstream for, what seemed to me, an inordinately long time.

He is lying below the surface and drifting back with the food to examine it closely," Wilson remarked. "This fish is not swimming directly up to the fly," he added.

I watched Wilson wipe the last two feet of his leader clean so that it would not lie on top of the surface film. Releasing line slowly and keeping the tip of his fly rod to the side in order to keep a low profile with the rod he began to cast and slowly release line. Each cast placed the fly approximately one foot further upstream. Wilson did not false cast to dry the fly. The trout took the Condor and Grizzly on the fourth cast. Wilson positioned the rod to one side, rod tip about one foot above the surface of the water and then tightened-up to set the hook. The trout began to bore upstream with a steady and dogged determination. Suddenly the fish changed direction 90^{0} to the left and surfaced. I say 'he' because I caught a glimpse of the hooked jaw. I also noted the long wide flank and enormous tail. There was a wave of water the like of which I have rarely observed in fresh water fishing. Wilson's reel steadily released line and he began to wade upstream—following the trout.

About twenty yards above the location where the trout rose, a little riffle spilled between a large boulder on the left bank, and an abutment of rock on the right bank. Just downstream of the rocky abutment on the right bank there is an over-hanging ledge of no small proportion. The water is deep here—perhaps twelve to sixteen feet. It is also shaded on this side of the stream bank by coniferous growth, much of which growth overhangs the top of the high bank.

The trout turned and headed for this deep and sun-protected pool. Wilson managed to retrieve the backing and considerable of the fly line.

It seemed appropriate for me to walk through the trees away from the north side of the stream. I knew that Wilson would not object to my watching the play. But I made certain not to distract his attention from this trout. I sat quietly on the bank, some distance behind my companion, and unsnapped the flap on the camera's protective case.

The fish sought depth in the pool. This move by the trout enabled Wilson to retrieve more of the fly line as he waded to a more appropriate position.

I glanced at my watch. It was 1:49 p.m. Wilson's rod remained in a static arc. As accurately as I could observe, the line was not moving in any direction. I leaned back and settled to a more comfortable position.

A porcupine revealed his presence by changing position on the left bank about fifty feet upstream. A Queen Bee made overtures to the toe of my left wading boot. Bugs made soft summer sounds.

Wilson had braced his feet for a long battle. I observed him—from time to time—exert a side-pull to see if the trout could be induced to move. And this fish did move occasionally but not more, according to Wilson later, than twelve inches. He was stubborn and dogged in attitude and, who knows, how much he weighed. My watch announced that the time was 2:03 p.m. with a quiet impersonal dignity. And then I heard Wilson's groan of disapproval and observed his rod return to the straight position. He reeled in slowly and, after examining the fly, waded across stream and sat on the bank beside me.

"Take a glimmer at this," Wilson requested, handing me the tippet of his leader.

The barbless hook was almost straight. It was a case of one of those hooks that evades detection by the hook maker and the fly dresser. I muttered some comment to the effect that once again the concept of zero defects failed to recognize that people are not perfect.

"Well," I said, "two down and one to go."

"Two down and what to go?" asked Wilson.

"Two Condor and Grizzlies lost, and one remaining in my fly box," I answered.

"Really," replied Wilson, "this experiment was interesting. But the evening rise will likely be to March Brown's." Wilson left to return to the cabin and the tying vise to prepare March Brown's for his evening fishing.

With the faint hope of matching Wilson's recent performance I opened my fly box, selected the remaining Condor and Grizzly, and tyed it to a 4X tippet. Wading slowly upstream and surveying a glassy unbroken stretch of water, I began by working the tailwater of the pool. Several casts later an eight inch rainbow greedily attacked the fly and hooked itself. I could not, I suppose, expect a repeat performance. But in the process of dreaming about another spectacular fish I allowed this little fellow full rein. It was—to put it mildly—a mistake. I knew that the log was there. And I was reminded about the deadfall after he wound my leader through some branches mid-way along the underwater obstruction. I finally had to break off and, in the process, lost the third Condor and Grizzly. Three strikes and you are out, I chided myself.

There were no rises now and I therefore changed the reel spool to facilitate use of a sink-tip line and tyed a nymph to the tippet. For about half an hour I continued upstream, half concentrating on fishing, casting mechanically, and reminiscing about the loss of Wilson's giant brown trout. It would be wise to start back to the city a little early, I decided, and avoid the traffic.

Arriving back at the cabin I disjointed, wiped, and packed my rod. And there was Wilson, visible through the front window, hunched over the tying vise. The expression on Wilson's face resembled that of a Bulgarian Werewolf.

I entered the cabin to collect a few unmentionables. "Leaving now," I announced, "see you next weekend."

"Fine," Wilson replied absently. "These tails are too short."

"What are you tying?" I asked, easing open the screen door on my way out.

"Oh, er, I thought that I would er try my hand at a Condor and Grizzly," admitted Wilson sheepishly.

"Be careful," I remarked in a cautioning tone. "Remember, they come in high." The spring tension on the screen door protected me from a well-aimed damp wading sock.

I walked through the reddish glow of the late afternoon sun to the car parked beside the old sand road.

CHAPTER 10

The Hackle Fiber Spinner

It was early evening when a brook trout slashed at the spinner in the fast water of the small stream in the Wilderness Lake area of Northern Ontario.

During 1972 I made a pilgrimage to Alexander Lake, Northwest of Temagami, Ontario, to flyfish for the Aurora Trout. The Aurora is a color variant of the brook trout, and it represents a unique fish that, until recently, was presumed to be extinct.

Fishing the small river during the journey had proved an interesting sidelight. The trout fought bravely in the fast water, its resistance highlighted by leaps and surface splashing. I gently released the fish from the linen net, and removed the rotunda spinner with its reddish-brown body and hyaline wing which offers the challenge of imitation for the fly dresser.

It was June 3 according to my fishing diary, and time to keep an appointment with Dr. George Hale during the following three days at the club water in Québec.

I had dressed a round dozen of E. rotunda spinners in preparation for the fast water stream in La Belle Provence. Experience has confirmed the appetite which trout have for the six-sixteenth inch mayfly body when the spinner fall occurs.

Memories of flyfishing are as bright as a riffle over pale sun-washed gravel. Such memories recall past years hatches of Ephemerella rotunda. Its nymphs are found in the fast-water areas of the stream. My guest at the Arundel, Québec club water remarked about the many long, glassy-surface type pools. And I replied by recounting memories about the difficulty of observing the fully spent spinners on the water; particularly during twilight. Success in anticipating the spinners generally depends upon estimating how long their molting will last in the bordering streamside vegetation. The hatch of these graceful flies had been prolific during the past two days.

There are also memories of rewarding evenings in the West on the Railroad Ranch stretch with this pattern — but dressed on a size twenty up-eye hook. The size twenty version of the Ephemerella rotunda was eagerly accepted by trout of twelve to fifteen inches during July.

My guest's fly box contained the described imitation of the spinner which we have found productive. The major challenge is to imitate the translucency and/or light pattern of the natural wing. And, if possible, to dress an imitation which approximates the delicacy of the E. rotunda.

We proceeded along the barely discernible path which borders part of the stream. There were wildflowers along the grassy verge of the river, and nuptial swarms of mayflies were in evidence. The spring air had that chill which you are never really conscious of when you are involved in this engrossing sport.

Fly patterns which have been found to be productive are best when shared. If you have occasion to fish the imago of this mayfly, I think you will find this pattern productive when the spinner of E. rotunda is the trout's diet of the moment.

Before describing the procedure I employ for dressing this delicate three-quarter spent wing mayfly, I should emphasize that this pattern is particularly appropriate for quiet flats and glides. I frequently observe the slow and deliberate rise of the trout to these spinners, and considerable of the trout's feeding occurs in the pools and glides on the stream.

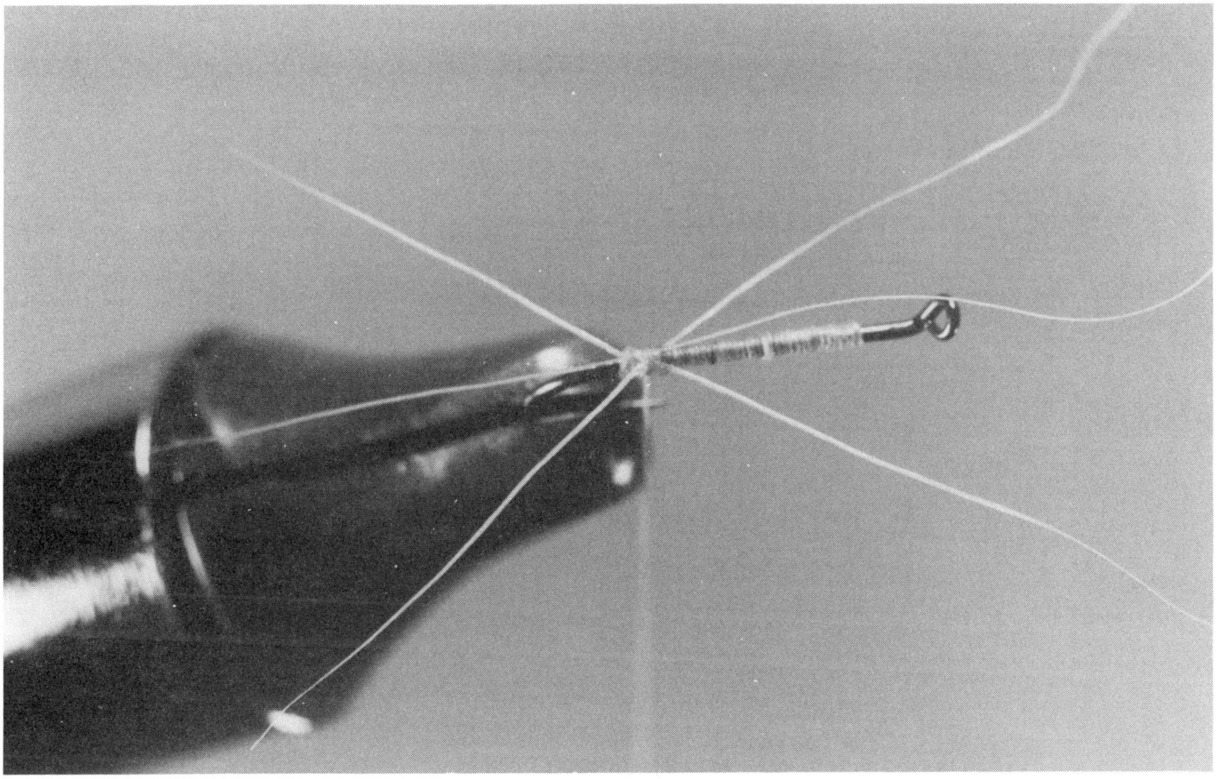

STEP 1 Illustrates a size 14 fine wire hook in the vise with three 15 mm. tails mounted as shown. Three polar bear hairs have been selected in which the tips are straight, and each tail has been mounted separately. An up-eye hook has been chosen because if the hook-eye penetrates the surface film, it may distort the light pattern as perceived by the trout. The tying thread is started one-eighth inch behind the eye of the hook.

There are dressers of flies who prefer to commence by mounting the wings. My experience, however, is such that when the wings have been set on a small hook, and the tail assembly follows, quite often the wings will be moved, before the spot of varnish dries because of accidental contact by hand or finger while mounting the tails as a second operation.

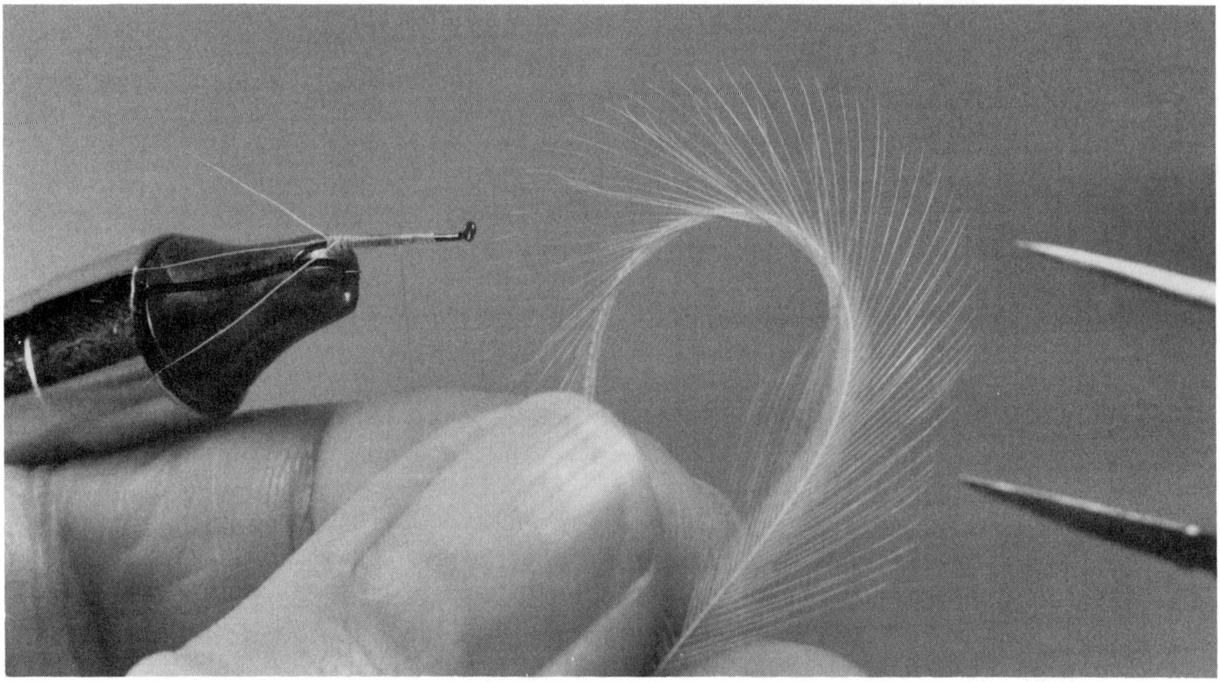

STEP 2 The excess polar bear hair has been removed at the tie-in position. Wood duck flank feather or spade hackle for the tails do not contribute as effectively as polar bear hairs for the purpose of floating the fly consistently in the film. The tying thread has been advanced to the position shown.

In order to imitate the iridescence and amber tint of the natural wing select a sandy dun cock hackle on which the fibers (barbs) are STIFF. I cannot overemphasize the need for stiffness for this application. There have been two occasions when I have used spade hackle for this fiber spinner wing; realizing about one and one-half turns around the hook shank for each spade hackle. The result was a finished wing, which while not very dense, stood-up admirably and took a number of trout.

The sandy dun hackle should not be too tapered, and should include a large number of barbs of the same length; in this case 12–13 mms. This is not difficult to realize because, for one, the lower third of the hackle is removed. This serves to eliminate the softer (webbier) fiber, and provides for winding a thinner part of the quill around the shank of the hook. In this step I have opened the selected hackle in my fingers, and set the dividers (a very useful tool for fly dressing) at 13 mms. You can see that there is a considerable length of fine quill with fibers of the same length. All of these barbs measure 12–13 mms.

STEP 3 It should be emphasized at the beginning of this step that the objective is a three-quarter spent wing design, and not the (usual) full-spent dressing.

Prepare the hackle by removing the lower third which consists of down or flue. This will provide for winding a thinner quill which requires less space on the hook shank. And, consequently, the fibers will adopt a position in which they are more likely to be perpendicular to the shank of the hook. In order to achieve a neat start cut six or seven barbs from the side of the feather quill that leads into the wrap. Leave a tiny length of very short barbs, cut by scissors, to give the tying thread a good grip on the quill. This will help to prevent the hackle from pulling free when the hackle is wound.

Tie in the hackle by the butt, bright side facing the eye of hook, and clip off the excess stem. Make five turns in the direction of the eye of hook so that each turn is as tight as possible against the proceeding turn. Do not overlap these turns of hackle. Wind the balance of the hackle in the center of the five turns. This operation will serve to spread the hackle barbs. I have stopped here to photograph step three so that the viewer will see the results. Note the amount of hackle fiber required to form, in the next step, the delicate wing characteristic of the Ephemerella rotunda spinner.

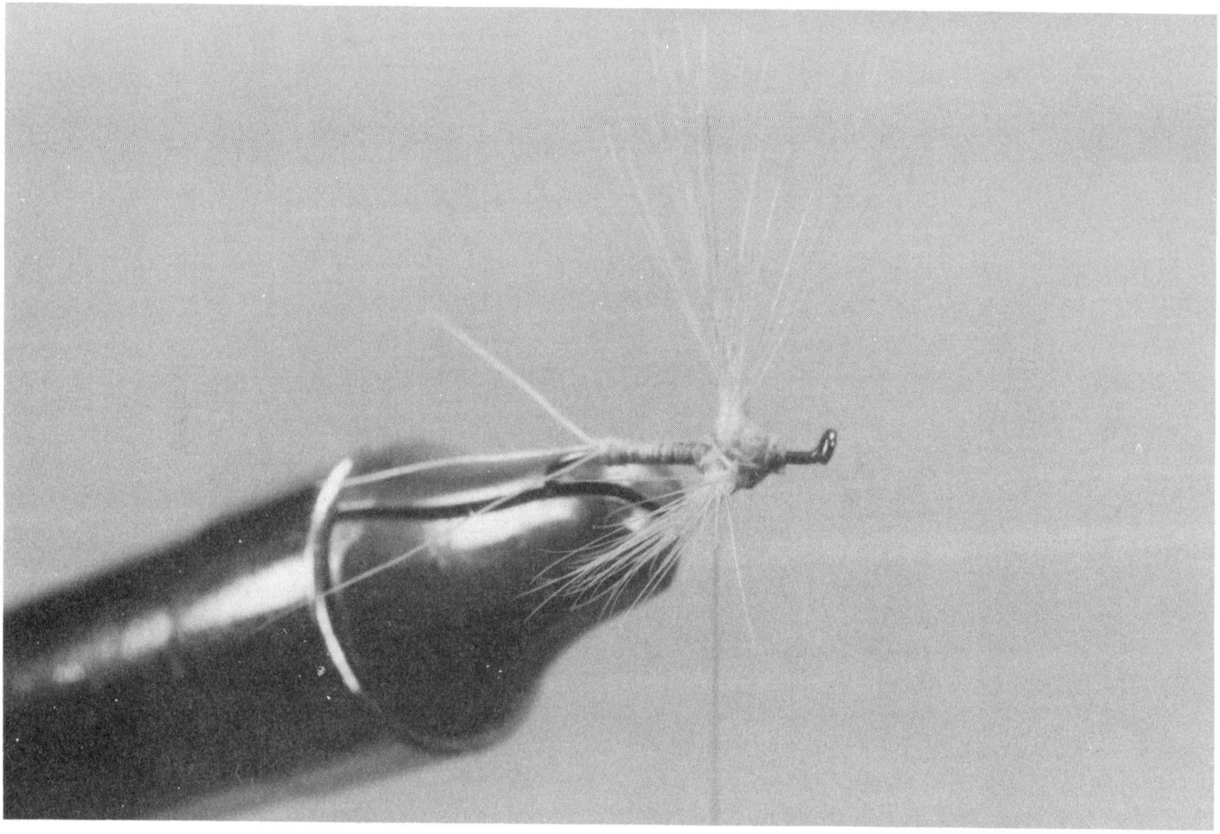

STEP 4 When the hackle is tyed off in the centre of the windings in this step the hackle fibers will spread, because of the method of winding described in the previous step.

Gather one-half of the hackle below the shank of the hook with the tying thread, and reverse direction of thread by passing behind the hackle and then over the top of the hook shank. Raise this mass of fiber to the three-quarter spent position on one side.

Then pick-up the other half of the fibers from the opposite side below the shank of the hook, and carefully raise these barbs to the three-quarter spent position. Now secure with three firm turns of the tying thread, and then divide the top (above hook shank) hackle with X turns, position, and secure at the three-quarter spent position. This operation requires a small amount of practice in order to set a wide flat wing with good hackle fiber separation. Place a tiny drop of cement on the X windings. Note these features and the density of the wing in step four. The result is an amazingly durable wing, light in weight, and capable of transmitting natural light in very much the same pattern as the linear pleats of the natural wing.

STEP 5 Change the tying thread to a medium brown. Dub the body a medium brown with slight reddish tone. One can use light rust-colored mink underfur. During recent years, with the advent of polypropylene fiber and its property of a very low specific gravity, I prefer to dub with this material. If white polypropylene is used for dubbing, the body can be touched up with a permanent marking pen. Pantone Permanent marker No. 181-M will yield a close rendition to the body color of the natural which—to the eyes of some—is chestnut.

A small head, with clear varnish over the brown tying thread, produces a finished head which is very much the shade of the natural spinner.

The accent for this dressing is delicacy. And its design and low weight result in an imitation which will float in the film persistently. I often fish this spinner on a 5X or 6X leader tippet.

SPINNER DRESSING (Ephemerella rotunda)	
Hook:	MUSTAD 94842, size 14 PARTRIDGE L3B Captain Hamilton Up-Eye, Size 14
Thread:	ivory 6/0 and brown 6/0 in that order
Body:	underfur of mink, dyed a rust color (reddish brown) or polypropylene dubbing tinted reddish brown.
Wings:	light sandy dun hackle tyed three-quarters spent; 13 mms. long
Tails:	three well spread fine polar bear hairs, or light tan spade hackle barbs; 15 mms.
Head:	clear varnish over brown tying thread

CHAPTER 11

Battenkill Bounty

"Some trout streams are important for their trout, almost all for their beauty, a few for their associations and memories."[1]
from *Upstream and Down* by Howard T. Walden 2nd

We had almost finished dinner with George, Melanie, and their daughter Megan. "You should write the story about last year's pilgrimage to the Battenkill for the club paper." George treated himself to another helping of Lasagna Verde.

I sampled a little more of the Chianti and admired the fire in the dining room hearth. The wood coals had burned to a bright tangerine-colored glow. It was warm and pleasant in this room with good friends. Dr. and Mrs. Hale, I reflected, were that special breed which fostered courtesy and friendship, without a hint of apathy about important matters. They were ardent fly fishers and photographers.

It was Melanie who proposed that we have coffee in their hobby room and, after coffee was poured, we watched George work on an unfinished Hendrickson. "You should write last year's Battenkill experience for the club paper." George suggested.

"I am not certain that I can do justice to describing the events of that day," I replied. "It is impossible for me to write about an unbelievable day on the Battenkill and make it sound plausible and acceptable."

"Should you decide to write this story," George responded, "be sure to include the episodes that occurred at the large pool below the place where that cold brook enters the main river. Make certain that you

---

I am thankful that we fished the salmon river together last year which was, it developed, Dr. Hale's last year.

In putting these words on paper I shall try to capture the essence of George's insight and knowledge about hackle. For he was a person who lived each new fly fishing experience with the wonder of a child, the manners of a gentleman, and the inquiring mind of a scientist.

describe the complete scene, including the deep water at the foot of the rock shelf. That deep water was where you took a brown close to sixteen inches on the Algonquin Streamer."

The Battenkill is a storied river where, during early morning, trout often feed greedily on Tricorythodes nymphs. This kind of fishing calls for light weight tackle, and double taper floating 3 and 4 weight lines are suitable when fishing the imitations of these tiny insects on the flats.

The Septophlebia nymph is also worth fishing on the Battenkill during May near Cook's Falls. These heavy gilled nymphs such as the Septophlebia cupida, sometimes referred to as the Early Black Quill, are best imitated on size 14 3X long nymph hooks. I dress this nymph with tails of one-half inch pale woodduck barbs, the body a brownish-black, and imitate the gills with closely wound dark olive marabou. The pronounced gill structure is reinforced with fine gold wire. During recent years I have used a wire called Schurer Art 2702. This extremely fine twisted filament gold wire is enormously strong, does not tarnish, and is identified on the 200 meter spool as "Night Oxydiereno". The L. cupida is completed with a black thorax, brown feather section wing cases, and legs of an olive brownish cast.

I have also fished the nymph successfully on Penn's Creek, and Big Fishing Creek in Pennsylvania.

It is an important hatch, and Melanie Hale had captured two fat brown trout on the Battenkill the previous year by a careful approach near the banks. I admired the technique, and her depth of knowledge about this nymph's habits of emergence, which are sluggish, and include migration to slower currents.

Now, watching Dr. Hale dress the Hendrickson, my thoughts returned to reflection about the many years I have fished the Battenkill. Each Spring I would use one week of vacation and, leaving Montreal, drive the pleasant scenic routes of Vermont. The weekdays were best because of the solitude available on many parts of the river. I frequently fished streamers during the evening until dark. There was a beautifully tied Algonquin Streamer on George Hale's tying bench that evening, and it recalled to mind the classical patterns of the New England region. New England is the genesis of many of the bucktails and streamers. Wil-

---

[1]Reproduced here by the kind permission of Elizabeth W. Hyde and Ernest B. Walden.

liam Edson, Herb Welch, and Carrie Stevens produced classic patterns. Small fish are often the targets of large fish, and the innovators of such streamer flies were well aware of this condition.

But my intent that evening with Dr. Hale centered upon drawing on his extensive background with hackle. George had raised game cocks for several years, and had often commented upon the value of the stiff cock's hackle. I asked him, while he was tying the Hendrickson dun, about this feature of dry fly design.

''My experiments with the floating dun in flowing water,'' George answered, ''indicate that the legs of the dun on the surface film do not appear to the trout as six dots. Rather they produce a pattern of distinct streaks, more often six in number. These streaks or brightly lit ''flowing spots'' resemble tiny lenses, and they magnify the intensity of the light. Clearly these patterns can be seen by the trout on the underside of the surface of the water for some considerable distance. When the trout observes the approaching light pattern, he can move to the right or to the left, as we have frequently seen, and intercept the food form. If the trout is concentrating on a particular pattern of light on a very smooth water surface, he has the time to let the floater enter his window where he will have sufficient time for visual inspection before acceptance or rejection. The fast current forces the trout to rise to the light pattern, very often without inspection, before it reaches his window. This, in my view, is why the color of a food form which is riding a heavily disturbed surface film, fly tying aesthetics aside, is often unimportant to the trout.''

George had now positioned the tails, made from spade hackle, to his preferred location on the Hendrickson. The forked tails had been split at almost a right angle to the shank of the hook in order to achieve maximum spread. I recognized the reason for this design. Repeated pickups of the fly force the tails backwards and thereby considerably reduce the spread, as Vince Marinaro so correctly asserted in his superb book, *In the Ring of the Rise*.

''How do you measure the quality of a dry fly cape?'' I asked. ''And what constitutes quality insofar as imitating the floating dun?''

''The stiffness of the barbs is of vital importance.'' George stated. ''Of equal importance are the number of barbs per centimeter or inch. A fly prepared, or wound, with a hackle which has a large number of barbs per inch will result in a larger number of support points on the surface of the water. Remember that a fine quill or center stem is desirable. Aside from disposing of the lower third of the hackle feather for reasons of soft material and web, you will be left with the thinnest portion of the center quill for the purpose of winding the hackle. Good hackles also have a luster and resilience to the barbs like the Metz and Hebert genetic capes you are now inspecting. I noted these same excellent qualities in the Pardo hackles you received from Spain, through the efforts of your friend, Dr. Angelo Droetto, of Genova, Italy. During my experience as a serious breeder I was concerned about hackle shape. Good shape and stiffness usually go together. It is the web and the length of the barbs which governs the shape of a hackle."

I watched while he selected two exactly matched hackles, removed the bottom third, and tied them in with the dull side facing out. He then wound the quill of the first hackle close together with the dull side facing the hook eye, tying off on the underside. Gripping the second hackle with the hackle pliers he made one turn against the rear of the first hackle, working the second hackle through the first one by moving the hackle pliers back and forth (from side to side). The result was a beautifully hackled fly characterized by barbs which flared at a right angle to the hook shank. The medium blue dun rooster hackle used for this fly in the vise prompted me to ask about what colors of hackle fly tyers should possess.

"Brown, grizzly, ginger, light ginger, black, and blue dun are essential." George replied. "Try to select a cape, or hackles, which have a quill that is flexible enough to be wound without twisting. Choose a neck which has a range of feathers for the hook sizes you tie. It is no longer true that wild birds produce the best dry fly hackle. Quality hackles are obtained by genetic breeding, which produce the kind of overall good quality features that we require for fly tying. The blue dun cape is of exceptional interest to the fly tyer because of the variety of shades. My breeding experiments resulted in medium to dark shades, and some capes were a medium greyish-blue with a light brown overtone. No two capes were exactly alike. There was, at the very least, a subtle difference in shade. A very dark blue dun can be close to black, however, the dark blue dun which is close to black will almost always have stiffer barbs, and less webb than a true black. Really outstanding black dry fly necks, like rusty blue duns, are difficult to find. If you should find a rusty blue dun cape you will be very fortunate. They are characterized by a sprinkling of rusty spots on top of the blue. They are very rare and very beautiful.

Hen hackles, saddles, and spade hackle should also be in your collection of materials. The hen's hackle for wet flies, and saddle hackles of various colors for streamers and salmon flies. Spade hackle is good for tailing dry flies and if offers an infinite variety of colors. I must admit, however, that synthetic Microfibbets are superior when used for the tails of dry flies, where the fly design calls for tail support of the fly on the water."

Dr. Hale removed the completed Hendrickson from the vise. "Your turn Megan," he prompted, and we watched the young lady while she skillfully dressed an Algonquin Streamer.

As we finished our coffee I reflected upon the tumbling music of the Battenkill. The river is not unlike many other great rivers of North America. There is a need for the nymph, caddis, the dry fly, and the streamer. All have their time and place in order to meet the challenge of the trout. Since that evening at the Hale's I continue to use the Algonquin Streamer. Perhaps it is not more productive than some other streamers, however, it has produced exceptionally. And I have made only two modifications to the original dressing during the past twelve years. I refer to the addition of a bright gold tag and a wing topping. The fly has proved useful for brown trout, and it has produced some fine catches on the Battenkill.

This year in Algonquin Park it took more than its share of black bass. Nearly all of the bass were released. The following are the recommended materials and construction steps for the Algonquin Streamer.

Hook:	SEALEY 1734-B size 6 6X long or, MUSTAD 9575 size 6 or, MUSTAD 3665A 4X long
Tag:	flat gold tinsel—medium
Tail:	golden-pheasant crest
Body:	black rayon floss
Ribbing:	flat gold tinsel—medium
Throat:	english grouse feather
Wing:	ginger deer hair
Topping:	Crystal Hair™ CHO4 (yellow).

STEP 1 Position hook in vise and hone point, if necessary, to sharpen. Commence working (gray) thread and tie in the tinsel (for tag) at position illustrated. Complete tag and set golden pheasant tail crest as illustrated.

STEP 2 Ensure pheasant tail crest is secure and tie in tinsel body ribbing. Then wind working nylon forward and tie in black body floss at the location shown. Remove excess ends of pheasant tail crest.

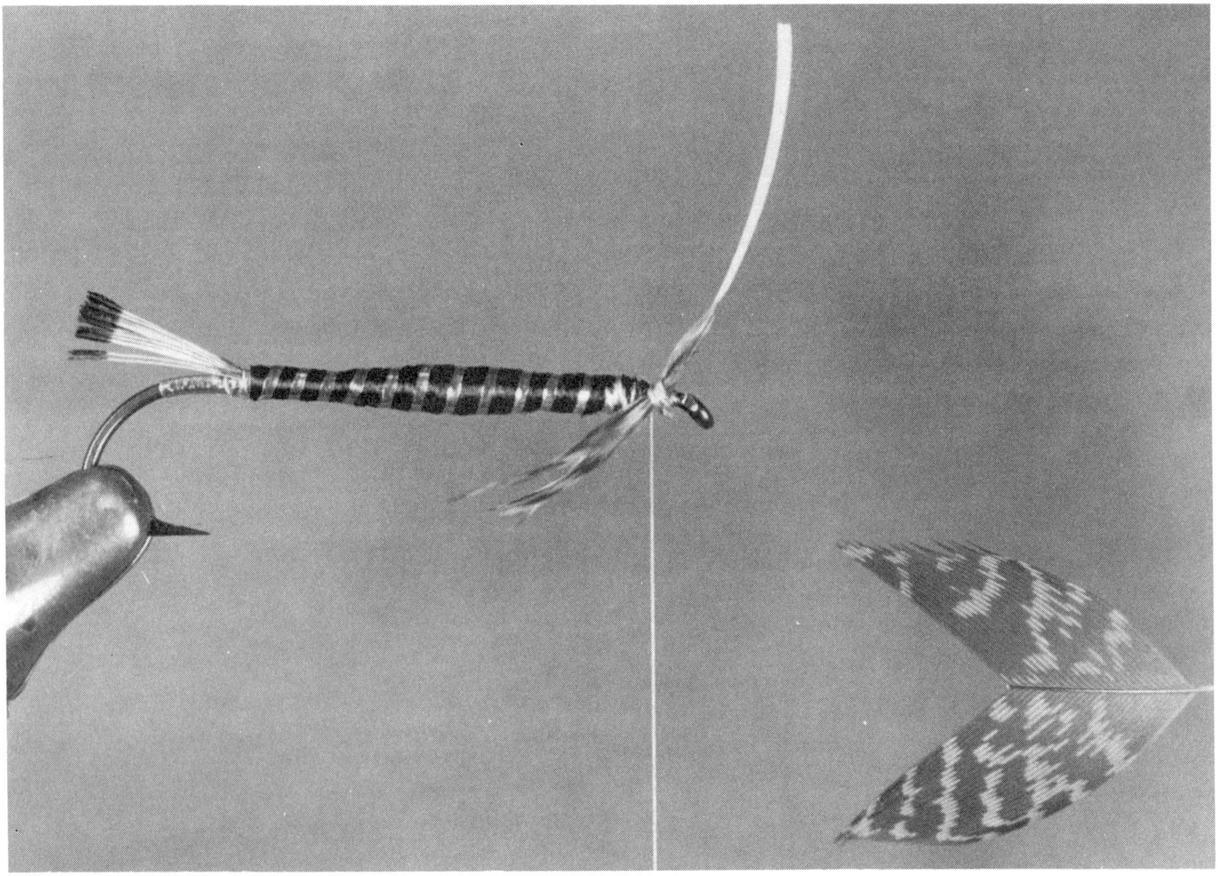

STEP 3 Wind body floss and taper as shown. Then wind body tinsel forward and tie-off. The lower right-hand corner of the film frame illustrates a prepared Grouse feather section. Note the light mottling of the feather which is now secured at the location shown.

STEP 4 Remove excess floss and tinsel. Mount deer hair wing to length indicated. Five or six strands of Crystal Hair are now applied as wing topping.

STEP 5 Clip off excess deer hair and Crystal Hair ends. Form head to profile illustrated and apply clear varnish or cement to complete.

As this pattern developed over the years I discovered that "short takes" were largely eliminated by fixing the wing so that it does not extend very much beyond the hook bend.

CHAPTER 12

The Golden Shiner
(Notemigonus crysoleucas)

The galaxy of bait-fish patterns have been widely used by North American anglers since the turn of the century. Some historians assert that bucktails have their genesis in the Bumblepuppy patterns developed by Theodore Gordon on the Neversink in 1880. It is certain that the Scripture Bucktail was developed prior to 1990. William Scripture often dressed his bucktails with a down-wing, tight along the top of the hook shank. Paul Young tied a split-wing bucktail for use on Michigan rivers about 1924.

Bucktails produced superbly on the watershed of the coast of the Pacific, and continue to do so today. The original fly patterns developed by Jim Pray, Gary Howells, and Polly Rosborough are now American classics. These flies are often effective for large trout, bass, pike, and pickerel. In my experience large fish which attack bait-fish are often defending their holding lie or territorial section of a stream. The shared motive is plain simple hunger. The proof of such hunger lies in the result of autopsies on the stomach contents of large Labrador brook trout, which frequently contain bait-fish. Labrador waters are not always treated to hatches of Litobrancha recurvata subimagos, a (realistic) fly dressing of which the dun is illustrated in the color plates.

During the past forty years some of the bright colorful patterns have given way to less ornate dressings which seek to imitate bait-fish which exist in the specific waters being fished by fly anglers. The Muddler Minnow may be the best known development of this kind of expert craftsmanship, as it imitates the sculpins and madtoms of many American rivers.

I am reasonably certain that it was the hair-wing salmon fly which influenced my preference for the hair-wing streamer fly in the lakes of the Laurentians and the Adirondacks of New York State. Many lakes support Golden Shiner minnows (the correct term is bait-fish; a member of the family Cyprinidae). Very often these same lakes contain black bass. That magnificent gamefish is strongly attracted to the streamer fly. Experiences with the Micropterus dolomieu (small mouth) further suggest that the presence of rocky shoals with deadfalls as natural cover, and an imitation of the natural food form combine to yield above average success. I prefer, as do many persons, to use a seven weight or eight weight rod/line, and a nine foot leader with a tippet of approximately five pounds test. Because I often fly fish for bass during the evening (when the light is decreasing), and on lakes where there is frequently wind, I do not use the barrel knot for attaching the tippet to the end of the leader. A quick, easy, and secure procedure is simply to form a small loop at leader's end, and a small loop at one end of the tippet. Pass the leader loop through the tippet loop and draw the tippet through the leader loop. The two loops, when pulled slowly and firmly, are now interlocked. I prepare some tippets with a loop at one end beforehand. The credit for this innovation belongs to Lefty Kreh who described the technique to me over coffee several years ago. It really is preferable to tying the barrel-knot in a stiff breeze under conditions of very low light.

Because I have found the Golden Shiner imitation to be productive just above the natural cover which bass prefer I carry, and often use, a sink-tip fly line.

The illustrated fly is very lightly weighted. Its sink rate is designed to be about the same rate of speed as a slow sink fly line. This results in a taut or straight line between rod tip and fly. Such a condition is preferable to having too much "belly" in the line because there is a need to set the hook quickly with bass. The Golden Shiner[1] has a flattened body. The head of the natural is long and pointed. It is, of course, not difficult to imitate these features with the (described) dressing. But if we proceed with the view that color is important to the underwater fly, then imitating the color is a different matter. Matching the color is somewhat more challenging because it is necessary to observe the imitation when the fly tying materials are wet and compare the imitation with the natural. It is not difficult to see this bait-fish in the water and compare its appearance with the "finished fly" when the imitation is drawn through the water on a short piece of monofilament. The color is brassy (or golden) with brownish back.

This bait-fish is worth imitating because it is found in virtually all of the Eastern provinces of Canada and many American states.[2] The Golden Shiner is frequently observed to be feeding below the surface in mid-water, or on algae. The dressing described has proved to be very effective for bass. And it was developed with many adjustments to materials during a period of about nine years.

---

[1]Also known as chub, windfish, bream, roach, and butterfish.

[2]*See About Bait-Fish in Ontario* by R.G. Wallace, Biologist, Commercial Fish and Fur Branch, Division of Fish and Wildlife, Ontario Ministry of Natural Resources, 1976.

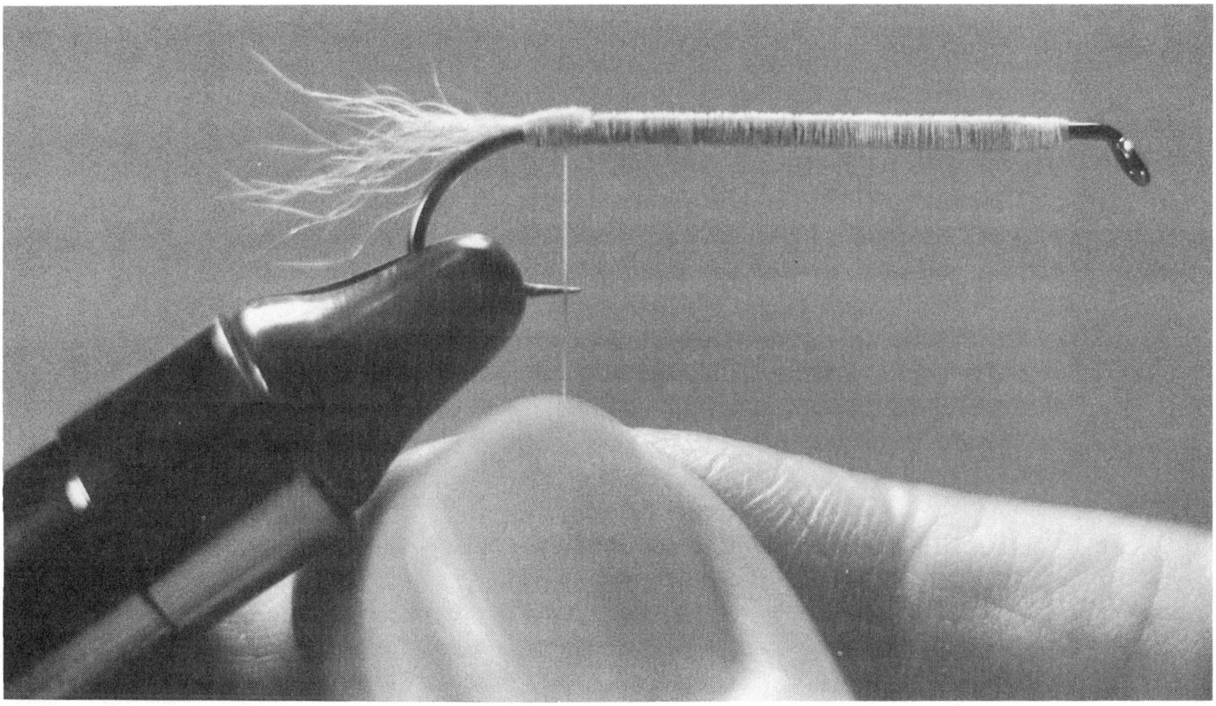

STEP 1 Select a size 4 or 6 6X long streamer fly hook. There are a variety of hooks available, and one should select a hook which has features which ''blend in'' or match the characteristics of the finished fly dressing. Position the hook in the vise and, starting the white tying thread three-sixteenths of one inch from eye of hook, cover the hook shank to the beginning of the hook bend. Now secure a strip of (preferably) flat lead wire about .020 inches thick to the underside of the hook shank. Wrap the tying thread forward and then back to the bend of the hook. Apply a coat of waterproof cement to the thread windings. The tying thread should now be located at the hook bend where a section of light yellow calf-tail hair is positioned and secured. The butts of the calf tail have been cut at an angle (tapered) to achieve a smooth juncture. Apply a small drop of clear cement to the thread windings.

If you observe the completed imitation as it moves through the water, it will be noted that the tail (the caudal fin is yellowish) is more life-like when the calf-tail hairs are dressed with a small application of silicone floatant material. I do this just before fishing the fly by pressing the calf-tail hairs between my fingers to apply the floatant.

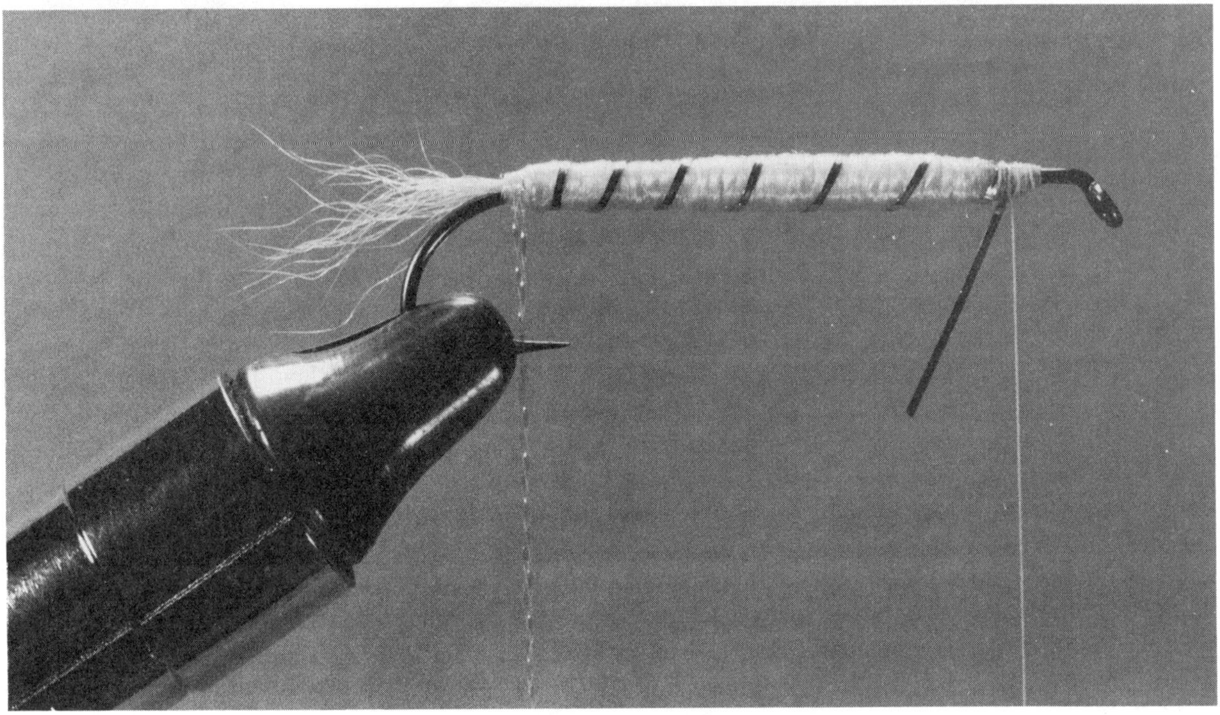

STEP 2 Three kinds of material are now secured at the beginning of the bend of hook. First, a length of unwaxed floss by splitting (or unravelling) the end to achieve a neat non bulky tie-in. Second, a ten-inch length of gold tinsel by advancing the tying thread two or three tight turns which do not overlap one another. And, third, a ten-inch length of CHO4 Crystal Hair which has been doubled and loosely twisted. Advance the tying thread to front end of body location. Contour the body to the illustrated shape with the floss. I use floss which is made from cotton or wool. Both of these materials are hygroscopic (they have the ability to absorb and retain moisture), and aid with sinking the fly. Tie-off the floss at the front and remove the excess floss. Now segment the floss body with the tinsel with turns which are progressively wider, proceeding from the rear to the front of the tapered body. The spirals of tinsel will not slip if no extra turns of the tinsel are used at the beginning and the end of the segmenting operation. The Crystal Hair remains hanging at the rear of the body.

Apply one brushcoat of fine clear varnish to the body.

STEP 3 Clip off excess tinsel. Apply a second coat of clear varnish to floss and tinsel on hook shank. Before the varnish dries spiral the Crystal Hair towards hook eye by winding between the spirals of tinsel. This material, applied with tension, will imbed itself in the floss. The body now reflects a golden or brassy hue. Remove the excess Crystal Hair.

The tying thread is still located three-sixteenths of one inch from the eye of hook. And it is at this location that a medium sized bunch of natural polar bear hair is secured to the length shown. The hair-wing material butts are later cut at a slant to allow the material to be layered by the tying thread. This technique for construction has, as one purpose, the goal of a longer, slimmer, pointed head; a characteristic of the natural. The polar bear hair-wing should extend to the end of the bend of hook. When this wing is secured, raise it slightly with two turns of tying thread around the base of the hairs. Then make two more turns with the thread in the usual manner. Remove the excess hair which extends toward the eye of hook, cutting it so as to create a steep, downward angle. This procedure will assist in facilitating the long pointed head. Tie in a few strands of CHO4 Crystal Hair (the same length as the polar bear hair) on top of the polar bear hair. This material is topped by a small bunch of brown bucktail—about the bulk of a wood match. The bucktail hairs are three-quarters the length of the polar bear hairs. The Golden Shiner has a brownish back and brassy sides. Step 3 illustrates the length of the winging materials. Note the space for length of head.

STEP 4 Trim, with small needle point scissors, the butt ends of the remaining winging material from the position where the head will be located. Mount and secure the jungle cock eyes at the location shown. When I first began to use this pattern during the Autumn of 1979, the jungle cock eyes were mounted in line with the body. During 1985 I discovered that the wing action was improved by fixing the eyes against the edge of the wing. This resulted in more accent in water for the rear portion of the wing. This design also results in improved visibility of the body and, therefore, a better ''flash of gold''. The stripped quills of the eyes extend forward, and are locked in under the long tapered head. It is a simple operation to mount the throat feather at this time. Because the underside of the head of this bait-fish is grayish-white, I use a grayish-white feather, of the size illustrated, which

also represents the gill color of the natural bait-fish. The lower (plain) portion of the Amherst tippet neck feather is ideal for this component. This portion of the shoulder is mounted so that the Amherst neck feather aims at the barb of the hook. It extends slightly rearward of the jungle cock eyes.

If the profile of the relatively long and pointed head is to be represented by this streamer fly it is wise, when securing the eyes and throat feather, to give attention to each turn of tying thread. in this manner the head of the fly, when varnished white, completes the operation to produce the Golden Shiner imitation.

This shiner may be the most popular bait-fish in North America. Culturing of the Golden Shiner has been successful in many American states, and in ponds in the Province of Ontario, Canada.

When fishing this bait-fish, the natural of which the author has been observing for about forty years, I retrieve the pattern in not too rapid increments of approximately ten or twelve inches. Then a pause prior to the next move. This technique may be accomplished by retrieval against the current when stream fishing.

The Golden Shiner was developed as an imitative food-form. It is sized to a scale which imitates the average growth of the species. The pattern may be dressed slightly larger for use on big brawling waters where this shiner has measured as long as 4.5 inches. Clear weedy lakes with extensive shallow areas are prime habitat for this bait-fish. The spawning season commences during June in water about 70 degrees F. and lasts several weeks (in Michigan June to August, and in New York State May to July). The rate of growth varies considerably, and depends upon temperature and the availability of food. Most golden shiners, however, may be expected to mature at approximately 3 inches.

On days when there is nothing hatching, large trout will sometimes roam the shallows in search of bait-fish. It is often at this time when the darting rhythm of the imitative bait-fish is worked across the current, that the value of fishing the streamer fly will excite you and prove to be rewarding.

THE GOLDEN SHINER

Hooks:	PARTRIDGE bucktail/streamer (D4A) hook or, Size 2 or 4 6X long ''MUSTAD STINGER'' hook, or PARTRIDGE Trevor Housey Dog Knobbler (K9A) L/S hook
Weight:	srip of .020 flat lead wire lashed to underside of hook shank
Thread:	white or straw
Body and Rib:	gold tinsel over unwaxed (find) dental floss, or white cotton or wool floss
Second Body Ribbing:	CHO4 Crystal Hair
Tail:	yellow calftail
Wing:	natural polar bear hair and strands of CHO4 Crystal Hair
Overwing:	natural brown bucktail
Throat:	small gray-white feather
Head/Throat:	white varnish and jungle cock eyes

CHAPTER 13

A Creelfull of Rain

The sky was old. Strong gusts of wind turned the leaves at streamside and, in the flashes of lightening, the oak leaves resembled Chinese lanterns swinging in the wind.

It had rained relentlessly during the Friday evening drive on highway eleven. The rain tapered off to a drizzle by the time I arrived at the cabin on the club water. After transferring supplies from car trunk to camp the rain stopped, and I rigged up, walked to the stream, and began working a stonefly nymph well down in the deeper pools. But now the storm was spattering large drops of rain again. Lightening flashed in forks which appeared to be signalling personal attack. It occurred to me that I was inviting one of two dangers; pneumonia or electrocution. Now the unctuous bowing of trees weighted by wind. The water was high and roily. There were no rises and the one light tug-and-release I experienced on the upper water was to a size ten Black Ghost streamer. The trees rustled, giving off the scent of resin as the wind increased in tempo. The rain swept-in heavy and on cue with a bang of thunder. Wading ashore I found the footpath through the dense growth of maple trees and headed for camp. The sweep of car headlights could be seen through the trees as I approached the cabin. It was the Friday evening arrival of Forsythe. I hoped that he had remembered his commitment to bring the oil for the lamps, and the fly repellent.

For some years I have been disposed to avoid this account about conditions which are integral to the milieu of the fly fisher. But events which include Forsythe seem to precipitate episodes which constitute a candid profile about fly fishing. First, however, I should request that you do not accept certain material set forth here as criticism of Forsythe. For aside from a propensity to "borrow" my pipe tobacco, some inclination to drastic measures, and the constant ability to misplace essentials such as fly repellent, no finer chap has cast a fly line. Forsythe was a gentleman in a world which appears to have decreasing use for a gentleman. He was also an anachronism of our time; a non-complainer.

According to Forsythe it was not going to rain this weekend. The pronouncement was made in contradiction to the latest data from the Weather Office. As usual Forsythe marketed the concept of idyllic conditions on-stream for the week-end. "It will clear during the night" Forsythe announced with all of the panache of the practiced optimist.

As I awaited sleep in the top bunk across the room from Forsythe I remember listening to a vivid account about the interpretation of barometric pressures, moon phases, wind direction, cloud streaks, et all until, mercifully, sleep clasped me to her bosom.

I awakened Saturday morning to a dull gray light and a harmony of rain drumming on the windows of the cabin. The whine of attacking mosquitoes was partly obscured by the noise of the rain. Rarely does one appreciate a surplus of mosquitoes so fully as when descending from a top bunk. They get you when your clothing is scanty. And as the intensity of the light increases so, it seems, does the frequency of attack during mid-May. I could not locate the fly repellent. And so I settled for the addition of two more logs on the fire.

Whoosh, whoosh I detected and, sure enough, through the front window of the cabin facing the stream I observed Forsythe approaching the Home Pool. He was using the soft whippy fly rod. You know, wide loop and more of a fishing tool than a casting tool. If this sounds like a value judgement allow me to add that Forsythe was presenting the fly with delicacy. There was small delicacy however about Forsythe's opening statement as, drenched with rain, he entered the front door. "We have to obtain some dynamite," he announced.

"You are an extraordinary fellow," I replied. "The stonefly imitations that you have been using should produce in this water."

"I am not referring to the trout," countered Forsythe, eyeing the scrambled eggs with obvious satisfaction. "The water downstream is lower than it should be because the beavers have repaired their dam upstream below the forks of the river." Forsythe accentuated this last remark by sweeping a hand in the general upstream direction and grasping a homemade corn muffin as his hand returned. "We should blow the dam as soon as possible," he concluded.

"Sit down, have breakfast, and we can discuss the matter over coffee," I offered. Following some discussion Forsythe finally agreed that the beaver dam would not be detonated. I explained that the sudden rush of water would cause the release of silt. And the silt could settle on redd's with a possible disastrous result prior to the hatching of new trout. He further agreed that we would dismantle the beaver dam by small increments during June. And obtain the services of a skilled trapper in order to cage the beaver and transport the critters out of their location upstream.

That matter being settled I masked a sigh of relief and reflected upon the many years I had fly fished with this man. Forsythe was a chap who possessed an affable disposition and a sense of humour. Black hair, a bushy mustache, brown eyes, and an enquiring mind were also characteristics of Forsythe. He possessed that special ability of large men; the surprising capacity to move quickly. I had learned to respect his skills at identifying hatches and his ability to match the hatch at the fly tying vise.

And now as he divided the last corn muffin between us I found myself listening to a narrative about why he had forgotten to purchase a fishing license. The story was a familiar one to me because I had made the acquaintanceship of Forsythe many years before under conditions which involved a misplaced fishing license. I remembered that he had taken a risk in fishing at that time, and he eventually purchased a license on the return journey to Montreal.

''Take a drive over to Arundel,'' I suggested. ''The general store and post office issue fishing licenses. Eddie Graham will supply you with a license and the fly repellent which you seem to have forgotten or misplaced.'' Forsythe's answer was a nod of approval as he extracted a tin of my pipe tobacco from his pocket.

The rain continued its thunderous roar of applause. Forsythe began to describe the Spring fly fishing he had recently experienced in New York State. While residing near Phoenicia for a few days he had fished the Stony Clove for spring rainbows just below the confluence of Warner Creek. ''What imitations proved to be effective?'' I asked.

''The water was a bit murky,'' Forsythe replied. ''But,'' he continued, ''I had some success with size 18 dry's in the faster water. The dry's were dressed with parachute style hackle mounted under the hook shank.'' Forsythe elaborated upon this adventure including all of the attendant beauty of the Catskill's and Route 214. It was his considered opinion that two decades of fishing for Rainbow and Brown Trout proved that Brown Trout = bank, and Rainbow Trout = rapid water. ''Yes, that is it,'' Forsythe concluded with a Solomon like pronouncement. ''The Browns love the bank cover and the Rainbows are almost always found inhabiting the faster water away from the banks.''

''And speaking of trout,'' I replied, ''the only item we will likely capture today is a creelfull of rain.''

Forsythe made a preliminary move to sort fly tying materials in the streamside kit which was his constant companion. Soon he was tying flies and I watched his manual dexterity with admiration.

Morning progressed to afternoon and the intensity of the rain increased. A brief visit to the stream resulted in one take by a wild speckled trout which succeeded in throwing the fly almost at the net. I watched an admirable addition to Sunday breakfast swim confidently away. Looking at the leaden-like surface of the water I had the impression that I was being attacked by molten lava. The level of the water in the stream appeared to be five inches higher than it had been seven hours earlier. I returned to the inviting warmth of the cabin and removed raincoat and hip waders.

''While you were fishing in the Catskills,'' I remarked, ''Vermont was charming me with scenic splendour and trout. There is an idyllic town called Weston and a river runs nearby. The area is a classic example of peaceful New England. An old gristmill rests on the bank of the river. There is a country store and folks gather beside a pot-bellied stove. Jars of candy compete for shelf space with freshly baked loaves of whole wheat bread, dill pickles, maple syrup, and pipe tobacco. I found a winding road which led me to an inn at Weston. It deserves many stars in a reliable guide book. And the inn was refreshing because of its special warmth, excellent home cooking, garden, and superb old elm trees. After a day on-stream one returns for a before-dinner aperitif to the inn's hayloft which has been converted to a bar with fireplace. When you are tired of the city, and I am quickly tiring of cities, it is a special tonic.'' ''Perhaps,'' I continued, ''the paramount ingredient of the tonic is courtesy. The area abounds in courtesy—by any standard. I met a chap the second day I was wading the river. This flyfisher described the natural food in the stream available to the trout. He perused the contents of my fly boxes and made discreet suggestions about specific imitations which proved to have an appeal for the trout. No one seems to be in a hurry. People are more interested in spending time than in saving time. I have made a mental reservation to visit the area again.''

''It sounds magnificent,'' Forsythe concurred, ''but is this rain ever going to stop?''

''We can drive to Arundel and obtain your fishing license,'' I suggested. ''And besides,'' I continued, ''I need pipe tobacco.''

''Forsythe extracted another familiar looking tin of tobacco from his fly fishing vest and proffered the tin to me with an air of special dispensation.

''That tin looks vaguely familiar,'' I remarked. ''I have to deduce that you are not enthusiastic about obtaining your license today."

"I'll obtain the license tomorrow," Forsythe replied. "It looks like we are in for the kind of weekend rain which you described about this time last year in the Singer Reserve."

Forsythe was correct, however, it did not daunt the Singer Reserve trout from attacking a variety of flies. Rarely have I observed trout in such quantity. Reflections about the Singer Company's woodlands stir memories of almost unlimited woods in an area which is close to Montpellier in Québec province. From there, if you possessed a permit to fish, issued and approved by the Singer Sewing Machine Company, you could proceed to the company gate and gain admittance to the Reserve. The area kindles remembrances of wood-scented trails, flushed partridge (pa'tridge if you reside in rural Vermont) deer, and bear.

"Yes," I continued, "I described the rain to you but not the mystery under the elm tree. That weekend at the Singer Reserve is really the experience of the trout under the overhanging elm tree. I watched that fish rising regularly for at least fifteen minutes. But the trout came to my attention by another means. You see I had approached the shore of this particular lake quietly and was surveying the terrain. The Singer Reserve, as you know, contains several trout lakes. The fly fisher working from shore must select a position which accommodates a backcast. The person who is proficient with the rollcast has an advantage. I stood approximately ten feet from that elm tree. And suddenly I realized that you must use your ears as well as your eyes. I heard a 'slurping' sound. I knew that this sound confirmed a surface feeding trout, however, all of my previous experiences with this unique sound had occurred on streams. Here was a fish surface feeding at the shore of a lake under an overhanging elm tree with gourmet abandon. You have style, I reflected. But I had the desire to discover why this trout was feeding on the surface. And so I placed the rod aside, removed my hat, and crept on all fours to a position where I could carefully part the long grass and look over the bank. There was a sharp indentation in the shoreline about four feet wide across the mouth, and the elm tree leaned over this indentation in the bank."

"What was your next move?" enquired Forsythe who had temporarily abandoned the art of dressing flies in order to extract one of his wife's gastronomic creations from the car cooler.

"My next move was to examine two small green worm-like creatures which fell on my forearm out of the tree." "I have never identified this particular dietary source for that trout. But I watched her rise and continually feed, as I stated earlier, for about fifteen minutes. The trout was approximately twenty inches in length. She would rise to this nourishment and then slowly sink four or five inches below the surface, fins sweeping gently. It was a beautiful sight.''

Forsythe mumbled something almost indistinguishable about forgetting to bring the oil for the lamps. I lit two more candles which cast a flickering glow against the cabin walls. Suddenly, in the late afternoon, it had become almost dark. The rain continued its monotone of sound on the pitch roof of the cabin. I placed more wood in the stove. Forsythe was now dressing a streamer fly large enough to present to a baby tuna. ''What was your next affirmative action with this trout?'' Forsythe asked.

''After easing out of the close viewing position I removed my fly fishing vest and found two more of these small green insects on the back of the vest. It was, I think, at that precise moment that I determined to capture this trout. It was no dishonour to kill a few fish in the Reserve. Curiosity about the quantity and kinds of insects that the trout had consumed was paramount. Important, at least, for the purpose of identifying the food form being consumed. First it would be necessary to locate a position from which the cast could be made. I did not anticipate a problem with imitating the insect. There were a number of dressings in my fly box which could be modified to represent a reasonable imitation of this natural worm-like insect. There were, for example, some small flies dressed with green bodies. It would be a simple operation to remove tails, hackle, and wings.''

''I located a casting position about thirty feet from where the trout was surfacing. It would mean a side case, low and parallel with the water, into a space about three feet in height between the surface of the water and the lowest branches of the elm tree. After setting up leader, fly, and positioning myself at the edge of the water I proceeded to cast.''

''What was the result?'' enquired Forsythe, scowling at the rain through the cabin window.

''I hung three flies in the lower tree branches,'' I replied. ''And there were only two dressings remaining in my fly box which were candidates for modification. The trout under the elm tree was proving to be the challenge par excellence! Fortunately Ed Delforge arrived on scene and he immediately asked why I was using a tree for a target. Ed was a superb caster and I requested that he try for this fish. Delforge used a shorter fly rod; about seven and one-half feet. He also reduced the length of his tippet section. I watched him make his first cast short, however, the fly and tippet did enter the space under the tree. His second cast was magnificent. The fly and leader entered the prescribed area with an accuracy which was astonishing.''

''What happened?'' asked Forsythe, pausing in his efforts to negotiate with the cork in a bottle of Hospices de Beaune.

''Nothing for about six seconds,'' I replied. ''And then the line and leader became a straight line. I watched Delforge position the tip of the rod low—just clear of the water. He tightened up on the line. Suddenly the rod bent and there was a tremendous splash beyond the tree. Water sprayed in all directions. The rod throbbed violently and the section of the leader which extended under the tree leapt up into the lower tree branches. Fortunately the leader fell clear. Then the trout plunged for depth. This fish fought with short, hard, sporadic plunges. Delforge eventually led the fish out to deeper water and the struggle continued with the fish seeking increasingly deeper water. This trout made one more attempt to head back under the tree. But Delforge stalled that tactic. We netted the fish and found a place where we could examine her closely. The trout was out of water about twenty seconds by now—but full of life. Delforge had not had to play her for too long because of the heavier leader. We noted that her mouth contained several of these little green insects. You had to assume she was stuffed with them. Delforge looked at me questioningly. Wordlessly I nodded an assent to his unspoken question. We released her and she moved away with surprising agility.''

''You fellows made the right move,'' Forsythe remarked. ''Listen to the noise that rain is making on the roof!''

''Time for dinner,'' I said. ''Do you think that this rain will continue tomorrow?''

''Not a chance,'' Forsythe replied.

The flash of headlights on a rain-drenched window provided a last nudge to my wake-up cycle. It was early; false dawn illustrated the eastern sky. There is an incompatibility about fly fishing and very heavy rain. Light showers do not present the same problems. Fly hatches seem to occur with startling regularity regardless of the temperature of the air. Perhaps, during a heavy and sustained rain, the commotion at the surface of the water inhibits surface feeding. I believe that under conditions of heavy rain trout feed in deeper water. Most of their feeding, for that matter, consists of nymphs, caddis, larvae, stonefly nymphs, and bait fish.

I pulled on some clothes before Wilson entered the cabin. ''The rain is easing off,'' commented Wilson, hanging up his raincoat and adding a log to the fire.

Forsythe came out of the bedroom pulling on a sweater, and announced that he was developing ombrophobia. His bouncy charisma was contagious and extended throughout breakfast.

Looking through the window while filling a pipe I could see that the rain had tapered off to a fine drizzle. Soft shadows fell over the quiet hills. Mist drifted and curled like long eerie fingers searching absently for something lost.

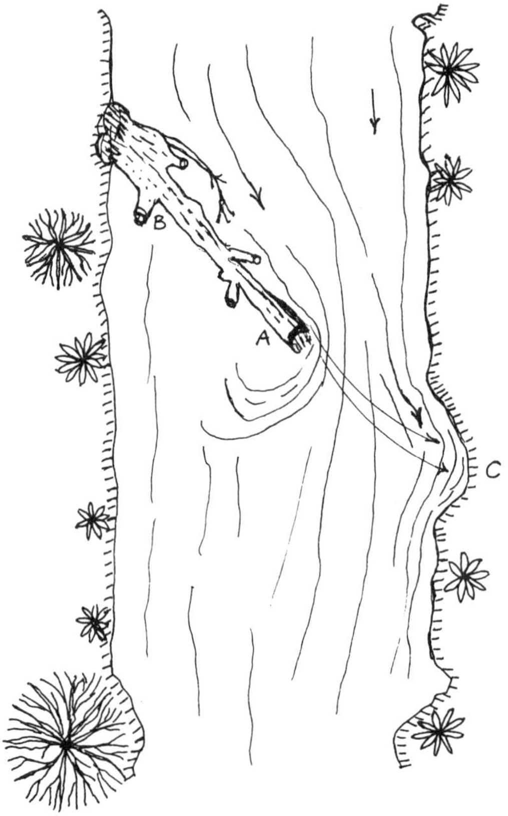

The tree referred to in the story could be a harbour for a trout at "A" or "B," however, the downed tree is a case for stream improvement.

The upstream side of the tree is clearly a catcher of debris.

The current is poorly deflected; witness the erosion of the bank at "C."

This situation, unless corrected, can be a causative factor in forming sand and gravel bars near "C," and downstream of "C."

I selected a nine foot rod for six weight, pulled on waders, a jacket, and walked to the river. I began to ease out line, aiming to position the weighted nymph upstream of a large boulder which broke the water's surface and was surrounded by reeds and the stems of plants. A downed tree in the water made a case for stream improvement. It was during the process of looking up to watch the leader and line straighten before falling to the surface of the water that my eye caught the movement of a silhouette upstream. I looked again; ignoring the cast now. Yes it was definitely the poacher we occasionally observed but could never confront. There he was, up to his fetlocks in the long grass about a hundred and fifty yards upstream. The rain, now approximating a fine mist, shrouded him in the mysterious appearance he traditionally created for us. Three years ago Wilson had dubbed this fellow "The Peerless Poacher." We knew it was Brewster, we knew where he lived and, in fact, were acquainted with two or three of his relatives. Only last year I had given a series of fly casting lessons to Brewster's nine year old granddaughter Holly. I performed this service in spite of her pronouncement that she preferred High Liner to trout. Forsythe summarized his feeling about the poacher nicely when he admitted that "this sly rascal did not harmonize with the pastoral side of his nature." But the matter of Brewster had become a game; a game which spanned many years. We had tried to catch him in the act, only to have him disappear like an elusive pimpernel. He knew the surrounding terrain. We knew that his appetite for trout was sporadic. And so the game continued with the same players. Brewster would not request permission to fish private water. And we, the members, could not catch him in the act of poaching.

I retrieved line slowly to minimize reel noise and waded quietly to shore. This time I would confront the fellow with the thatched-cottage-hairdo and we would have an eyeball-to-eyeball discussion about rules. Brewster's rules and bylaws were unacceptable to the members. I moved quickly and quietly, I hoped, through the cover of a heavily wooded area. At first I did not notice the failing light perhaps because of my travel through dense woods. What was that rushing wind-like roar? I emerged from the densely timbered area into a rain of Monsoon proportion. To make matters worse I discovered that the waterproof hood, usually attached to my rain jacket was missing. Then I remembered that Forsythe had borrowed the hood. Brewster was also missing from the scene. The will-o-wisp of the county had done it again!

I returned, soaking wet, to the cabin. Discarding wet clothes and standing with my back to the fire as I dried my hair, I surveyed the scene before me. Forsythe and Wilson were tying flies—no doubt in anticipation of stellar days to come. The rich aroma of coffee did not escape me.

"Some hot coffee on the stove," said Wilson. "We calculated that you would need it."

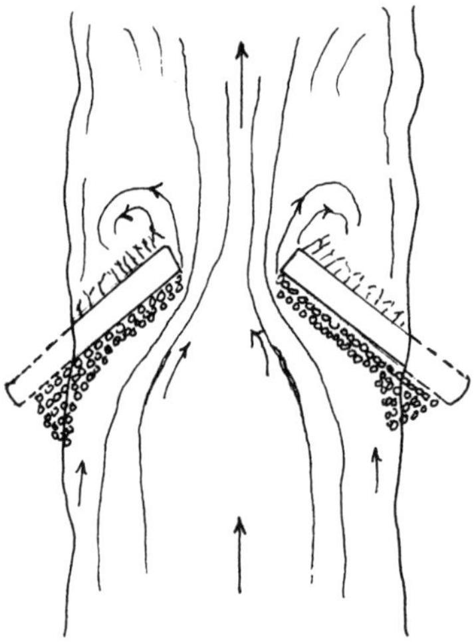

V Deflector

This kind of deflector is often employed to make beds for spawning trout. The "V" deflector, a stream improvement device, can be installed at the head (beginning) of a silty stretch of a stream. The "V" deflector creates a stronger current that sweeps the silt and sand off the gravel. This material deposits itself downstream of the deflector. Trout can now deposit their eggs in the gravel and cover them over. The faster current aerates the water. The bonus is the provision of a nursery for a supply of nymphs, caddis, midges, and damsel flies for the stream. Note that the support fill is rock.

"Thanks," I replied. "It's raining buckets out there." I walked to the window and watched the rain sweeping in over the Laurentian hills. There could not exist two truer friends, I reflected. The creel will always have to accept its position of lesser importance. "Just look at that downpour," I remarked, "will it ever stop?"

"Tomorrow will be a gorgeous day," Forsythe remarked. I turned to stare at him. He was concentrating on crushing a cube of sugar in the bottom of a cup of coffee.

EPILOGUE

Many years after the events surrounding this story fire destroyed the cabin. No cause for the fire was identified. It cannot be attributed to faulty electric wiring; we did not have electric power.

The following year we camped by tent during the trout season. And then I was transferred to another Province in Canada. But, as I suspected, the friendships survived. We keep in touch and I continue to see Wilson; occasionally we fish a river together. Forsythe lives on in good health. I cannot, in good conscience, report upon his sagacity as a weather forecaster.

Two years ago while researching a piece about my early experiences with Salvelinus marstoni (Red Trout) for an American publication, I visited La Belle Province (Québec). During that brief holiday I returned to the old site and its trout water. A row of cottages line what was once a secluded part of the river. The trees along the banks of the river had been removed. Two small boys were skipping stones across the Home Pool. I decided not to venture further up-river.

On my way to the main highway I drove past the Brewster house. The house had been abandoned. I continued along the old gravel road toward the main highway. Approaching the paved intersection I switched on the windshield wipers. It had started to rain.

Those rewarding years, filled with good companionship at the Arundel Water, included the use of many flies. But no pattern produced as well as the Anax junius in slow current water. The dressing given below has been matched to actual samples. The materials used to imitate this dragonfly nymph have changed with the passing of time to incorporate some modern synthetics. But the nymph's effectiveness has not diminished. The recommended tying materials result in a fly which, to the human eye at least, compares favorably with the natural—colorwise—when the materials are wet. The collected samples, approximately one and three-quarter inches long, represent the almost mature nymph.

GREEN DARNER DRAGONFLY NYMPH
(Anax junius)

Hook:	size 4–8, 3X long MUSTAD 3665A or 9672
Shaping wire/wood:	.012 inch diameter
Thread:	olive-green and dark olive 6/0
Body:	white floss, Fly-rite No. 13 (green) ribbed with Poly-Straw No. 105, or bright metallic green tinsel
Tracheal spinules:	short olive-green feather (hackle) barbs; 1/8″
Legs:	green hackle or mottled green wood duck fibers; 3/4″
Wing cases:	olive-green mandarin or wood duck 3/8″ long
Antennae:	green (feather) barbs; 3/16″
Head:	bright chromatic green; 3/16″

STEP 1 Select a size 4 to 6 3X long hook. (The nymph varies from one to two inches in length). Commence tying thread 3/16″ behind the hook eye, and cover shank with olive-green unwaxed 6/0 thread. This nymph is somewhat slender, however, the body is ovoid. In order to match this latter characteristic Wilson and I lashed a short length of .012″ flat wire to the sides of the hook shank. We used thin slivers of wood for the floating pattern. Position the wire(s) or wood strips, and advance thread to cover hook shank. The thread is now at the forward end of the wire (or wood).

STEP 2 Wind tying thread rearward to hook bend. Brush-coat thread windings with varnish or waterproof cement. Mount and secure four short olive-green fibers on top of hook shank. (Short barbs from a dyed green hen neck are ideal). These fibers represent the Tracheal spinules. They extend 3/16″ and are firmly attached. At this location (hook bend) secure a 12″ length of No. 105 Grannom Green Poly-Straw or metallic green tinsel. In front of this attach an 18″ to 24″ length (depending upon size of hook) of unwaxed dental floss. (White floss may be used to form the underbody). The floss is tyed immediately forward of, and after, the Poly-Straw or tinsel.

STEP 3 Illustrates the modified De Feo section of the mandarin or wood duck section which will be mounted on top of the hook shank in the next step. The material, when correctly mounted and secured, provides for excellent natural movement in water.

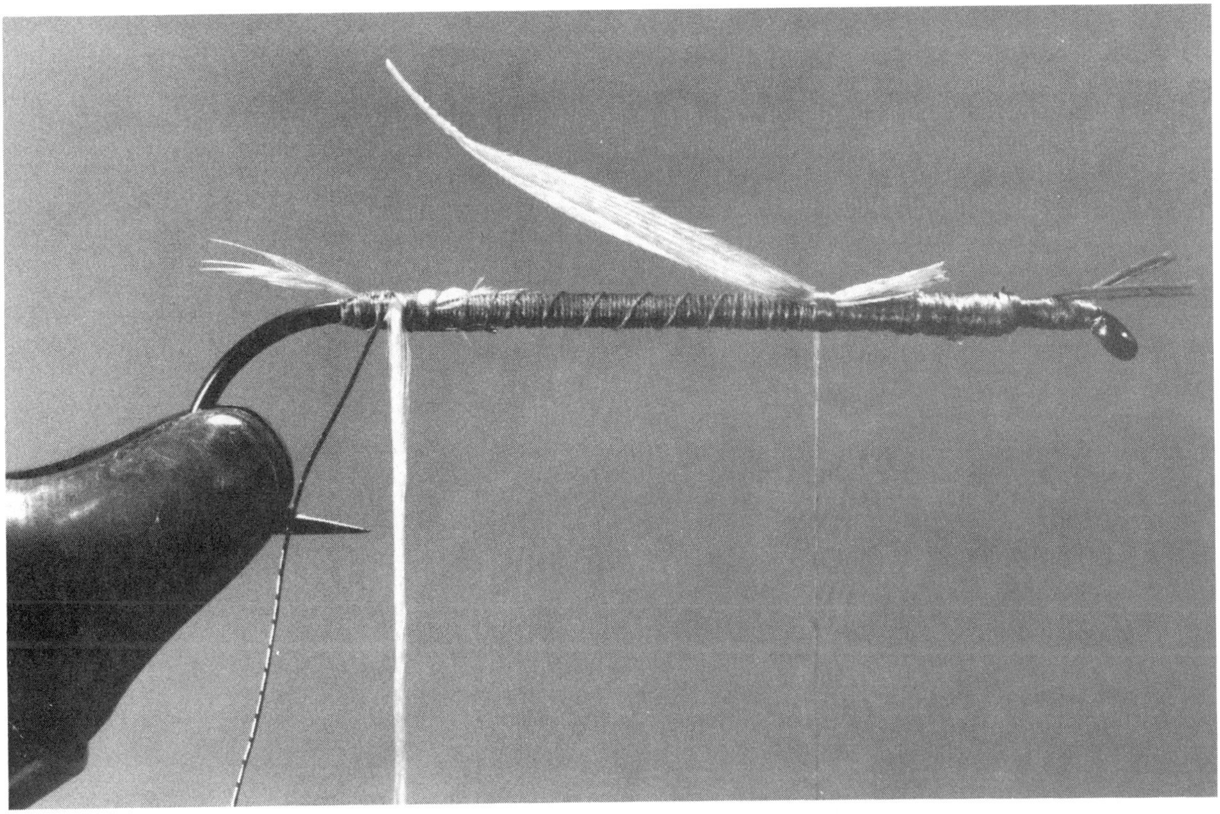

STEP 4 Advance olive-green tying thread to position behind the eye of hook, change thread to bright (fluorescent) green, and position the antennae. These two 1/4″ fibers are curved—as illustrated. Return thread to position shown (juncture of thorax and abdomen). Fasten the two tips of the feather shown in STEP 3—dull side up—at this position. This wing-case will later be folded forward. There is no need to trim the protruding barbs (shown); the floss will cover them. The thorax of this nymph is one-quarter the length of the hook shank—excluding the head.

STEP 5 The abdomen and thorax are now contoured with the dental floss or other white (fine diameter) floss.

STEP 6 Dub the body a bright green. (I now use Fly-Rite No. 13 Grannom Green). Spiral the Poly-Straw or metallic green tinsel around the abdomen and tie-off at rear of wing-case position. Remove excess material. Advance tying thread to front of wing-case. Select a dyed green hackle and use that portion for the legs on which the barbs measure approximately 1/2". Secure underneath hook shank at wing-case tie-in position, by the end which has the slightly shorter barbs—bright side up. This will assist the barbs to adopt a rearward slant. Make two or three turns of hackle. Lock-in and remove the excess hackle.

Advance thread and tie down wing-case leaving slack in wing-case as shown. Form head and whip finish. I use green No. 16 "Cellire" (Unitit) varnish. It has the property of excellent gloss. The head of the natural nymph is a bright chromatic green. This completes the dressing for the Green Darner Dragonfly Nymph.

Over the years I have experimented with several imitations of this Anisoptera nymph. None have been as productive for trout and bass as the foregoing dressing.

The riseform may be likened to a symptom, or fingerprint, which determines the angler's approach and presentation.

Chapter 14

Streamside Studies of Rise Forms

Some years ago after attending the Tangleweed Music Festival in the Berkshire Hills, we drove through the beautiful countryside of Massachusetts via Route 28, and fly fished part of the Mashpee River. The water was low in the Mashpee and the trout were "picky." There were no rises, and we fished the sinking form of the nymph exclusively for the first hour on the river.

Austin and June Amos had recently returned from Nevada. Their search for the Moriah Trout (Salmo behnkel) had proved to be fruitless, but their stories of creek fishing were fascinating.

Following about one hour of fishing time we changed to the nymphs of the Sherry Quill (a Cloëon), and a Neocloëon the Tiny Gray-Winged Yellow, both dressed on size 22 hooks. The weather was drizzly and the fishing unproductive. There were three or four half-hearted takes to the nymph of the Sherry Quill.

About 4:30 p.m. the clouds cleared, and the sun shone on a sweeping bend of the river characterized by some vigorous currents. It was near the bend of the river where the current was swifter, that I saw the first WEDGE-SHAPED sub-surface rise of the day. The configuration of this kind of rise is quickly lost in the fast current. But if one observes it in slow moving currents the rise is distinctly wedge-shaped, and the apex of the wedge faces upstream. With this kind of sub-surface nymphing the dorsal fin penetrates the miniscus, as does the tail of the fish. I would like to be able to describe a stellar catch that afternoon, but Austin captured the one and only trout. His nymph was taken just below the surface film, and I watched the wedge-shaped rise form, once more, quickly disappear in the fairly strong current.

On the return journey to Montreal we drove through Vermont, and experienced the identical kind of rise form on the White River. There is a section of the White River between Rochester, Vermont and West Hartford, and that was the section we fished. The three trout caught

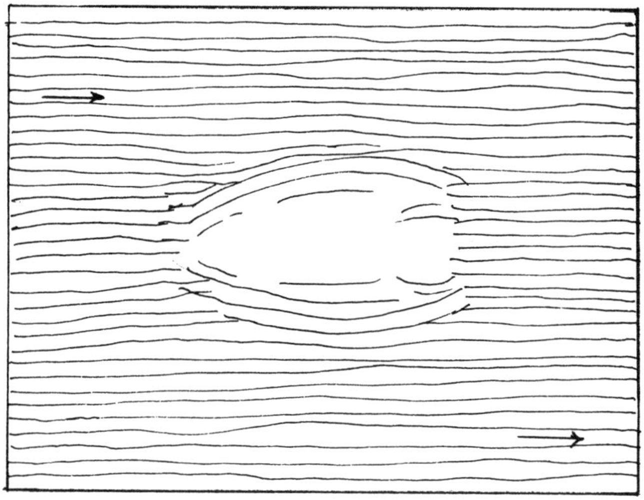

The wedge-shaped sub-surface rise form varies in configuration with the speed of the current. Fast current compresses the form illustrated into a tighter shape, with a more emphasized apex into the upstream current.

This kind of subsurface rise is formed by trout positioned under the surface and intecepting nymphs. The dorsal surface and tail penetrate the film, but not the head.

were all holdover stocked fish, however, they were perky fighters and one of them measured eighteen inches before it was returned to the water.

It is necessary to take note of the speed of the current with this rise form, because its size and shape are determined by surface water speed and characteristics. It nearly always indicates that the trout are taking nymphs.

Any discussion about rise forms related to trout fishing should be preceded by the understanding that, very often, there are differences in rise form behavior between hatchery stocked fish and native trout. The hatchery (stocked) fish are less skillful when feeding in a current. Their rises are "showy" because they do not have the skills that wild fish practice, that is, acceptance of the fly with a minimum expenditure of energy.

One contrast in feeding style is often observed when a good sized trout is lazily feeding in a slow smooth-surfaced pool, or under a protective bank. The execution of a SIPPING RISE by a native trout forms a tiny ring, and the victim disappears. Occasionally a small bubble appears on the water's surface, however, more often there is no bubble. This can mean a good sized trout. If it is a hatchery fish, and not a two or three year hold over, the rise form would very likely be vigorous and the fish smaller. One can, however, be mistaken about such a rise form because some native trout will feed on small insects riding the surface film with a fast penetrating force. This swift thrust-like motion often occurs with ants, tiny spinners, and small floating wasps.

Very often the fluttering adult caddis will be taken in a manner described as a SWIRL. The object of the trout's attention is either in, or just above, the surface film. Because the food form is often to one side of the trout's feeding station, the fish must move out of the line of drift it is occupying, and take the fly with a sidewise turn which creates the swirl. I have watched many hundreds of trout rising, and it is incredible how the actual point of interception is made so frequently. This is often the case with fluttering caddis just above the surface film. But then the trout cannot afford to miss very often because of the amount of energy expended on each occurrence. The interesting aspect about this kind of rise, and the resulting rise form, is that it can mislead the fisherman about the trout's actual feeding position. If the trout's actual feeding position is not observable to the angler, one must try to determine from which side the fish has moved, and place the next cast accordingly if the first fly drift has failed to induce a take.

Some years ago I recall fishing a large pool on the Beaver River in Southern Ontario. The pool is twelve to fifteen feet deep, and about sixty-five feet long by forty-five feet wide. The surface is glassy smooth, and the tail of the pool slopes to a depth of one to two feet—culminating in a four foot waterfall. It was almost twilight and two large trout, one a brown trout, and the other fish a rainbow, had positioned themselves in two separate lines of drift. Both trout were on the far side of the pool about ten feet above the waterfall. Both fish were feeding at a regular rhythm on green drake spinners. While in the process of knotting on a three-quarter spent hackle fiber green drake spinner, I saw the flash of car headlights on the trees bordering the huge pool. Turning, I recognized Bud Hoffman's station wagon. Bud Hoffman operates a very successful fly fishing school in the valley, and is a dedicated fly fisher. Seeing me he parked and turned off the car lights and engine.

"Come and take a look at this." I called out.

"You smooth talking devil." Bud rejoined, opening the rear hatch door of his station wagon and withdrawing one of his permanently set-up fly rods. As he joined me on the river bank I pointed to the typical HEAD-AND-TAIL rise, which is characteristic of trout feeding on spinners in the film. The top of the head, dorsal fin, and tail break the surface film successively. This motion is quite fast and the take is not as subtle as the sipping rise, which creates only the faintest disturbance on a calm surfaced flat, or mirror-surfaced slow moving pool. "You take the closest one," Bud volunteered, "and see if you can do it without disturbing the other fish." The nineteen inch brown took the green drake spinner on the first cast and proceeded to go wild. He was all over the pool and three of his four acrobatic leaps cleared the water by two to three feet. The second trout stopped feeding, and Bud saw his wake heading upstream towards the head of the pool. My companion moved up the shoreline of the pool, and stationed himself at a location where a break in the trees would allow for a backcast. His second cast with a hackle-fiber spinner captured a twenty-one inch rainbow. The trout made four runs, leaping at the end of each run like an Atlantic salmon.

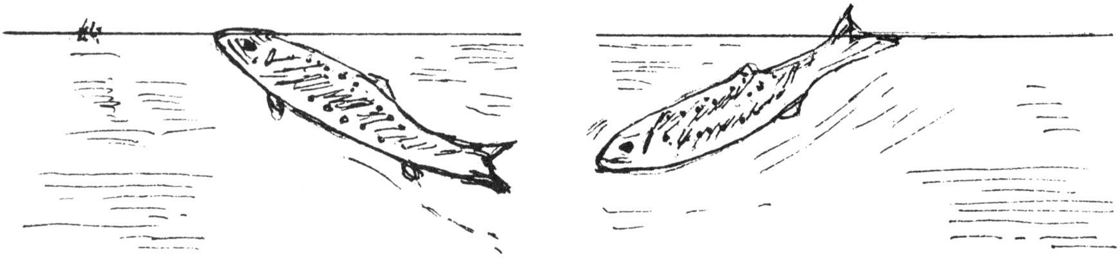

The *head-and-tail* is a frequent kind of riseform. The top of the head penetrates the surface film as illustrated at left. Following the capture of the food, which may be a spent spinner or some other insect trapped in the surface film, the head turns down. As this move occurs the tail angles up as shown at right, and also pierces the meniscus or surface film. Sometimes duns will be taken this was on a rainy day when their wings will not dry, and they are trapped in the surface film.

When the whole arch of the back is seen it is known as the "porpoise roll."

"Good fish." I exclaimed as I watched Bud release the rainbow.

The joys of such fly fishing thrills, often initiated by understanding the rise form, have their opposite in what I call the frustration rise. It is perhaps better known as the INSPECTION RISE, and it is just another instance of the trout's rarity for indulging in total exposure. This complex rise form may include a very long drift and refusal of the fly, unless a totally different approach is used; very often a change of position for the caster. But a debating attitude on the part of the trout will be observed by the fly angler. The trout may hang almost vertically under the fly. There is obviously doubt on the part of the fish about the food form. I have experienced this trout attitude many times, and it is often characterized by the trout drifting downstream in a placid pool, and delaying close inspection of the fly. He is uncertain! And no word in the English language seems to be more appropriate. It may be that excessive drag has destroyed the ability of the fly to imitate the natural. It may be that the size of the fly is not satisfactory to the trout. Or the leader tippet is too large in diameter for the wise trout. The fact remains that the fly and the trout continue moving downstream the same distance apart. Frustration often builds in the angler during this drift and inspection process. Dr. Alan Grove once described fly fishing as a pseudo-science. And he may have been correct, however, it is difficult to objectively rationalize the fly's ineffectiveness, or the trout's indecision. We are left with one of two results. The trout will either refuse the fly and return to its feeding station, or it will speed-up, chase the fly, and strike. During this kind of fishing experience I continue to allow the fly to drift, even if the trout begins to head upstream. For there have been many occasions when the fish has turned and headed downstream towards the fly. If this should happen, the trout will virtually always take the fly. There is no better reason than this for adopting the posture of allowing as full a drift of the fly as possible and then, ultimately, removing it quietly from the water. Should the trout return to his feeding station, I rest the fish and concentrate upon the next presentation. Experience has proven, with regularity, the value of placing the fly accurately in the required line of drift with a drag free float. The inspection rise is particularly noticeable on a smooth flowing flat.

During the process of observing the behavior of trout one cannot fly fish for very long without experiencing SPLASH RISES. Some seasons ago Frank Snow and I fished Slate Run in North Central Pennsylvania. This is back-packing and climbing country, wild, and not without rattlesnakes. But it is a lovely stream which boasts wild browns and brook trout, although I did take two stocked fish. It is a stream which demands a low profile, often casting from a squatting position. Approximately six miles of Slate Run was, at the time, restricted to fly fishing.

"They will not take any dry fly." I called to Frank who, ninety feet downstream of me, was into a twelve inch brown trout.

"Come down here," Frank called back "and be careful of snakes in the streamside foliage." Frank pointed to some small flies on the surface film, but he had quickly diagnosed that the trout were feeding on a small nymphal pattern. The splash rise usually consists of a demure approach to the floater and, very often, a break in the surface near the fly—creating a splash. Sometimes the fly will be lightly touched but more often this is not the case. Repeated resting of the fish and a fresh cast usually has the same result. Occasionally a fish will be lightly hooked.

But more often, even though the trout wants the fly, there will be no hook-up. The food-form is simply unacceptable. This can also be a frustrating experience, particularly for the novice fly fisher. The major feature is a splashy response to the fly and, very often, that response is matched by other fish in the area.

Correct diagnosis of a rise form can help remove the "mystery" from fly fishing which, in the past, too many of its devotees would have many of us believe. Fly fishing is within the capabilities of the larger majority of men and women. It has a fascination for persons who enjoy the study of form and behavior. And it rewards the analytical mind that is capable of observing and diagnosing the anatomy of the rise.

The "slash" riseform is characterized by a fast moving fish at the surface after a fast moving food form. The fly could be a fluttering large caddis fly or a mayfly. There is usually a "surfing" of water and a cascade of spray. This kind of riseform is not to be confused with the slash rise discussed above.

The Late Season

If an occasional trout is retained for the table, it should not be taken from a no-kill area.

CHAPTER 15

The Trout of Euphrasia

Exploring some new and old techniques in an old and rich region of heritage.

The river flows through the valley with a casualness which obscures its splendid deep holding lies. It seems to be more alive when fishing the riffles or white water during July and August. My predilection for the Beaver River is the product of many years and the challenge it offers me as a fly-fisherman. I have listened to the claims of many persons who have reviled the difficult fly fishing. There is—in fairness—some truth to their admissions. The Beaver embraces currents which are difficult to read and not all feeding channels are readily discernible. Successful anglers are adept at reading the bottom of the stream, determining current path velocities, and placing their submerged flies at the juncture of faster and slower currents. Fishing this "boundary" on the slower current side requires the capacity to evaluate each unique situation. The sections of the river which cannot be waded, often accompanied by high banks, have almost no bank cover. This condition requires expertise with the side cast and the maintenance of a low profile. The river is a mecca for simultaneous hatches. To provide for further challenge the trout of the Beaver frequently change their food preference when several hatches are on the water. The majority of the water originates at Lake Eugenia near the South of the Beaver Valley and flows to Georgian Bay at the North of the valley. Small farming communities predominate, and the valley is sparsely populated with people whose ancestors have been residents of Euphrasia Township for generations.

This spring I observed a flyfisherman persistently working water downstream of an old stone and wood bridge (circa 1924). This man was casting a forty to forty-five foot line upstream. He consistently placed his fly close to a feeding station occupied by a sizeable trout. The fly alighted, each time, about two feet above the riseform; leader thrown to one side. And in the fading light of day it was unlikely that the trout could discern the profile of the seven and a half foot rod or the flyfisher kneeling on a low section of bank. The man had been there for about one hour—the trout rising—but without acceptance of the artificial. The five and six minute wait periods which I observed, during which time he rested the fish, were because he was consistently putting the trout down. I noted that this flyfisher had acquired a perplexed expression which revealed his frustration. His fantasy of conquest had been shattered.

But the truth of the matter was that this trout could see the leader. For this fish was positioned in the eddy of a pool, head to the current, facing downstream. If the fly is placed on that part of the current which is turning upstream it will be floated to the fish in the natural process. The progress of the artificial will follow the natural insect if some loose tippet material is placed on the water below the fly. Clearly this was a situation where the angler should have been dropping the fly two feet below the fish, and slack leader below the fly in the water which was turning upstream.

SUB-SURFACE FEEDING

In the very early spring when the water is cold the sport of fly fishing may offer its maximum challenge in fresh water rivers. If trout are feeding in water below fifty-five degrees Fah. they are usually holding near the bottom and may be feeding on nymphs.

The first prerequisite should be the use of a thermometer. I have rarely experienced good fishing during early spring if the water temperature is below forty-seven degrees Fah. The migration and feeding habits of trout are affected by the temperature of water. Generally speaking trout will be actively feeding in water that measures fifty-five degrees Fah. to sixty-seven degrees Fah. When the water temperature exceeds seventy degrees FAH. to seventy-five degrees FAH. trout nearly always migrate to spring holes (colder water), or to the junction input of colder creeks. This usually means that good fishing can be anticipated in strictly defined or prescribed sections of the river. This condition, in my experience, is often forgotten or ignored. If, for example, one fishes the Firehole River (Wyoming) when temperatures are high in midsummer, the majority of fish tend to remain near such feeder creeks as Sentinel and Nez Perce.

DIAGNOSIS AND PRESENTATION

The second objective is diagnosis. What kind of food is in the river? Are the Hendricksons, for example, about to hatch? Are the trout feeding on stonefly nymphs? Seining for samples of food forms does not guarantee an answer to the trout's current diet. Examination of the first trout caught usually answers the question. If trout are feeding heavily in a specific section of the river, seining may be helpful if the samples are taken just upstream from the active area of feeding.

I remember being unable to diagnose a hatch of Pseudocloeons one late spring evening. There were other hatches emerging and, finally, in the fast fading light I took a fourteen inch brown on a grey fox variant. Before releasing the brown trout I saw the tiny two-winged mayflies in the mouth and gullet. Saving two or three samples for analysis, they proved to be Pseudocloeons with the light olive-green body and no anterior wings. The experience was frustrating because my fly box contained imitations of the nymph and adult.

The third factor is correct presentation. If trout are feeding along the river bottom it becomes mandatory to get the artificial "down there." This kind of fly fishing is most demanding. Presenting the offering at the correct depth and on the required line of drift requires knowledge about stream currents, speed of water, and familiarity with the characteristics of one's equipment.

A decade of fly fishing the Beaver has established that the majority of trout are taken with imitations of underwater food forms. Plate 1 illustrates two dressings which have produced good catches on the Beaver. The stonefly nymph illustrated on the left of one of the color plates, Pteronarcys dorsata, imitates one kind of natural food in this river, and also many tributaries of the Saugeen (a nearby watershed). The black stonefly nymph is particularly effective when fished during early morning. Its peak time of emergence is mid-June. I have found it effective in shallow water when fished at the beginning of daylight. Because this nymph is often worked in shallows it is lightly weighted with a fine lead wire bound to both sides of the hook shank and not the heavier brass pins which, for some situations, cause the imitation to sink too quickly. This nymph is large, often one and one-half inches long. It can be dressed on a size two to six 4X long hook.

HARMONIES OF THE EVENING

Mist shrouds the forest floor of the valley. It is close to the end of twilight. The surface of the flowing river reflects the evening light as a soft metallic sheen. The limestone bluffs which enclose the valley can be sensed rather

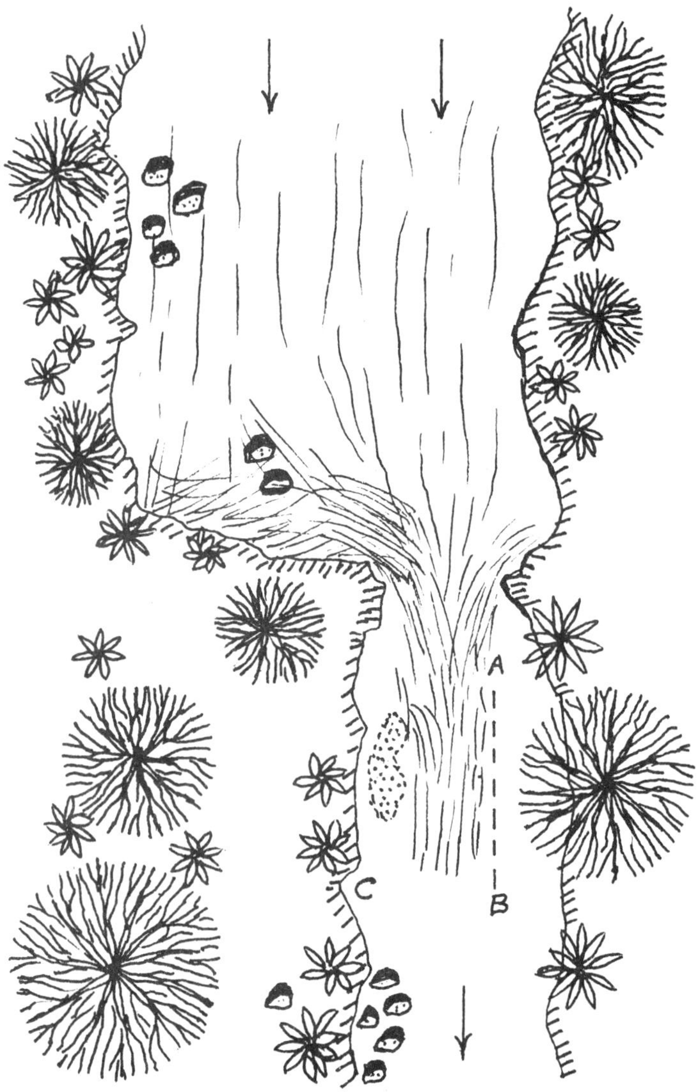

The funnel pool of the Beaver River is part of the fly fishing only, catch and release section of the river.

The author has fished this pool for sixteen years and, inevitably, trout are found just to the right of "A"---"B." The current is slower under the overhanging tree—which affords protection from predator birds.

There is usually a trout at "C," just below the gravel bar where there is an indentation in the bank of the river.

than seen. At this time many of the larger trout leave their protected lairs and enter the shallow areas of flat and pool. It is June and a few sulphurs (invarias), now spinners, are in the riffles. Frank Snow, who has fly fished in most of the Western world, stands beside me at streamside. Frank is a water biologist and entomologist. We have been turning rocks and rubble on the river bottom during the past twenty minutes and observing trout indulging in sub-surface feeding. When he reaches for one of his fly boxes I know that he has diagnosed at least one potential food form. Because our seining had revealed the presence of many crayfish, a favourite food of Beaver River trout, I anticipated the selection of an artificial crayfish.

The Isonychia bicolor

I watched my companion firm-up a barrel knot to secure a new leader tippet. "Did you see that flash of colored flank in the shallow water upstream of the bridge?" asked Frank.

"It looks like a good fish," I agreed, "and a difficult cast from downstream of the bridge." The underside of the bridge is approximately four feet above the surface of the stream at high water. The observed trout, feeding on nymphs, was not bulging but intercepting naturals well below the surface—two or three feet upstream of the bridge. I noted Frank's nymph selection—an Isonychia bicolor. I also admired my companion's approach; quietly kneeling on the river bank. He was achieving a low profile and avoiding the probability of wading through recently formed redds.[1] The side cast was placed across and upstream—flowing smoothly under the bridge. The ovoid shaped nymph weighted with two brass pins, one on each side of the hook shank, submerged rapidly. The acceptance by the trout was immediate, and the fifteen-inch brown fought as long and hard as a much larger fish. "Bright spots and beautiful coloring," I remarked as I watched him gently release the trout.

"A wild, stream-bred fish," Frank answered, "nothing quite like them and too valuable not to release."

---

[1]The "recently formed redd" has been made by a rainbow trout which had "overspawned" a brown trout redd formed during the preceding autumn. Such cases are not infrequent in streams which contain brown and rainbow trout. The frequency of overspawning is larger, with consequent loss of brown trout, in river sections where (spawning) gravel sites are scarce. In this case a spawning rainbow trout had disturbed a considerable portion of a brown trout redd prior to the hatching of the brown trout fry.

The Isonychia bicolor nymph, illustrated at the right of one of the color plates, measures three-quarters of one inch. I dress this nymph on a size ten 3X long hook. Although the great leadwing drake nymph constitutes a small hatch, the ovoid body (weighted) pattern is always in my fly book when fishing the Beaver during June. This nymph has taken many large rainbow and brown trout during very early morning and during the two hours following sunset.

RESPONDING TO THE RISE

The Beaver River supports a significant cross section of Ontario's mayfly hatches. The hendrickson, blue winged olive, green drake, sulphur dun, and the march brown (gray fox) are followed by many other hatches. On occasion a surprise ensues and a cloud of cream colored duns, the size fourteen Ephoron leukon will emerge during early June, in addition to their usual August appearance. The almost white dun is often a large hatch which coincides with the emergence of the green drake. And the trout feed prolifically on the spinner fall. This kind of surprise reinforces one's resolve to replenish fly boxes with suitable imitations during the winter.

The technique I have found to be effective for the purpose of determining current trout diet is to follow the floating path of one particular fly. If the fly can be seen and its drift continuously monitored, and the fly is accepted, there can be small doubt about the preferred food form of the moment. One feature is immediately discernible from observing the drift of the natural insect. That feature is the absence of drag. The opportunity to use the "dry" fly[2] has frequently established that fine, supple tippet materials are less likely to induce drag. And I am reasonably certain that while the flyfisher may not discern drag from a distance of thirty-five or forty feet from the fly there may, in fact, be drag observable to the trout. Such drag has been confirmed by a companion angler who has watched the drift of the fly from a close vantage point. Not infrequently this difficult to detect drag occurs during "retarded drag." This kind of action takes place when the fly is drifting faster than the leader, the leader having been thrown to one side and the fly in the faster current is held back, or retarded, by the slower moving leader. This

[2]I use the term "dry fly" with hesitation. Dry fly referred, historically, to a fresh (dry) fly taken from one's fly box. The term was employed during an era when it was likely more difficult to float a fly. The term "floating fly" seems to be more appropriate.

is a strong argument for ensuring that slack in the leader tippet is downstream of the fly. I am also convinced that it is preferable to have the leader tippet just under the surface film. Leaders are subject to smaller magnification and are less noticeable when viewed from under water in strong sunlight. Trout have frequently surfaced to the knots in leaders when the knots are lying on the surface of the water. But I have rarely observed this frustrating condition when the knots are under the film.

Although considerable has been written about the floating fly during recent years, my log book reveals some interesting observations. Aside from the importance of the correct size of fly, there is a distinct advantage in number of fish caught, under certain conditions, when the high floating fly is used on smooth water surfaces. I refer to a style of dressing which ensures that the fly rests upon the water on its hackle, tail, and with the hook bend either above or just touching the surface film. The fish taking potential for the high floater is enhanced because of its ability to cock during drift. The Beaver River includes water which flows through meadows. The water surface is smooth and the current speed is constant. On meadow water, aside from good summer fishing with imitations of the cricket and grasshopper, the high floating fly is often susceptible to wind. This style of fly will frequently be cocked by a light breeze during the fly's drift. I believe this action to be of vital significance. Trout, on many occasions, backing slowly downstream of the fly and examining it closely will suddenly, when the fly has cocked on the water, strike with alacrity. The vagaries of the current will sometimes cause the fly to cock and prompt a rapid strike. Whatever the reason for this simulation of life-like behavior it must be meaningful to the trout. The high floating fly, shown in one of the color plates, is dressed with finest grade (cock) hackle. The hackle is oversized (similar to the design of the Gray Fox Variant) and the tails are longer than normal. The tail fibers are tilted down so that the fly sits on hackle and tail on the surface film. Flaring or spreading the tail whisks (barbs or hair) results in a more balanced float, and allows for efficient drying during false casting. The fly is dressed on fine wire hooks with a very slim body. The body should be composed of the lightest possible material. One barb from the long side of a Condor feather and, if unavailable (or illegal), the quill from a gray goose wing satisfies the requirement for minimum weight and a realistic mayfly body. The imitation at left of the color plate has its body fashioned from one barbule of a Condor feather on the shank of a size fourteen hook. The fly at the right will also float on the surface film. It is dressed on a size ten regular shank hook.[3] The barb is wound around the hook shank on its narrow (thin) edge. The body segmentation takes on a translucent appearance when two coats of varnish have been applied. Because this fly must be as light in weight as possible the wings are omitted. Hackle is offered as a simulation of the profile of the wings—cut wings may be advantageous with very selective trout. When dressed with a minimum amount of material the fly will descend gently to the surface of the water. The effect is much like the kind of delicate presentation achieved with a spider-hackled fly which has been dressed on a small hook.

Some experiments appear to confirm that hackle color should imitate the color of the natural wing. Thorax silhouette may or may not be important because the hackle windings often obscure a portion of the thorax. The resulting light pattern, when viewed from below, results in a profile of abdomen, thorax, legs in the surface film, and tails. Wings may be necessary on some rivers but, are not necessary on all rivers. If we concede excellent vision to the trout, and observe that most imitation midges are wingless, we must acknowledge the efficacy of wingless flies. There have been too many selective trout caught on wingless fly imitations to adopt a rigid posture about the need for wings on every fly cast to a trout.

THE GREEN DRAKE

The Green Drakes emerged during the last two days of May and the first three days of June.

I arrived in the valley on Saturday evening to stay at the Talisman resort near Kimberley. We were part of a small group of early diners and the sumptuous buffet included roast pheasant, Pacific salmon, jugged hare, and Coq au Vin de Bourgogne.

Twilight was almost at an end when I walked to the river. There were swallows wheeling and flashing over the river in the failing light. The Green Drakes were fluttering off the surface accompanied by a mix of

---

[3]The relatively large green drake dun can also be tied on smaller (size twelve or fourteen) short shank hooks with an extended body made from a small feather.

This style of dressing usually includes cut or hair wings. Aside from the abomination cut wings can become if misaligned (usually after some use) the extended body pattern is more fragile than the style described. And the cut-wing dressing—usually tied with parachute style hackle—sits in the surface film.

Keeping a low profile can be vital for success.

March Browns and Blue Winged Olives. The volume of the March Brown hatch was, in a word, incredible.

On Monday I went up the river to join Bud Hoffman and fish the gorgeous water that flows through his property. The river is sixty to eighty feet wide here and the river bottom contains a scattering of boulders. When I arrived Bud was releasing an eleven inch brown trout near the bank of the river, and we talked about the hatches and compared fishing strategy. The fishing was good with an emerger pattern for the Green Drake. The yellow/olive body color is always deadly. We released several beautifully spotted browns in the ten to twelve inch range.

THE GIANT POOL AT THE SKI CLUB BRIDGE

It was during the following two evenings that we experienced rises by some magnificent fish proving, once more, that the return of the Green Drake spinner predisposes the larger trout to rise. Bud and I fished the enormous pool below the bridge on the ski club property. The pool is almost eighty feet long and the tail of the pool flows to a shallow glide which culminates in a waterfall. From between two small trees near the tail of the pool I watched Bud Hoffman play a magnificent twenty inch rainbow. His cast was perfectly timed and positioned to a repetitive rise-form and the fly was immediately accepted. Bud handled the rainbow with that innovative kind of skill which is the product of many years of fly fishing. His leader tippet was of sufficient strength to enable him to net the trout and release the fish before it reached a state of exhaustion.

''Beautiful rainbow,'' I commented, as I watched the trout being returned to the water.

''Small head and firm fat body,'' Bud confirmed.

I returned to a position where I could observe the tail of the pool. Two large fish were rising regularly to Green Drake spinners. The location demands a cast from the bank. The large deep pool cannot be waded. Trees prevent casting across and upstream. The challenge, over the years, has remained constant. Achieve a drag-free float for the six or seven foot drift to the edge of the waterfall. The two trout were in different feeding lanes. They were rising, slowly backing downstream, and finally sipping the spinners two or three feet from the edge of the waterfall. Crouching on the bank I took the closest brown first, a lively nineteen inch fish that jumped four times in quick succession. On the last leap, very close and right at me, the trout cleared the surface of the water by close to three feet. The brown re-entered the water; in the process falling on the leader tippet and breaking-off. The fish was close enough for me to see the brilliant spotted sides. It had accepted my standard dressing for the Green Drake spinner, as did the second fish, a lively twenty-two inch rainbow. We used a dressing which has produced exceptionally good results. The body of the spinner is dubbed with Phentex, and the three-quarter-spent wings are well marked gray deer hair tips. The partly spent wing design has proved to be far more effective than the fully spent wing. The fly is dressed on a size ten hook. If an extra fine wire hook is used the fly will persist in floating in the film very much like the natural imago. You can see this design in one of the color plates.

There is a magic about the valley. The Bruce Trail follows the crest of the mountain which includes a high limestone cliff towering seven hundred feet above the sparkling river. The wooded base of the valley is nourished by the winding river. The clover laden fields and grazing cattle enhance the impression that all this is a picture postcard.

It has been a long time since the hotel Condy opened at Kimberley, and James Thurston operated a "temperance hotel."[4] Still longer since Albert Barnett Peterson, whose grandfather was a leading Euphrasia citizen, won the honor of being Louisiana's "First Citizen."[5]

But the character of the valley has not changed. Euphrasia was named after an English officer's wife. It is a Greek word meaning delight . . . or much more appropriate as the name of a plant used as a treatment for sore eyes. "The beauty of Euphrasia is such as to treat any eyes, sore or healthy."[6] And those analogies are as appropriate today as they were in 1840 when David Eaton and his family came from Pennsylvania to settle the valley.

The Beaver River provides the challenge of fly fishing for stream bred trout. This challenge includes spotting and stalking trout from the bank. And the satisfaction of detecting and casting to the inconspicuous rise.

---

[4]See *A New History of Grey County,* written and edited by Davidson, Arthur T., Published by the Grey County Historical Society, Chapter XV, Township of Euphrasia, p. 135.

[5]ibid p. 141.

[6]ibid p. 133.

CHAPTER 16

Some Thoughts and Observations About Mayfly Impressionism

We have been reading with increasing frequency, every year, some very imaginative philosophy about imitating and fishing the various characteristics of natural mayflies. Considerable of this material has been framed in convincing rhetoric and presented as new discovery. We have seen the dun (subimago) sitting in water with vertical hackle, without hackle, and with parachute style hackle. The parachute style hackle has appeared with the turns of hackle above and below the shank of the hook. Each advocate of a particular style seems convinced that a specific design will qualify as an improvement. And the result of this experimentation and variation will, inescapably, lead to improved fish-catching. We have been advised by some persons that cut-wing dun patterns are essential for selective trout. This hypothesis has been advanced although chalkstream fly fishers have been taking selective trout for decades on the "traditional" hackled fly dressed without wings. Such anglers continue to do so today. In order to allay the reader's presumption that I am biased, let me quickly add that I dress (imitative) subimagos with and without cut-wings. I also dress them with stiff (genetic raised) hackle and hackle which is not so stiff in the barb.

I am not decrying the need for new and improved patterns. Let me emphasize that I am in favor of experimentation, and the creative use of new materials.[1] I am, however, advocating the need to match the manner in which the natural presents itself on stream or river. In this sense I am convinced that form and behaviour are far more important than rigid imitation to color on flies fished above the surface film.

For more years than I wish to count the fully emerged subimago has been floating by me on the meniscus. I remember a discussion about

---

[1]I refer here to polypropylene yarns for dubbing, prismatic mylar, closed-cell foam, Microfibbets, and other materials which have features which are advantageous to the fly tyer.

this some years ago with Art Flick. This great angler remarked to me that "the Gray Fox Variant is a high floater, and there seem to be few patterns like the Gray Fox Variant for raising them." I believe Art Flick—and with good reason. For here is a dry fly pattern designed to emulate a characteristic of the dun, that is, the ability to float on the surface film. I refer here to the floating (fully emerged) dun prior to its leaving the surface of the water. Trout sometimes feed at this stage of emergence of the aquatic insect. On relatively smooth water the ring is circular, and this suction-type rise often leaves two or three air bubbles riding the film and, if one is close enough to the trout there is often a distinct sucking sound to the fly riding on the film.

Forty-five years of fly fishing have resulted in some observations about the floating characteristics of the subimago. (Entomological characteristics do not have the propensity for change that some humans experience). That is, I continue to frequently observe the dun floating on the surface film. When wading hip deep in water, on one of the four rivers I regularly fish, these tiny "sailboats" keep floating by—on the film. Sometimes I observe a swirl to an insect in such a position. Very often the trout is capturing its food on the meniscus with a sidewise body turn.

During early June of 1986 I experienced a superb hatch of the Green Drake. One really has very small difficulty observing the details of the Green Drake. Its size precludes the possibility of making a glaring error of observation. If the Green Drake dun has one leg or two legs "locked" in the surface film, it is struggling to free its legs. The fly is above the film and obviously intent on drying body and wings in order to fly from the surface of the water. That is the dry fly. And the riseform that accompanies that phenomena is the dry fly riseform. Perhaps this is why top grade genetic hackle remains important. That stiff hackle, with its resilience, makes it possible to float the dry fly on the surface film. This kind of dressing, which guarantees a fairly long period of flotation on the film, is advantageous on days when there is a steady mist-like rain during cool weather.

I am not making overtures for the purpose of minimizing the value of, for example, the Paradun dressing. There is a phase during the escape of the mayfly from water where we observe the insect with its body in the water. The body is wet, the wings (not fully extended) are wet, the legs are below the surface tension, and the trout may be taking this aquatic food form as an emerging nymph under the film—or in the surface film. I have often fished the Paradun, a splendid imitation of an almost emerged dun, with success downstream of riffles during a heavy hatch of mayfly.

It is not difficult to observe the different position that the spinner assumes in the water after its fall. When one examines the natural imago there is no doubt that it is floating in the surface film. Perhaps initially (for a short distance) it rests upon the film. But in the streams and rivers that I flyfish the imago is awash in the film. And yet I observe "new and improved patterns," sometimes dressed with stiff hackle in order to, presumably, keep the fly well above the film. There is one characteristic which I frequently observe about the freshly fallen spinner. And that is its ability to strongly attract trout with its wings in the half or three-quarter spent position. But the body and tails of the (spent) spinner are in the film and, very often, a porpoise-type roll results, and the dorsal surface of the fish is exposed during the take.

The Green Drake hatch remains a significant attraction on many streams during late May and/or early June. Of all the mayfly patterns that I have fished none have been as productive for large trout as the coffin fly toward nightfall. The observations described below have been made over a number of years and, I believe, are valid because of their repetitive nature at streamside.

The writer has frequently fished over selective trout. I have taken selective fish with the "traditional" floating fly (a collar of hackle) and, very frequently, have not raised nearly as many trout with a cut-wing pattern. This condition has obtained during the same hours of the afternoon, with the same leader, tippet, and included casting from the same position. The natural light did not vary. This kind of experience has recurred frequently. It is difficult to determine why, impossible for me to explain. Did the "collar" of hackle refract the available light in such a way that the hackle substituted for, or was mistaken for a wing by the gamefish? Was the "traditional" style of dressing more successful because the hook was above the surface film on the imitation of the dun? I used oversized hackles, somewhat longer divided tails, and floated the pattern high—much like the Gray Fox Variant. Did these frequently fished over, or selective trout, not see the cut-wing on the pattern? On a number of occasions I have alternated my casting between winged, and dry flies dressed with only hackle.

It is likely, I believe, that one of the first observations by gamefish are the flashes of light created by the hackle points as they indent the surface film. Is it only the non "highly selective creature" that responds to these pin-point flashes of light? I do not believe this to be the case.

There is, to my knowledge, no empirical evidence to support such a hypothesis. But it seems virtually certain that the light pattern triggers the beginning of the rise.

Some selective trout wait until the fly has floated directly above them before accepting the offering. At this point the trout may see the cut-wing profile because the wings on the dun are normally mounted at a viewable angle—even from directly below the deceiver. But parachute style hackle may obscure the profile of the cut-wing when the trout is almost directly under the fly. Such is often the case when the hackle has been applied too liberally, and the barbs are excessively long. Selective fish do not always back downstream and closely examine the fly. And, if they do allow the fly to pass them, and then turn, my experience has been that they will take the fly.

Surely one of the first features of the cut-wing pattern to be observed by trout are the upright wings at the edge of the trout's mirror. Because of distance, in this case, the cut-wing silhouette does not always induce the selective trout to change its position and accept the fly. In my experience the selective trout does not move too far from its feeding station if the fish is of fair size. And at this point, when the wings appear to float over the rim of the mirror (before the wings are seen as integral with the body) the fly is still some considerable distance from the trout's feeding station. Remember at this point in time the fly is still being carried towards the trout's window. And yet the wings (cut-wings) still do not trigger a "take." Does this situation occur because the fly is too far away from a station that the selective trout will not abandon? Is the trout too far below the surface of the water and not hungry enough to be interested? Or did the trout see the leader or the fly dragging? A fly, that is, with or without wings. If the foregoing finds acceptance with the reader, it may explain why taking the appropriate fly to the fish is, very often, successful. I refer, here, to a direct prompt cast to the fish, upstream of the ring of the rise, because the ring is downstream of the fish after the rise.

As a brief digression from the floating fly consider why Sawyer's nymph presentation is effective. The fly is taken to the fish. But that is only part of the technique. The drama of this induced take includes, when casting across current, the action of the water upon the fly and the leader to result in animation of the nymph. Raising the tip of the rod so that the nymph pattern responds by rising immediately in front of the trout, often triggers a response by the fish because of this life-like action. Now what occurs here applies to an underwater technique which is effective at the correct depth of water and, hopefully, without any slack in the line.

But I believe that this same phenomena (life-like motion or action) is important to the floater. There have been many occasions when I have watched a selective trout backing downstream, not taking my floater, and then a gust of wind, or some vagary of water current has caused the fly to cock. Then the trout has seized the fly with alacrity! These occurrences are readily observable on smooth flats or pools and not, I emphasize, on turbulent water surfaces. I am also certain that most fly fishers have experienced the immediate take of a large (selective) trout to the most esoteric pattern, when that pattern was presented with accuracy, delicacy, and without drag on a fine leader tippet. That small diameter leader tippet seems to be most important on a bright sunny day. But then I concluded, many years ago, that success in taking the selective trout often results from going finer and darker in color with the leader tippet, than from changing the fly.

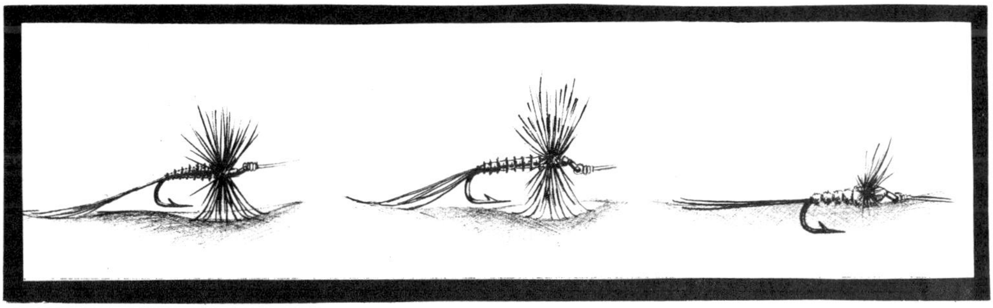

Courtesy of Larry Largay, AMERICAN ANGLER

Fig. 1 and 2 (from left) illustrate the Hendrickson and Green Drake duns which sit on the surface film. Note the hook is above the film. Very light weight durable bodies can be made from the first primary of a goose wing quill. These quills are suitably tapered. The body of the Green Drake dun is creamish yellow fur. The flies float on or above the film because of oversize hackles and slightly longer tails made from suitably colored microfibbets.

Fig. 3 illustrates the Green Drake (coffin fly) floating inthe film. The body and thorax are Kapok reinforced (ribbed) with white waxed tying thread. The wings are badger hair or well marked gray deer hair—22 mms. long. Tails are 3 dark moose mane fibers.

Are trout always able to discern a particular characteristic about the floating fly on one of our typical North American rivers with its heavily rippled or turbulent surfaces? This also raises the question as to whether there is a preferred kind of dressing for a particular kind of water surface. I think that the answer to this question is yes. A particular kind of dressing is likely to suit a water surface with unique characteristics. Observe how well the Wulff patterns float, and reward the fly fisher on tumbling, cascading river surfaces. The merits of fine quality hollow deer hair used for fly flotation has been firmly established.

Now let us examine another situation relative to trout which have been frequently caught and released. There is a place with special appeal for me on a river in Southern Ontario. I find the fly fishing rewarding here, particularly during May and June. The fly hatches are varied, and the quantity of mayfly is prolific. I often fish just downstream of an old wood and stone bridge, circa 1937. The trout at this location indulge in a voracious appetite for spinners during the evening. Here we have a situation where the brown, brook, and rainbow trout, over many years, have experienced catch-and-release. And the river contains stream-bred fish. I dress the Blue-Winged Olive and Green Drake spinners hair-wing and cut-wing style. I give attention to contour and size for both of these styles of mayfly dressings. Very often the spinner wings are hackle fibers, and, more often, the wings are dressed three-quarter spent. Both fly styles float in the film. And so the variable characteristic became type of wing; hair-wing or cut-wing. There have been many occasions when I have caught and released trout on the hair-wing flies; practically none on the cut-wing. And alternating between the two styles of dressing has confirmed the preference of the trout. In this case the hair-wing (made from stiff wide spread deer hair tips for the coffin fly) must "trigger" a response that the cut-wing is not doing as successfully. That is to say the hair-wing may present, to the trout, characteristics, or a characteristic, which more nearly resemble that of the natural. *Please note that I say to the trout.* Both dressings appear similar to me when they are wet. These observations, by the way, have been made over a period of years, with a variety of different conditions of light. The dressings have remained the same, and the imago is presented like the natural—floating in the surface film—and with three-quarter spent wings.

I have to suggest that there is considerable that we do not know about the predilection of trout for imitative food forms. But imagine for a moment, if you will, the satisfaction to be achieved in wrestling, from a very reluctant nature, one or two of her closely guarded secrets.

CHAPTER 17

The Bluntnose Minnow

A Dressing for Bass and Brown Trout

This is an account of investigative work in order to deceive black bass with a dressing to imitate the Bluntnose Minnow (Pimephales notatus).

The bridge arcs high over the winding river. A rumble of traffic resonates in the summer evening air. But after parking the car, assembling one's fly tackle, and proceeding a mile upstream, the rewards are considerable. The valley is heavily wooded, plant life abounds, and the tranquility makes you feel that you are a hundred miles away from that concrete approach to the city.

I frequently wade upstream during the long July and August evenings. The river is twenty-five minutes drive from my home. July is the time of the small mouth black bass. The bass arrive after the rainbow trout have migrated from the lake to spawn in the river. Many of the bass, however, remain in the stream during July and the first three weeks of August. The salmon swim upstream in the Autumn but it is not their time now.

During these summer evening pilgrimages I experimented with nymphs, dry flies, various streamers, and wet flies. Retaining the occasional bass for the table gave me the opportunity to analyze the stomach contents. The bait-fish that I found in a significant percentage of the bass were identified as Bluntnose Minnows, and were about two inches long. Some areas, I have since learned, produce a slightly longer (average) minnow. Bluntnose minnows (Pimephales notatus) are found throughout the Great Lakes area, with exception of the West end of Lake Superior. They are common in waters adjacent to populated areas. The body is tubular (not flattened from side to side). The snout is rounded, or blunt, and the dorsal fin (top fin) begins above the pelvic fin origin. The back of this minnow, when immediately taken from the water, is brown with just the suggestion of a green hue. The sides have a dark lateral band which extends from the caudal fin base to the snout. The belly is silvery-white. All of the fins on the samples that I examined had a yellowish or olive cast. There is a conspicuous black spot at the base of the caudal fin (where the tail and body meet).

With the preceding information I sat down at the tying vise and dressed the following bait-fish (streamer) imitation.

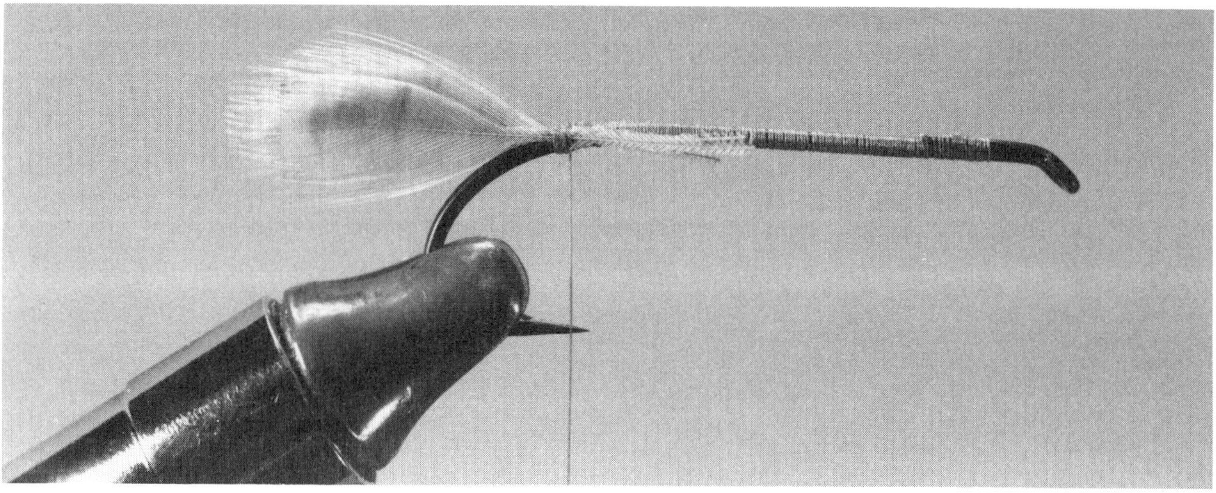

STEP 1 In this step you see a Partridge S.E.B. size 4 lure hook in the vise. Select four small olive hackles of the size illustrated. Trim the centre quills of the four hackles with scissors in order to leave short barbs on the stems. This will afford a good grip for the tying thread. Start the olive 6/0 tying thread three sixteenths of one inch behind the hook eye, and cover the shank of the hook to the start of the hook bend. Tie-in the four olive hackles, two on each side of the hook shank, with the dull sides of the hackles facing one another. Lock in the four hackles just forward of the hook bend. Note the contour of the hook bend. The position of the hackles is such that they (the caudal fin) can move laterally. If you examine the result of employing the four (olive) hackles in this configuration, and have the opportunity to examine the natural bait-fish, you will see the similarity of marking on the caudal fin. There is a darkened central mark which extends longitudinally on this fin. This darkened area is more pronounced when the bait-fish has immediately been removed from the water.

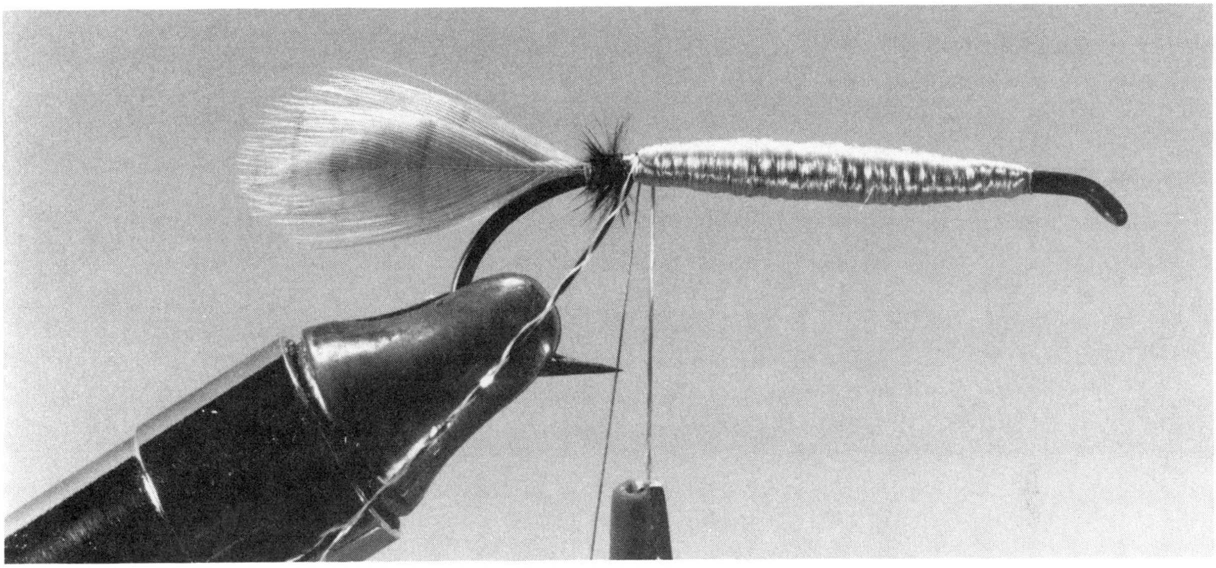

STEP 2 Clip off the four excess pieces of quill.

Position and tie-in two twisted black maribou strands about two inches long. Make three or four turns with the maribou and tie off. This material, which forms a small BUTT, imitates the black spot at the base of the caudal fin. It should be about the size illustrated.[1]

Advance the tying thread three turns and tie-in a twelve-inch length of Lusterelle. The color I use in this non-tarnishable nylon reinforced metallic yarn is Rainbow Opal No. 310. The Lusterelle is positioned on the hook shank with two turns of tying thread to the rear. Then tie-in the single strand brown floss with two more turns of tying thread also to the rear. You are now ready to form the profile shown with the floss. The floss is wound in layers, each layer shorter by one width (or diameter) of floss in order to obtain the tapered tubular shape shown. The final layer of single strand floss should end where the Lusterelle yarn was locked-in, and it is at this location where the floss is tyed-off. The resultant body surface should appear wavy or slightly ''ridgy'' as does the natural bait-fish. This effect can be achieved with floss.

[1]The only adjustment to this fly dressing, fished frequently since 1981, has been to make the BUTT (spot) smaller in diameter.

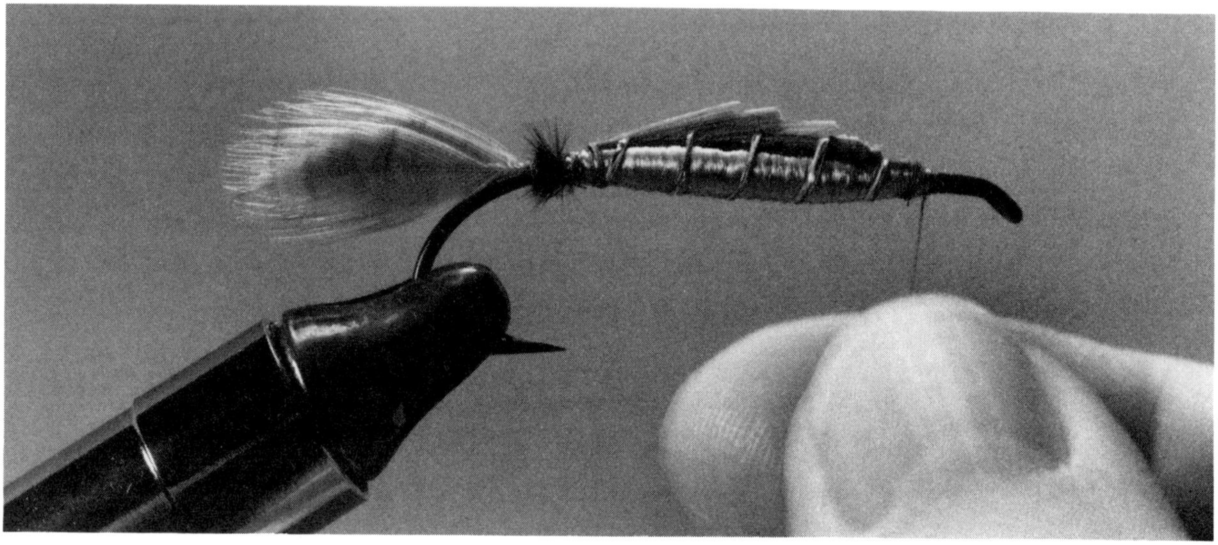

STEP 3 Remove the excess floss. Most minnows have a dorsal fin and the Bluntnose Minnow is not an exception. When the Chinese Biot is flexed the ''spines'' become obvious, and this material can be used to simulate the dorsal (top) fin. A short length of the Biot is selected, and the flared ends of the ''spines'' are tapered (cut) at an angle. Apply a very light coat of cement (I use ''Cellire'' Unitit No. 1 clear fine) or varnish to the bottom of the Chinese Biot section. Place this section on top of the floss body. The tying thread is now passed over the rear of the Biot section two or three turns. This procedure will open the Biot section slightly. (It opens a bit more and ''works'' when the streamer is retrieved through the water). Whip finish, or make three half-hitches to secure the Biot at the rear. Place a tiny drop of cement at this location. Make one turn around the shank of hook with the Lusterelle in front of the Maribou (BUTT) in order to provide for contrast and, therefore, emphasize the black BUTT.

The Biot section is bound (ribbed) to the top of the floss body with the Lusterelle yarn and the tying thread—simultaneously. This segmenting effect should result in equidistant spirals, and provide for firm positioning of the Biot section. Whip finish the Lusterelle one-quarter inch from the eye of the hook. When performing this operation arrange the ribbing so that only three or four of the ''spines'' at the rear can spring upward. The front third of the Biot section is also lashed to the top of the floss underbody. Place a small drop of cement at this location, and trim off the excess Lusterelle.

The combined effect of heavy wire hook shank (this hook is

ideal for this streamer) floss body, and the section of Biot will result in the tubular body profile which is characteristic of this natural bait-fish.

The other purpose of the Biot section is to create a lateral band from the snout. This ''line,'' caused by different light reflection of the two materials (floss and Biot), is also apparent on the natural bait-fish. This line is also observable in the photograph.

STEP 4 Rotate the hook 180 degrees in the vise.

Select a bunch of Polar Bear hair approximately the diameter of a wood match. Align the butts; not the tips of the hair. When the material is secured this procedure will ensure less mass of hair towards the rear where the tubular body is smaller in diameter. Mount and secure this slim profile of Polar Bear hair for the belly. The Polar Bear hair is intended to imitate the silvery belly of the natural bait-fish. The tips of the Polar Bear hair extend rearward to a point which is in vertical line with the point of the hook. The butt ends of this hair are secured under the shank of the hook, three sixteenths of one inch from the eye of the hook. After binding the hair at this location, place a drop of cement on the thread windings.

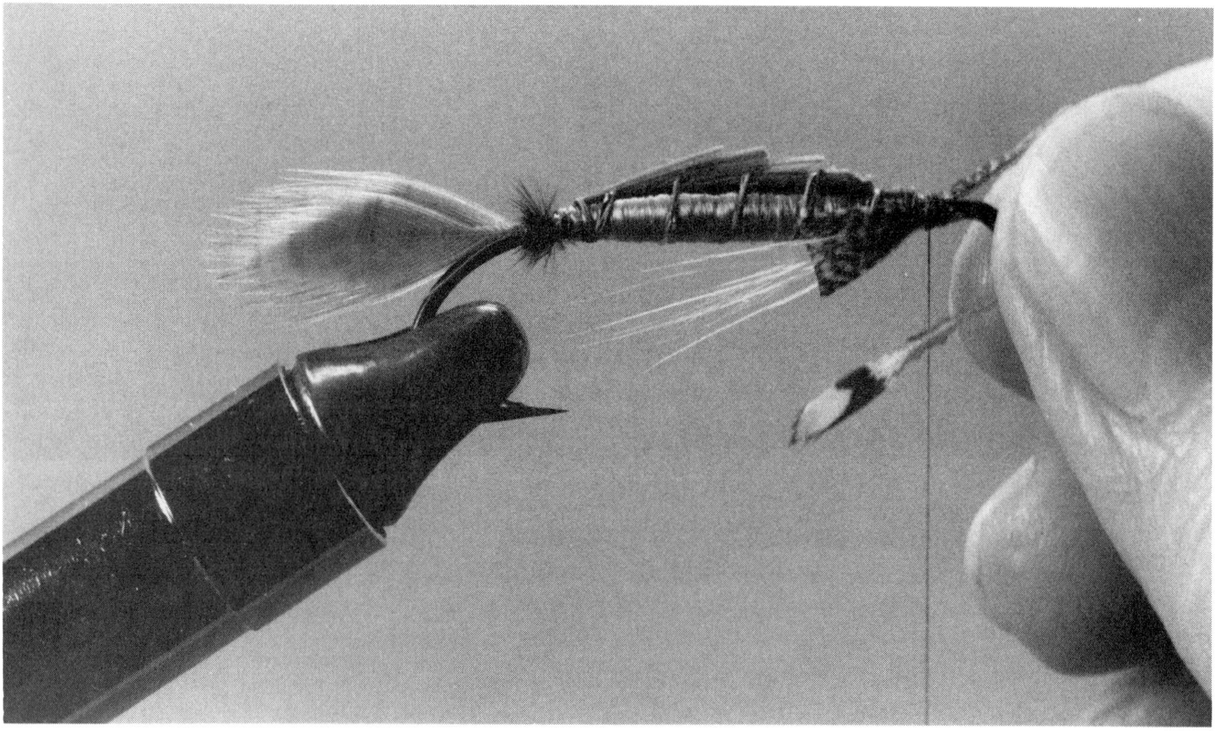

STEP 5 Trim away the excess Polar Bear hair which extends toward the hook-eye.

Prepare a pair of cheeks from olive-green wood duck. Then select a matched pair of Jungle Cock eyes. The eyes, shown held between my thumb and forefinger, should be of the size illustrated. The cheeks are positioned so that the lower edge(s) are in a line which is aimed at the point of the hook. This construction, when viewed under water, yields a blunt nosed appearance to the dressing. The position of the left cheek is shown in this step.

STEP 6 The Jungle Cock eyes are positioned over the cheeks and they are aligned with the floss portion of the body. The Jungle Cock eyes assist in supporting the position of the cheeks when the imitation moves through the water.

Form a head contour which is slightly "stepped," and which has its heaviest portion towards the rear. (It is usually preferable to whip finish the head at the rear). Cement the head with clear varnish and the bait-fish imitation is completed.

All of the recommended materials have been selected for color, texture, and markings to match the natural bait-fish as close as possible when such materials are wet.

I commenced testing this streamer fly during the Autumn of 1981. The fishing technique I use consists of a retrieval which moves the streamer fly with a darting motion. Its action in the water is lively when the fly is moved with quick bursts of speed. This year it captured a four and three-quarter pound bass from Drag Lake in the Haliburton Highlands region of Ontario.

The fly has also been effective on the Yellow Breeches near Allenbury, PA. (a limestone/freestoner stream). In 1988 this fly produced impressively at Falling Springs when fished under overhanging banks during the two hours before sunset.

MATERIALS BLUNTNOSE MINNOW	
Hook:	SEALEY Size 6—6X long 1734B or MUSTAD 3907B, or equivalent.
Thread:	olive.
Tail:	small olive hackles—webby; 5/8" - 7/8"
Body:	lusterelle No. 310 metallic yarn over light brown floss or pure silk twist.
Dorsal fin:	chinese or goose biots (brown).
Butt:	black Maribou.
Belly:	polar bear hair or substitute P.B.H.
Cheeks:	barred olive-green wood Duck or green flank feather.
Shoulders:	jungle cock eyes or substitute.
Head:	olive tying thread under clear varnish or cement.

Chapter 18

The "Dry" Fly and Salt Water
(Davis Bonefish Dry)

In a previous article about flies for bonefish I emphasized that sink rate is important.[1] Such is the case with the wet fly fished in three to five feet of water. At that time, however, I did not anticipate capturing bonefish on the "dry" fly.

The fly for bonefish is very often cast from a platform mounted on a skiff. But I have often felt conspicuous "up there," head and shoulders approximately nine feet above the surface of the water. Conspicuous, that is, to the bonefish. To compound the problem the wet fly may suffer from being inconspicuous. By this I mean that the sinking fly, when fished in shallow water, where the bottom is characterized by hills or troughs will, when the fly sinks into one trough, not be visible to a bonefish routing in a trough three or four feet away. To further compound the problem the sinking offering may hang-up on turtle grass or coral. This condition, even with the so-called weedless hook, prevents putting any "action" on the deceiver. All of the tribe Anomura, any of the crustaceans, are capable of movement, hence a need for "action."

This year during a falling tide I fished Bahamas flats covered by about ten to sixteen inches of water. I decided to give the floating fly a try. And I made the decision to wade in dark gray light-weight shoes with rubber soles. Conditions the first day were almost perfect for the floating offering. The bonefish were zigzagging, the sun provided for side-

---

The reader will note that the word "dry" is in italics. I prefer the term floating fly because the word "dry," historically, referred to a dry, recently unused fly taken from one's fly box. It was, usually, more difficult to float a fly historically, than is the case today. The dressing described in this chapter floats in the surface film.

lighting, and there was almost no wind. It is a rare day when there is practically no wind on the flats. Do not be misled; most days on the flats require the use of an eight or nine weight rod and line for bonefish.

But the large floating drake fly was almost obscured by reflections of sunlight. I therefore changed to a bright yellow floating Muddler Minnow which captured a six and a half and seven and a half pound bonefish. (Streamer flies of the hair-wing type were among the first successful flies used for bonefish.) Then the wind strengthened and made casting nearly impossible with the six wt. rod.

Two days passed before we had the opportunity to try the ''dry'' fly illustrated. A type of small crab rises from the turtle grass and weeds in Bahamas waters and moves about near the surface before descending. Such crabs move slowly with erratic motion as we perceive the action.

The imitations were dressed on low water (Wilson) black finish salmon irons—size two and four. Stainless steel and cadmium hooks have better resistance to corrosion, however, they also flash more in the sun.

This time I used a ten foot graphite (four piece) fly rod made by Gold-N-West in Vancouver. It casts a WF8F line with excellent control. The optional butt extension is a useful feature. The nine foot leader is eight pound test. I prefer the control of line offered by the ten foot rod because it is possible to keep more line out of the water when playing the bonefish. With rod held high during the bone's first long run, more line out of the water on shallow flats means less grass and weed will adhere to the fly line.

The ''white fox,'' which is the Albula vulpes (bonefish) is as skitterish as the brown trout at high noon in shallow water. It requires care to stalk one in ten to sixteen inches of water. They fight like the permit, that is, until they are exhausted. When a bonefish is *selected* (it is like chalkstream fishing in the South of England) I concentrate on tracking that *one* fish. If that bonefish changes direction, or moves too far away for an accurate cast, then, and only then, will I abandon that fish and select another bonefish for tracking. The first cast is the important cast. It must be accurate; not always easy to realize. If the fish is ''smoking'' (the puff of mud that becomes visible as it searches the bottom) the cast

---

[1]See Surette, Dick, *FLY TYER PATTERN BIBLE,* SALTWATER (V.7.1.2 issue), Sea Sinker and Sea Venture, Edition 1, p. 115, by Davis, E.G.

should be placed four or five feet in front of that last "smoke." When I spot a bonefish that is thirty-five to fifty feet away, tailing or otherwise. I sink to a kneeling position. (Polarized lenses in sun glasses are indispensible.) My reasons for adapting this posture are twofold. First I am indulging in a silent prayer that the bone will come closer. And second I am endeavoring not to spook the fish. When the surface of the water is calm bonefish can be spooked by a seagull flying over the surface of the water. One must see this to believe it!

I describe below my dressing for the DAVIS BONEFISH DRY. The fly is dressed on salmon hooks because the pattern which was successful was dressed on these hooks. There is no problem when using black finish hooks on a ten day vacation. The flies and all tackle can be rinsed in fresh water after fishing. The fly tying materials must be durable; a necessity because the "action" of saltwater gamefish can be rough on flies. One of these flies took three bonefish during one wading session. I lost the fly in a fourth bonefish. Moral: After each fish check the leader tippet close to the fly for chafing or other evidence which indicates wear or abrasion.

One last very important point about technique. After setting the hook (firmly) the bonefish will make a tremendous initial run usually, but not always, toward deeper water. Three hundred foot lightening fast runs are not unusual. The reel must be good quality, well lubricated and, preferably, carry two hundred and fifty yards of backing. When the bonefish takes off hold the rod as high as possible; hands extended above the head. This is the hallmark position of the expert taker of bonefish. And keep the hands away from the reel handle. At the speed these fish travel any impediment to continuous line outflow will result in a broken tippet and loss of the fish.

Now let's look at a dressing to imitate one of the more mobile and surfacing types of food forms of the salt.

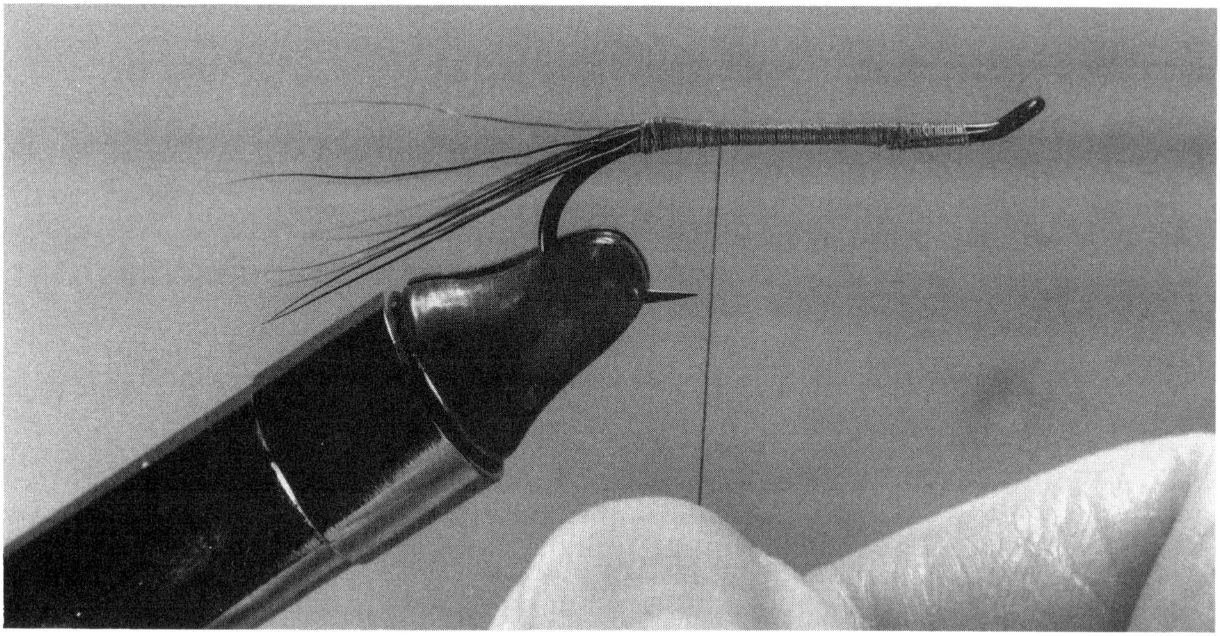

STEP 1 Place a size two or four (for Bahamas) hook in the vise and SHARPEN THE HOOK. The recommendation to SHARPEN THE HOOK is not intended as a criticism of the manufacturers of fly hooks. The quality supplied by hook manufacturers is very good. But the jaws of a bonefish are tough and a very sharp hook is advantageous to the flyfisher. Cover the hook shank (as shown) with 6/0 red nylon thread.[2] The tails (silhouette of short antennae) are divided and point down at an angle of approximately twenty five degrees from the horizontal (hook shank) plane. Each "fork" contains moose mane and porcupine guard hairs. Flair both forks of the tail to minimize capillary action of the fibers with salt water. The butt ends of the tail material which extend along the hook shank are trimmed at an angle (varying length). They are then cemented with waterproof cement.

[2]Because of the tenacity and rough action of saltwater gamefish many expert dressers of flies for use in saltwater double the tying thread.

STEP 2 Select a bunch of bucktail about the thickness of a lead pencil. The length of bucktail should be such that when the heavy ends are tied at the beginning of the hook bend, the fine ends of the bucktail fibers will extend one and a quarter to one and a half inches beyond the eye of the hook. Be certain to cement the butts and thread windings at the juncture of hook bend and shank of hook with waterproof cement.

STEP 3 While the (waterproof) cement previously applied to bucktail thread windings is still tacky, lock in a length of red floss at the hook bend. Advance the tying thread almost to eye of hook, and cover the hook shank with the floss. (The salt water will darken the red floss to a brownish-red.) Tie-off red floss, cement windings, and cut red tying thread and excess floss.

STEP 4 Attach 6/0 nylon green tying thread at hook bend. Select two cree hackles on which the barbules are almost the same length from tip to butt (not too tapered). The length of the barbules should be approximately one and a quarter times the hook gap. Tie the first hackle in by the butt as close to hook bend as possible, and palmer wind to mid shank position. Advance the tying thread through the hackle to reinforce and tie-off at the mid-shank position. Make three half hitches to lock-in and remove the excess hackle.

STEP 5 Position second hackle by locking-in by the tip at the mid-shank position. Wind the second hackle to a quarter inch back of hook-eye, reinforce with 6/0 thread as before, whip finish, and cement windings with waterproof cement.

STEP 6 The final operation includes folding (forward) the bucktail and tying securely one sixteenth inch from eye of hook. During this procedure divide the one and a half inch extension of bucktail in order to simulate the anterior pair of limbs which function as grasping pincers. As you do this many of the hackle barbules will be relocated to the sides. I have found it to be advantageous when none of the barbules are removed. During recent years I have reinforced the carapace (body) at two intermediate locations with nylon thread.

This fly simulates the action of a small crab on the surface, and can be twitched by moving the tip of the rod two to four inches. The bucktail configuration represents the flattened carapace and pincers of this member of the Brachyura. Because none of the hackle is removed and, in fact, extends to the sides, the hackle assists with the impression of the broader build which is characteristic of this crustacean. But of equal importance the flared hackle slows the rate of descent of the fly resulting in a softer land, a condition which is vital when casting to bonefish.

The capture of bonefish on the fly is not new. There is documented evidence of bonefish caught on fly dressings during 1924 and 1926; perhaps before this time.

The abundance of fish species in salt and brakish water will, in my view, continue to attract the flyfisher. And synonomous with that attraction we will witness a new era of creativity using natural and synthetic materials for our fly patterns.

DAVIS BONEFISH "DRY"
E.G. DAVIS

CRAB

Thread:	red and green 6/0 nylon
Hook:	VENIARD—WILSON type size 2 or 4 black finish salmon
Weight:	none
Body:	red floss
Cement:	waterproof
Antenna:	moose mane and porcupine guard hairs
Hackle:	cree cock hackle
Carapace and princers:	bucktail pulled forward, divided, and left extended 1 1/4" - 1 1/2"

NOTE: This imitation crab has produced exceptionally when the carapace and pincers are formed with green or natural brown/white bucktail.

Chapter 19

Mobile Crayfish

A few years ago when I had access to the private water at Camp Creek, Ontario, there was ample time for observations during the long summer evenings. There were only three persons who fished that water regularly. And it was a mecca for wild brook trout and large browns.

We enjoyed the facility of a small cabin with bunks, Coleman stove, lanterns, and a wood stove for those cold nights during early May and late September. We kept a stream log book for entering catches. All brook trout and brown trout were released unless they were injured, for example, a deeply ingested nymph pattern.

The cabin on Camp Creek. The home pool in the foreground always held a trout.

The Camp Creek water enjoyed excellent hatches of the major eastern mayflies which occur throughout the season. And also frequent hatches of caddis, stoneflies, and other trout food. The log book, referred to above, revealed an interesting profile of what trout took which fly and at which time, when analyzed at season's end.

But the situation which I am about to describe may not be familiar to some fly fishers. And that is the brown trout's appetite for crayfish.

For some time I had been releasing brown trout which showed evidence of snout abrasion. At first I speculated about the possibility of a parasite in the river. This condition, however, proved not to be the case.

During an evening in mid-July, after a very hot day, and the departure of Dr. Genyk, I jointed my rod and entered the water above an old iron bridge to wade slowly upstream. The water here is hip deep but shelves off on one side to a few inches. The stream bed at the shallows is populated by small stones and rocks about the size of a golf ball or smaller. It was here that I observed my first brown trout routing for crayfish. I froze motionless, thigh deep in water, rod held low, and watched a sixteen to eighteen inch brown trout nosing stones aside in her search for food. I made an attempt to get closer and raised the camera which is a fixture with me when fly fishing, and that motion spooked the trout.

Proceeding to the area where the trout was routing I began to turn over small rocks and dislodge stones. I counted eleven crayfish and two stonefly nymphs in an area of about nine square feet.

The concept of the crayfish dressing described below belongs, to my knowledge, to Dr. Ian G. Weeks, formerly of McMaster University, Hamilton, Ontario.

I have made two or three modifications to the imitation following some experimentation with casting and fishing this imitation of the crayfish.

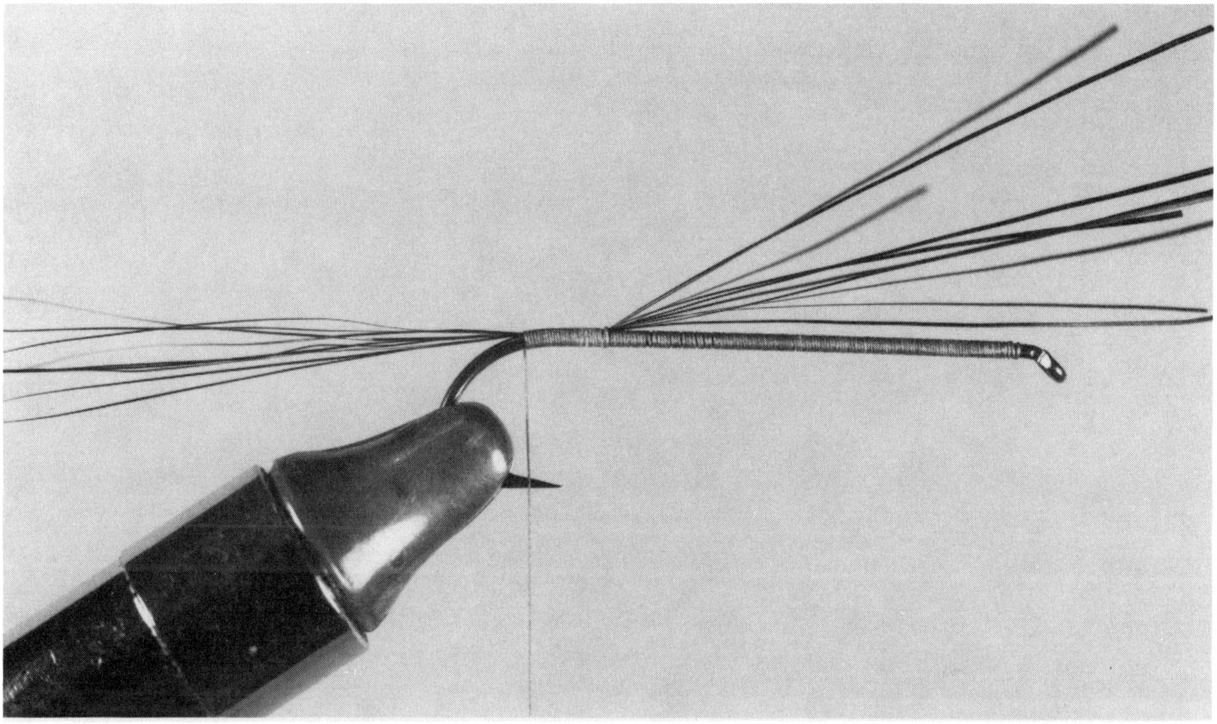

STEP 1 Position hook in vise and, starting 1/8″ from hook eye, cover shank of hook with brown tying thread to bend. Secure 6 to 8 European crane plume fibers, dyed black, with tips extending approximately one shank length from hook bend. Place a drop of cement on the thread windings to secure the antennules. More recently I have used Microfibbets for the antennules. These are a product of John Betts, and have excellent resilience and strength.

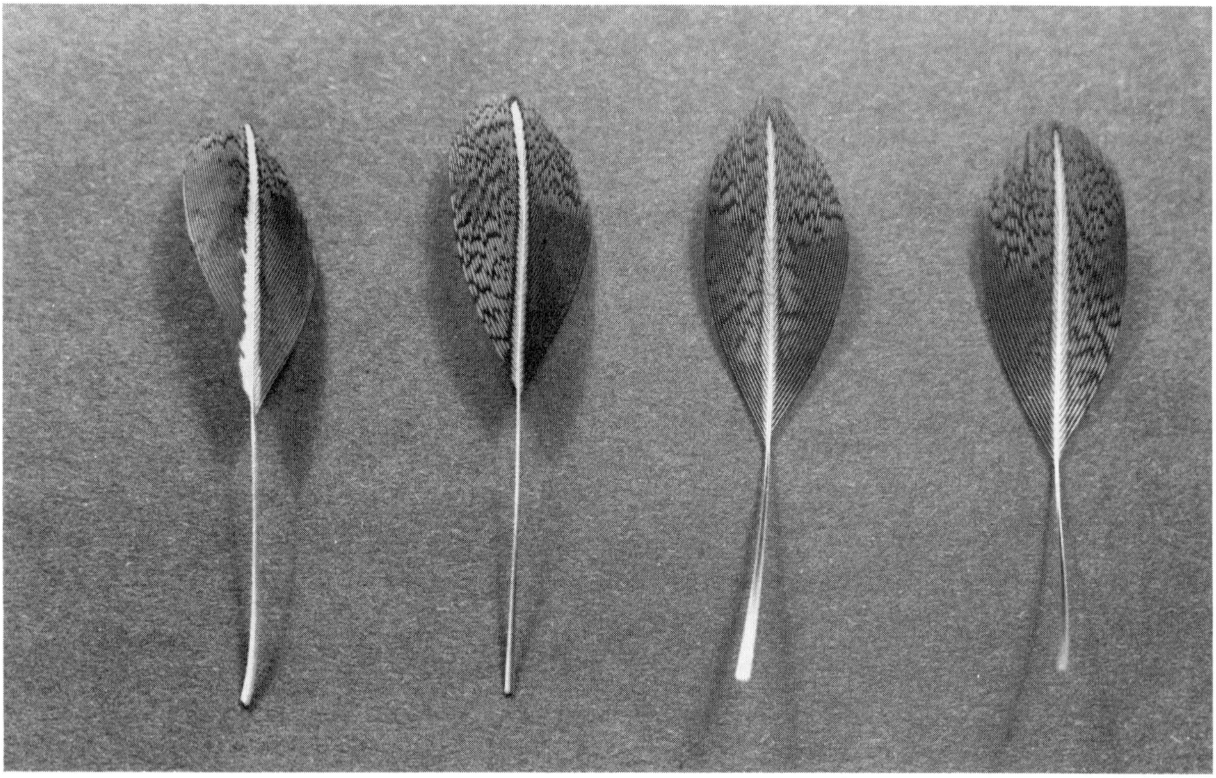

STEP 2 Illustrates two matched pairs of Canadian partridge feathers which will be used to represent one of the Great Cheliped (Mandibles). The two feathers at the left are face (bright) side up. The two feathers at right are dull side facing up. Note the dominant center quill on both sides. Also the mottled-brown characteristic. The dull (convex) undersides of the four feathers have been very lightly sprayed with (self-styling) hair spray. The feathers are then trimmed to the shape shown. They were selected on the basis of color and convexity of feather. The four feathers are sufficient for two imitation crayfish.

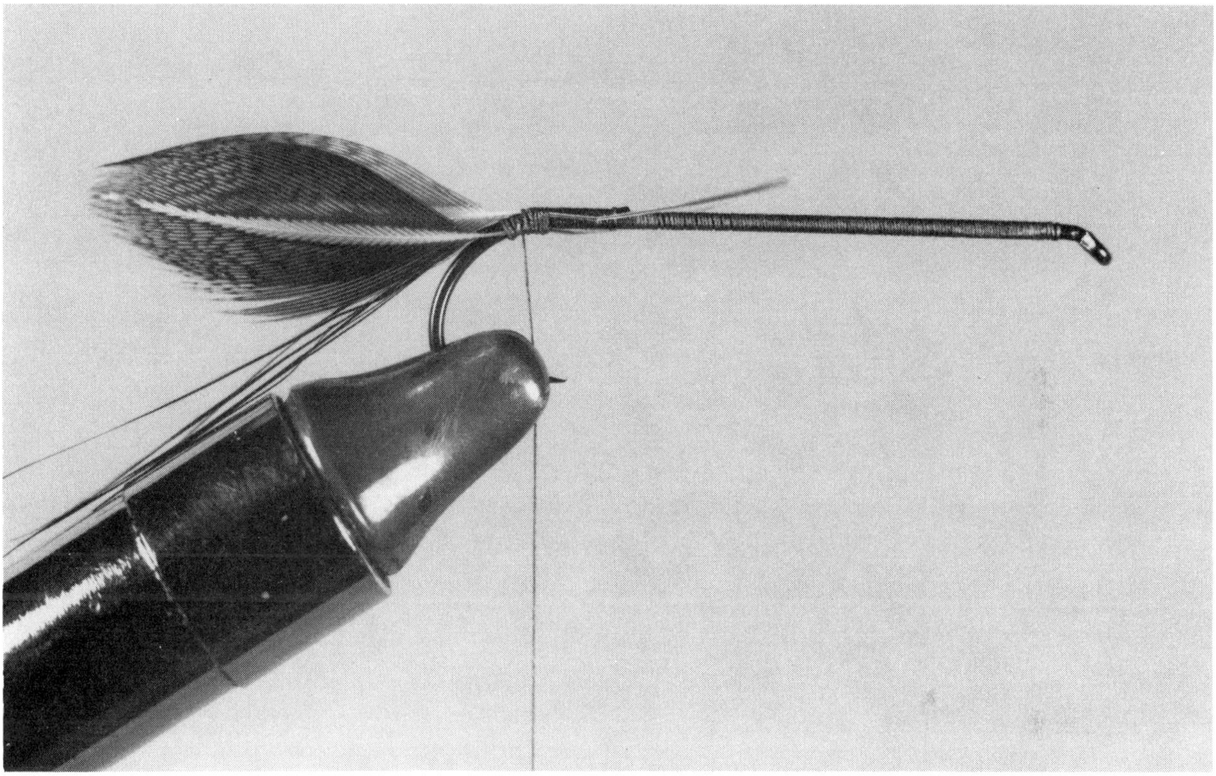

STEP 3 Remove the butt ends of the fibers. Secure the two feathers, one at a time, so that the convex sides face one another. The quills are positioned along opposite sides of the hook shank. When performing this step adjust the position of the antennules so that they angle downward. They "work" better in this position when the imitation crayfish is on the stream bed. Casting this imitation is not difficult when one Mandible is mounted instead of the usual two as on the natural anthropod body.

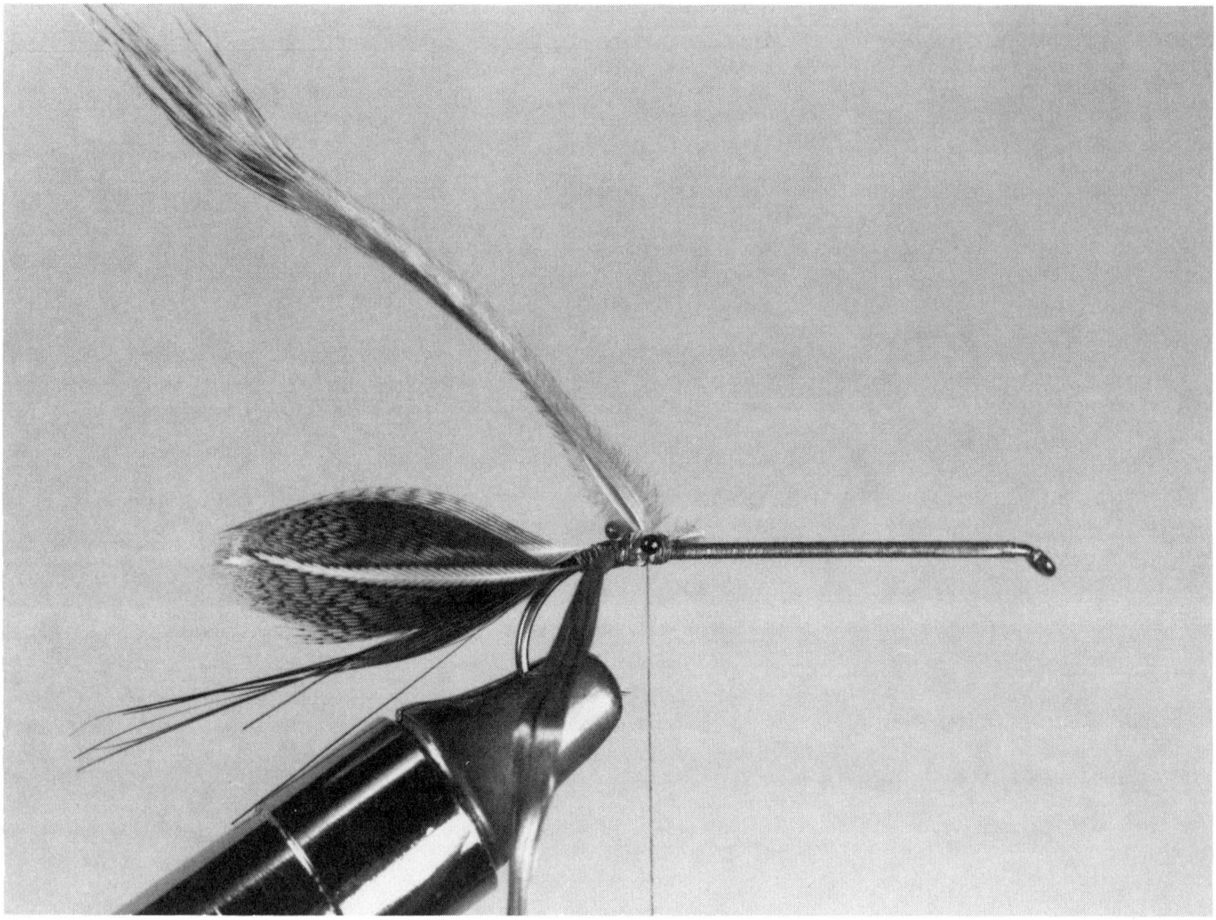

STEP 4 Remove butt ends of feathers. Secure a 20″ length of Poly-Straw (#107 Body Brown) immediately in front of the Mandible. Then prepare a 1/2″ length of 10 lb. test nylon leader material and secure this on top, and at a right angle to the hook shank. Nylon, an amide fiber, forms a hard black bead when melted. Mount, as shown, in front of Poly-Straw. Melt each end to form the two black beads. You can see the black beads in Step Four. They are now 5/16″ from one another. The piece of nylon is secured by ''X'' thread windings. Place a small drop of vinyl cement on the thread windings.

Now secure a 2 1/2″ length of 3/16″ wide tannish-brown owl feather plumage in front of the nylon strip. This material should be long enough, when pulled forward, to extend 1/2″ beyond eye of hook. (You can substitute the owl material with a lighter shade of brown Poly-Straw). But the outside edges of an owl feather include fine fibers ideally suited for the crayfish tail (Uropod). The tips of the owl feather barbs consist of fine wavy filaments which possess a ''willowy'' and enticing action in water.

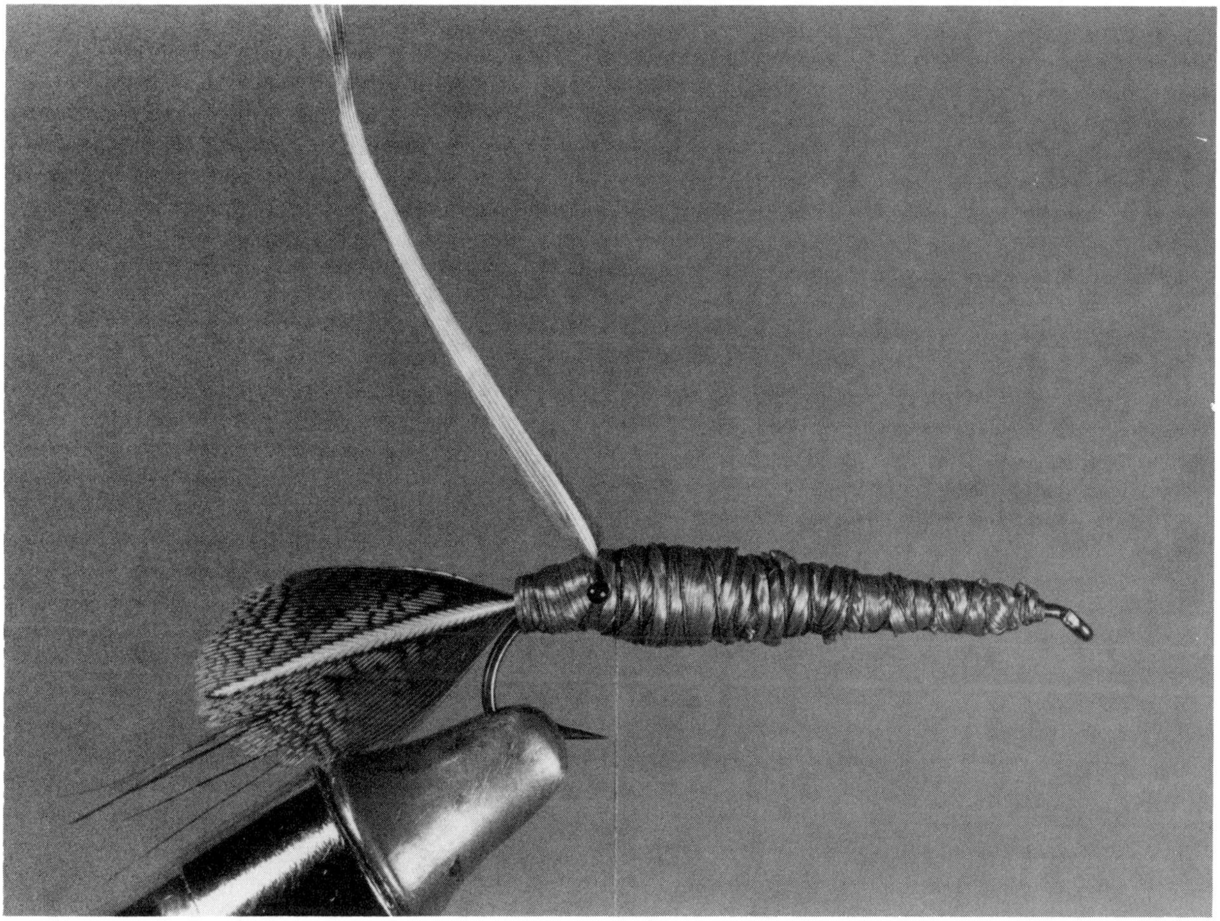

STEP 5 Contour the body with the Poly-Straw as illustrated. This material has the characteristic appearance of the natural crayfish body.

Because the eyes of the natural are on a movable stalk, part of which stalk protrudes, I taper the Poly-Straw at head so that the eyes protrude. Clip-off excess Poly-Straw. The 3/32" width of owl barbs now extends above the body. The length of this component is such that the fine (wavy) filaments at the tip will, when pulled forward later, form the tail of this crustacean. (If you have used a lighter shade of Poly-Straw the tail portion can be separated later with a needle).

STEP 6 Select an English grouse feather and prepare it as illustrated. Leave a short length of center quill at both ends. One can use any similarly shaped brown mottled feather here as a substitute, but the nature of the feather should be such that the barbs become progressively shorter towards one end.

STEP 7 Move tying thread in front of owl feather location. Mount the English grouse feather, longer barbs at rear, and position on top of body—dull side down. Use tying thread to separate (divide) small groups of barbs on both sides of the body to represent the appendages known as pereiopods. Secure feather with two or three turns of thread around protruding quill at mid shank. Now extend the owl feather forward and secure on top of the body at mid shank. Viewing the top of this dressing reveals that the owl feather barbs taper forward to complement the body (carapace) taper. The owl feather material will darken when wet.

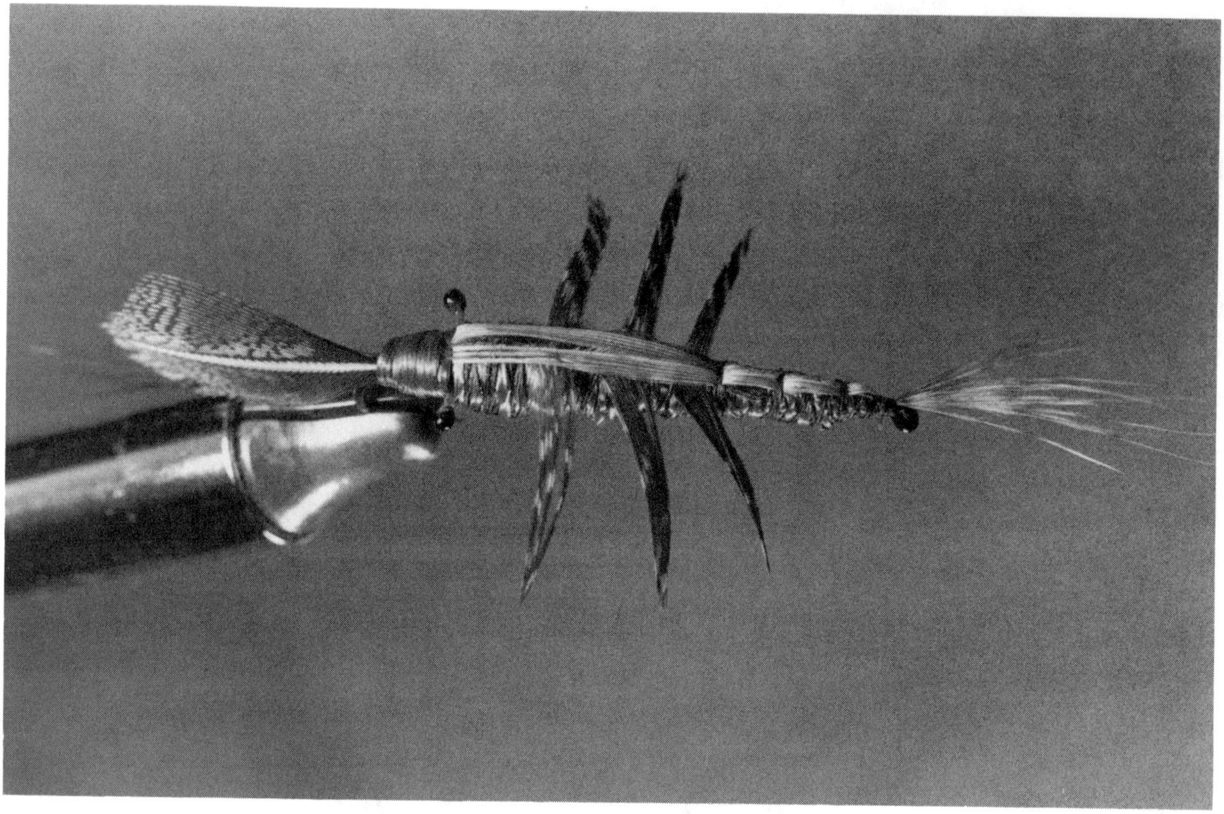

STEP 8 Complete this crayfish dressing by securing the feather section in the three locations shown, the last of which is 1/16" from eye of hook. The body segmentation is easily accomplished by advancing the tying thread around the body only, and progressively lowering the owl feather and making three or four turns of thread to segment. This method prevents cutting the thread until the last operation; the tie-down at the tail. Place a drop of cement on the tail location tie-off.

This imitation crustacean casts easily on a six to eight weight rod and sink tip line, with a tippet treated with leader sink material. When fished on the stream bed, and moved slowly and erratically, the Mobile Crayfish has produced superlatively for brown trout and bass.

CHAPTER 20

The Saugeen Streamer

The Saugeen and Sydenham watersheds of Southern Ontario have, historically, witnessed the skilled hands and inventive minds of many Canadian fly fishers. The late Jack Sutton, creator of the Despair, is one such outstanding personality. His dressings for the Despairs have often been displayed; more recently by the famous Bill Cushner of New York City. Bill and Phyllis Cushner now administrate the magnificent Fly Fishing Museum at Florence, Oregon. Their collections of mounted and professionally framed flies include dressings by Ted Niemeyer, Yas Yamashita, Jack Sutton, and many other famous artists and dressers of flies. Jack Smrekar is the Curator of the William Cushner Collection.

My collection of flies includes a superb group of dry flies tyed for me by Chauncy Lively. And a cluster of Despairs from the collection of the late Dr. Rowland of Toronto.

But my predilection for the Saugeen and adjoining watersheds was, originally, steeped in the time of the Hendricksons. Each fly fisher has his or her favorites. But on this cold winter day my thoughts turn to the hardy hatches of Ephemerella subvaria with its rusty markings, and its ability to survive despite the damage inflicted upon the ecology of rivers.

Mayfly patterns, however, are but one aspect of the wealth of dressings we possess. As important and soul-satisfying as the rise to the fly is, we are not always treated to hatches. There are occasions when the grasshopper and cricket are the order of the day. And there are cool fresh evenings and crisp mornings when the trout are roaming the shallows of the pools in search of bait fish.

The late Arnold Gingrich once described the streamer fly as "the fly fisherman's crutch for hatchless days." The rivers and lakes of Southern Ontario are no exception to the effectiveness of the streamer.

Our Saugeen River club-water holds stream-bred brown trout, brook trout, and rainbow trout. My optimum results with streamer flies have—in the main—occurred during early morning and the hour or two preceding dark. This situation likely obtains because the larger trout often feed on bait fish during these times.

Some years ago, in order to supplement established patterns such as the Mickey Finn and Black Ghost I developed this streamer fly. The Saugeen Streamer, I have been informed by other fly fishermen who have fished this pattern, has lively action in water, and good visibility under conditions of low light. There is also a translucency about the fly which is, in part, probably due to the natural polar bear hair which is used for the overwing. Observations of the minnows or bait fish in our stream confirm that they are predominantly one and three-quarters to two an done half inches in length. We do not kill the brown and brook trout. All members use barbless hooks for dressing flies and return trout to the water unless the fish is injured. Those of us who kill an injured trout and keep it for the table find an assortment of stoneflies, caddisflies, and mayfly nymphs which represent current hatches. Autopsies during July, August, and September reveal ants, grasshoppers, and crickets. Larger trout caught during the early morning virtually always contain bait fish and very often crayfish. The Saugeen Streamer is dressed as follows:

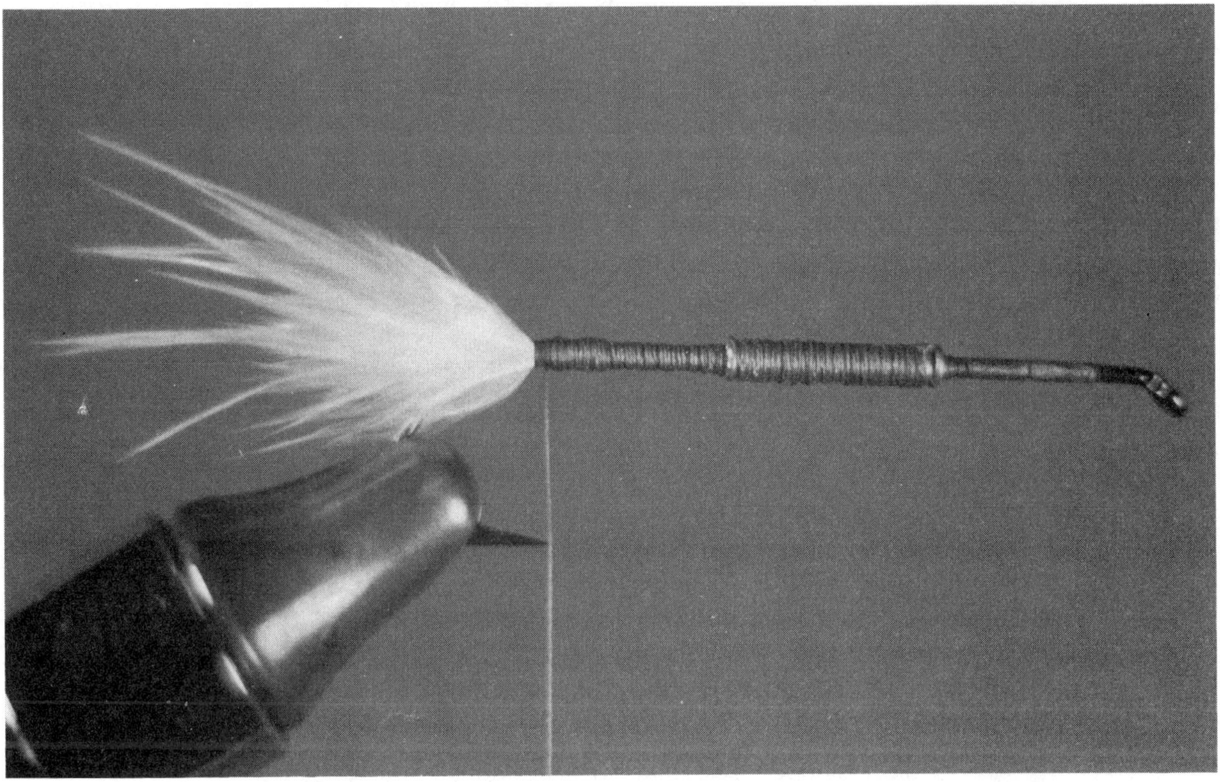

STEP 1 This fly is prepared on a size 6 6X long hook. The streamer is weighted with fine lead wire and I strongly recommend (flat) strip lead which facilitates a smooth body when overwound with floss. The shank of the hook is covered with green tying thread. Start the thread three-sixteenths inch behind the eye of the hook and continue close windings of the thread to a location on the shank which is three-sixteenths inches forward of the beginning of the hook bend. Mount and secure a piece of white maribou feather of the size and length shown. Then advance the tying thread one third the length of the hook shank and start the lead weighting at this location. Wind the wire forward to position shown. Now advance tying thread over wire and stop at forward end of wire. Then wind (return) tying thread to bend of hook. I have left the first and last coil of wire partly exposed to highlight the position of the weighting. The fly has a good action with the wire at this location. Apply a coat of varnish or cement to the hook shank. When dry apply a second coat. I prepare a number of these basic units in advance.

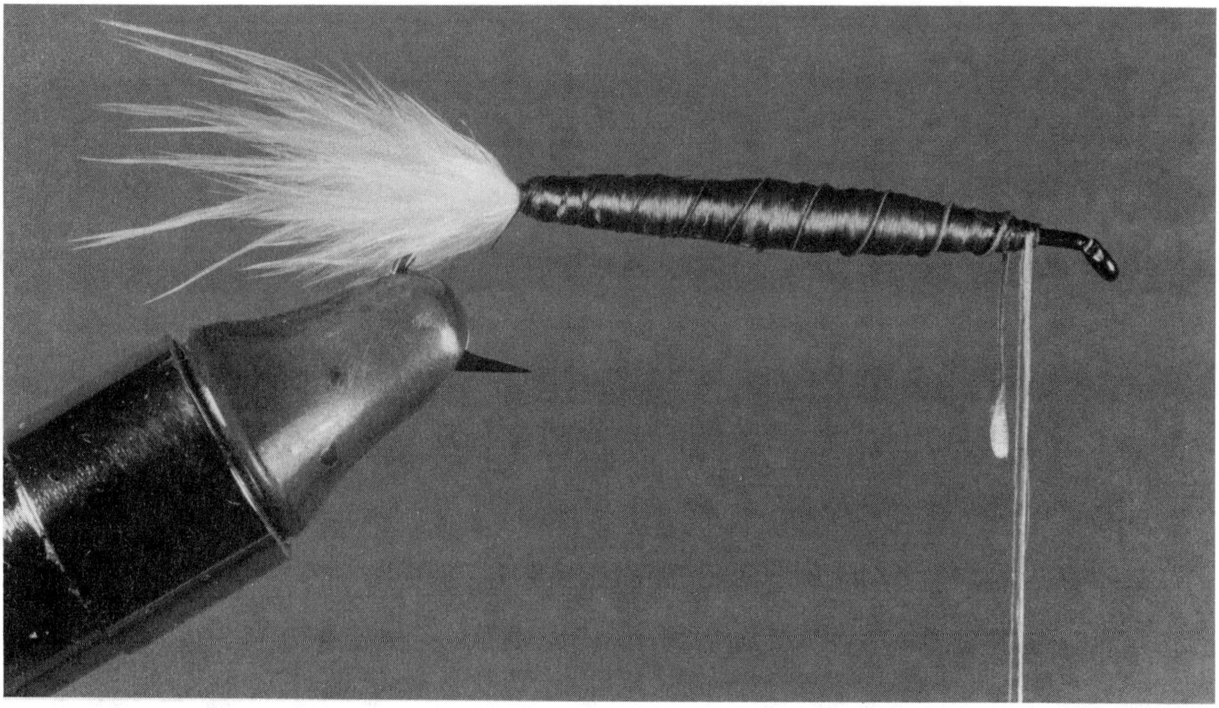

STEP 2 Advance the tying thread two or three snug turns and secure a black stripped quill from a hackle feather which has been soaked in water for twelve to twenty-four hours. It is preferable to use a quill which is not longer than four inches for a typical size 6 6X long hook so that the butt end will not be too thick when it is tyed-off forward. Leave the quill hanging free. Wind the tying thread two turns to the rear and secure the green floss. Because I use fine diameter floss there is no need to split the end in order to achieve a non-bulky tie-in with this material. Advance tying thread to a position three-sixteenths inch from eye of hook. Build the tapered body to the slim tapered shape shown. The fly is designed to sink slowly and can be cast with accuracy. Segment the body with the black quill. The quill will not slip if the winding is begun immediately at the rear and no extra turns are taken at the front; tying-off when the quill reaches the front of the body. Normally, when ribbing a tapered body, the windings become progressively wider when proceeding from rear to front. That is not the case with this dressing. When the quill is secured at front brush on a coat of clear varnish. I use ''Cellire'' Varnish No. 1 Clear (Fine) because it does not alter the color of the green floss.

STEP 3 Remove excess floss and quill material.

In 1982 I made a slight modification to the Saugeen Streamer. The fly works more effectively under conditions of low light when the under (bucktail) orange wing is mounted on the top of the hook shank to extend rearward so that the tips of the bucktail, when drawn through water, are in vertical line with the point of the hook. Place a drop of cement on the thread windings. When this wing material is secured raise it, and take a couple of turns of thread around the base of the hairs. Then make two or three more turns around the butts in the usual way. Trim excess bucktail from in front of thread windings. The underwing profile is shown in this Step. Considerable action of the fly will be lost if the wing material is too heavy.

STEP 4 Change tying thread from green to white. The sparse quantity of polar bear wing material, after alignment of the tips of the hairs, is mounted on top of the orange bucktail. The polar bear hair extends rearward to a position which, when the hair is wet and more nearly in the horizontal plane, the tips will be in line with the end of the hook bend. This hair is slightly longer than the bucktail underwing, and it provides for good visibility in low levels of light. Apply two or three drops of cement to the butts of the hairs. The two Jungle Cock Eyes are now positioned and secured so that the stripped centre quills of these eyes are locked under the head of the fly. The head is whip-finished and varnished blue. The hydrodynamic drag of this fly is such that it sinks slowly; an ideal rate of sink for shallow pools, riffles, or undercut banks.

I usually fish this streamer fly during daybreak or when the light is very low during late evening. If I am familiar with a stream bed, and fish the stream at night, I often use this fly because it has produced superbly. The technique I use is to cast across and upstream with firm presentation. Then keep the fly moving with a hand twist retrieve.

Designing attractor patterns can be rewarding. Two of the characteristics (colors) of this fly are based upon work done by Sosin and Clark. Their informative book *Through the Fish's Eye* describes conditions which reveal good light penetration depth at dusk and dawn in clear water—particularly for green. "At dawn," state Sosin and Clark, "when the fish switch to color sensitive cone vision, blue and green are the first colors visible in the early morning light . . ."

For those of you who fish Falling Springs in Pennsylvania (I make an annual pilgrimage which also includes Big Spring, the Yellow Breeches, and the Letort) this fly has been very effective when fished under the banks at Falling Springs. It has also produced superbly on the Yellow Breeches (a limestone/freestone river) near Allenbury.

There will always be something new to be learned about the use of fly rod and fly. Perhaps therein lies some of the fascination to be found with this intriguing sport.

CHAPTER 21

Shrimp on the Sawgrass

A cool tropic breeze entered the transom above the door. The impression is of rain when the evening trade winds rustle the palm fronds. Perhaps, I reflected, the coffee is keeping me from sleep. But the truth of the matter about not sleeping centered upon my anticipation of bonefishing. For there is something majestic about the ferocity with which these fish grasp the fly, and strip fly line and backing from your reel.

I had arrived that day in the country of the seven hundred islands. The flights were smooth and uneventful. This is an area of islets and reefs. The islets are often referred to as cays, and they exceed 2,000 in round numbers. The islands are, for the most part, flat. The highest elevation is Mount Alvernia which rises to 206 feet. The Bahamas islands are principally composed of oolitic limestone and coralline, and wind-blown deposits. The active coral reefs which fringe the coasts consist—in the main—of bright white coral sand. It is a land of few inland waterways; the exceptions being a large lake on Inagua and a river on Andros Island.

Richard Nelson called for me in the morning and shared a pot of coffee on the quiet terrace adjoining the breakfast room. The February sun bristled down on an aquamarine sea as we approached his small jetty.

Flies for bonefish (Albula vulpes) are best tyed on stainless steel hooks—sizes 8 to 2. Size 4 is preferable for most Florida waters; sizes 6 and 8 are predominant in the Bahamas. The hook size is related to the size of the fish. In lieu of stainless steel hook material you can use the cadmium plated hooks, however, they do not have the resistance to corrosion which stainless steel offers.

The major items in the diet of bonefish consist of mussels, small crustaceans, and copepods. The bonefish family (Albulidae) consists of two genera: Albula and Dixonina. Both genera feed on shrimp. Shrimp is the common name for any of approximately 2,000 species of the suborder Natantia (order Decapoda of the class Crustacea). Shrimps are characterized by a semi-transparent body flattened from side to side, and a flexible abdomen terminating in a fanlike tail. Shrimp larvae pass through five development stages before maturity. It is the shrimp deceiver that many flyfishers place before the bonefish. The common European Shrimp or sand shrimp (Crangon vulgaris), occurs in coastal waters on both sides of the North Atlantic. Its average size is 4 to 8 centimeters (1.5 to 3 inches). It is grayish-brown, with brown or pinkish-red spots. The salt water shrimp is likely one of the three or four most sought-after food forms by bonefish. Many salt water shrimp are a grayish-tan or off-white color. But some kinds of salt water shrimp do have a pinkish cast prior to being cooked.

For our purpose, or rather for the purpose of enticing the Albula vulpes, size, shape, and care not to spook the bonefish are the major criteria. There is, however, another plus for the fly angler. And that feature is visibility of the fly. Sunlight can play strange distortions on saltwater flats. A riffled surface can obscure vision unless sun glasses (a must) with polarized lenses are used by the fly fisher. A light colored fly on a dark (and frequently grassy) bottom is an advantage. The color photo illustrates a proven pattern for bonefish. Streamer flies were probably the first patterns used for bonefish. The small crab has captured many bonefish right in the surface film.

The mouth of a bonefish is a formidable crusher. It is difficult to penetrate with a hook. Setting the hook is preferable after the bonefish turns. And it is important to keep some tension on the fish after the strike. But there may be very limited opportunity to make a strike unless one

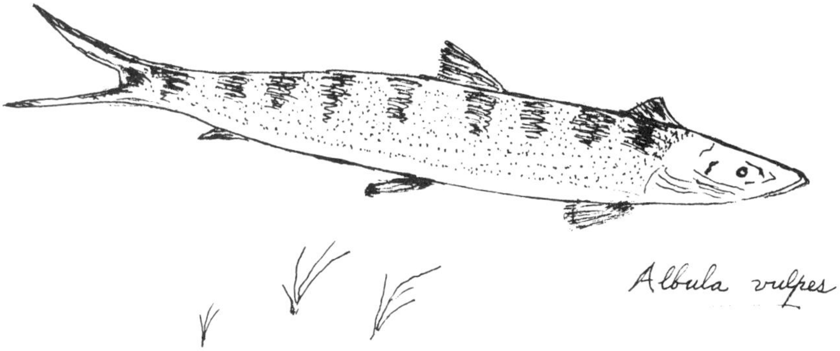

The "Fox of the Flats" is a fleeting shadow. In the glare of the sun, poloroid glasses and a wide brim hat (black on the underside) are indispensible. Go with a guide who knows the water, movements of tides, and who can read the symptoms of feeding bonefish. Be capable of casting accurately in wind with flies which have a specific sink rate in salt water.

can first command the attention of a bonefish with the proper motion of the fly. Bonefish are frequently nervous and it is imperative to place the fly with a minimum of commotion. One effective technique with a fly which is fished a few inches below the surface of the water is to action the fly in short abrupt movements. Try to ascertain the direction in which the bonefish is moving and place the fly three to four feet in front of the fish.

One of the illustrated shrimp-imitation flies is dressed, basically, of yellow and white materials and has proven itself to be a successful fly pattern. The visibility (contrast) is good. It does not sink too quickly, and may be presented quietly.

Use the clinch knot to attach the fly to an eight or ten pound test salmon leader of nine feet in length. Avoid joints (any kind of knot) in the leader to prevent picking up algae.

When the bonefish is hooked, hold the rod high to keep as much of the fly line as possible off the surface of the water. Then hope that the bone will run for deeper water instead of targeting a shoreline clump of mangrove or an abutment of coral.

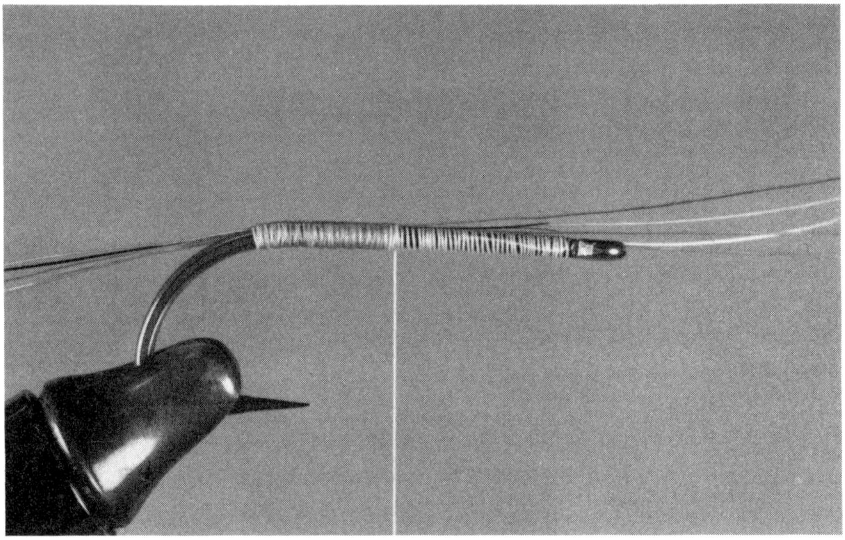

STEP 1 Select nylon working thread in preference to pure (animal) silk thread. Nylon has superior resistance to corrosion in salt water. Position the hook in the vise as illustrated and sharpen (hone) the hook point. Start yellow 6/0 tying thread close to hook eye and cover hook shank tightly to beginning of hook bend. Position six or seven Chinese boar hairs (a mix of brown, dark, and clear) on top of hook shank. Light and dark moose mane hairs can be used as a substitute. The hairs should extend beyond the hook bend for a distance equal to the length of the hook shank. These hairs represent the antennae and they will be bent downward at a later step in the construction. The antennae are bound tightly to the rear half of the hook shank. Brush on a coat of cement to the rear half of the hook shank. Tying thread is now located at mid-shank.

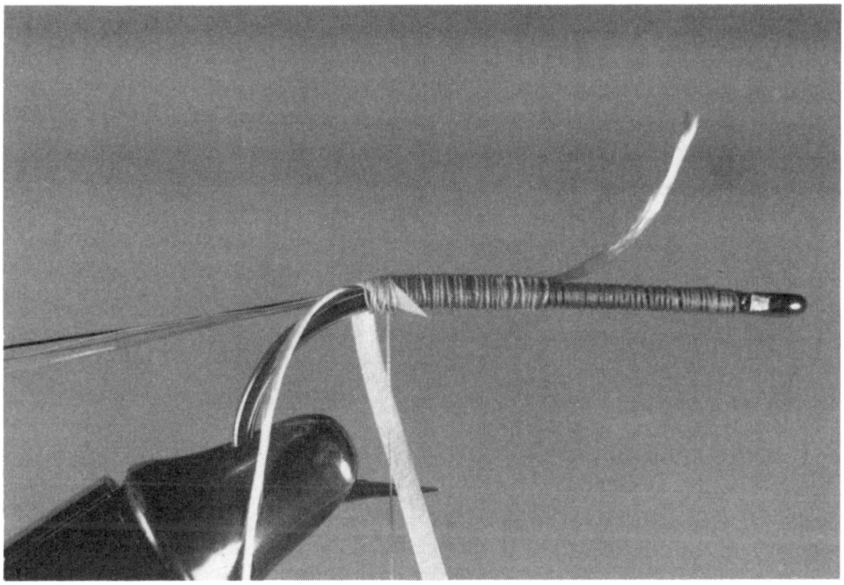

STEP 2 Cut off the butts of the Chinese boar hairs or moose mane hairs. The back, under-carapace, is formed with yellow floss. The floss is tyed in at the mid-shank position and on top of the hook shank. The floss is now bound tightly from mid-shank to hook bend by the tying thread. At this juncture—where the hook bend begins—firmly attach an eight inch length of yellow Pseudo-Quill-Medium. (Swannandaze Lace, Yellow No. 10 3/32″ wide may be used as an alternate). The end of the Quill is cut at an angle and locked in with four turns of thread to the rear. Remember that the shrimp swims with a "backward" motion. The head of the shrimp, therefore, should be located at the bend of the hook.

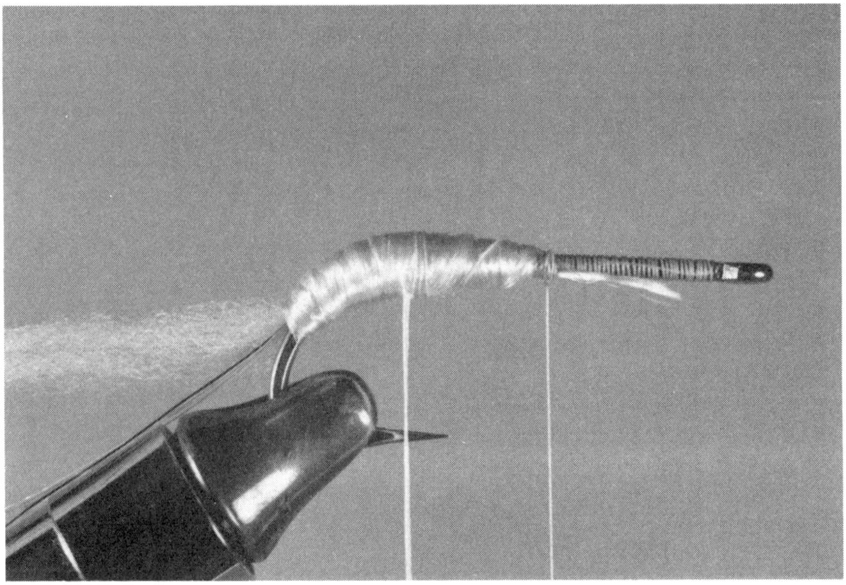

STEP 3 Clip off excess floss at mid-shank position. Secure a three inch piece of white 3-ply Phentex[1] (uncombed) at the hook bend. This operation will push the antennae down, thereby enhancing the resultant natural shrimp bend. The body contour of the shrimp is formed by folding and refolding the floss backward and forward on top of the hook shank, alternating between each fold by winding the floss around the hook shank. By reducing the length of each fold the typical profile of the salt water shrimp is achieved. You can see this profile in Step 3. Tie-off the floss with the yellow tying thread. The tying thread is now at the mid-shank position. The three inch length of white Phentex is half way around the hook bend. This has changed the position of the antennae. The six inch length of yellow Pseudo-Quill is in line with the beginning of the hook bend.

[1]This is one of the trade names for Polypropolene yarn.

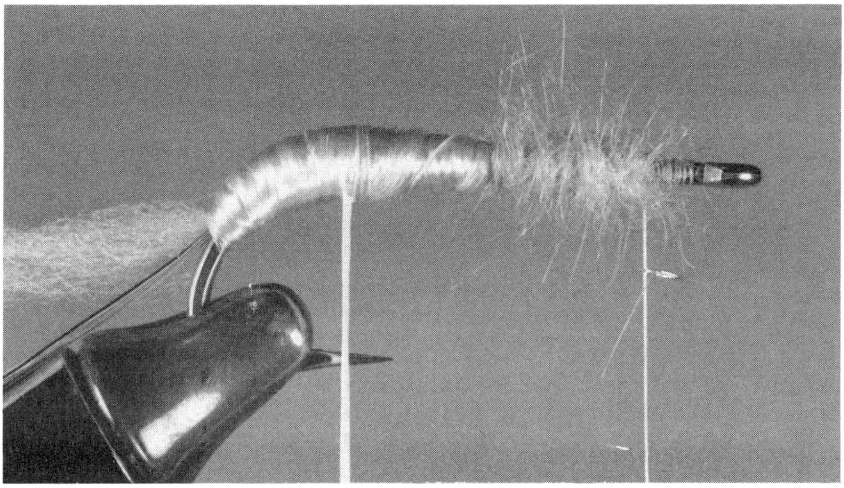

STEP 4 Cut-off excess floss. Bring the tying thread back 3/16″ (towards the Pseudo-Quill) and dub yellow Seal fur, or a substitute, (loosely) to the volume and location shown on the hook shank. Stop dubbing about 3/8″ from eye of hook.

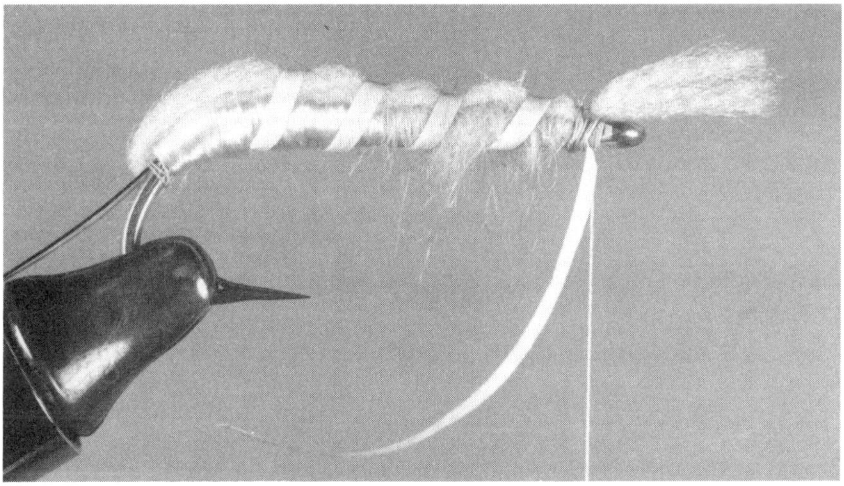

STEP 5 Pull the 3″ strip of Phentex, under tension, over the top of the shrimp body and tie down 1/8″ from hook eye. Place one drop of waterproof cement on these windings.

Now wind the Pseudo-Quill—evenly spaced—to 1/8″ of eye of hook and tie securely to Phentex and hook shank. Cement with waterproof adhesive.

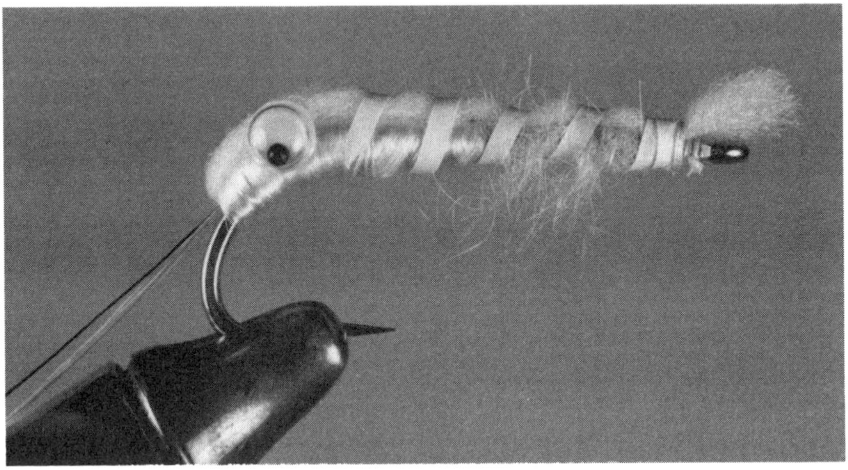

STEP 6 Cut-off excess Pseudo-Quill and cut tying thread. Leave a length of Phentex to extend 3/16" beyond hook eye. Pick-out dubbing to obtain the illustrated effect. The eyes are optional. I usually "spot" the eyes with black waterproof varnish then, when the varnish is dry, place a small "dot" of white varnish in the middle of the black "dot." These operations complete the Bonefish Shrimp. The materials have been selected to result in a slow rate of sink. The rate of sink can be adjusted by using layers and wraps of lead wire underneath the floss.

One final suggestion about technique. A long rod is an advantage when fly fishing for bonefish. I use a weight forward No. 8 line. This allows for additional backing on the reel compared with use of a double taper fly line of the same weight. Bonefishing requires a minimum of 200 yards of backing on the reel.

DAVIS VISIBLE SHRIMP	
Hook:	MARUTO –SS1930 size 1/0 to 4 (Stainless) O'Shaughnessy
Thread:	yellow 6/0 nylon
Under-carapace:	yellow floss
Carapace:	white 3 ply phentex
Antennae:	Chinese boar hairs
Ribbing:	Pseudo-Quill
Under hairs:	yellow seal fur picked-out
Eyes:	small rolly or dot of varnish
Tail:	white 3 ply phentex

The Aurora Pool—Newfoundland.

CHAPTER 22

Green Waters

A Scotch mist settled gently throughout the night.

The rain stopped at dawn and low scudding clouds drifted across the valley. I waded slowly upstream to the large pool located about two hundred feet below the abrupt ninety degree turn of the river.

I had fished the pool during two previous years but without success. It is a classic holding lie which contains two very large boulders of approximately the size of a card table. Looking upstream, on the right side of the pool is a sloping slate-like rock, its moss-covered surface reaching upward toward silver birches. The tunnel of trees overhead provides for a canopy designed to capture the fly which is allowed to ride too high on the backcast. The water had a metallic greenish hue and was remarkably free of sediment considering the recent rain.

I opened the Wheatley fly box and considered the contents. Today the Wheatley contained a mix of traditional flies, reduced patterns, and hairwings.

Charles De Feo was of the opinion that the salmon hairwings had their genesis in Newfoundland. And many of the patterns I carry are winged with reddish calftail, a characteristic of some early Newfoundland patterns.

My predilection for the hairwing is centred in pragmatism, that is to say limited time at the fly tying vise. The traditional flies came first and, many years ago, produced splendid catches for me on the Restigouche.

But there has always been room for experiment with the salmon fly. Certainly we realize this feature about salmon fishing when we examine Baden-Powell's Prismatic Fly, or some of the effective guide patterns frequently used on our rivers.

Wilson had moved close to my shoulder and was examining the contents of my fly box with the secretive look of the rare lemur of Madagascar. Wilson had also noted the three salmon in the pool.

"What do you think about this situation . . . any preference?", I asked.

"Try your green waters," Wilson suggested, "greenish water, green fly," he added.

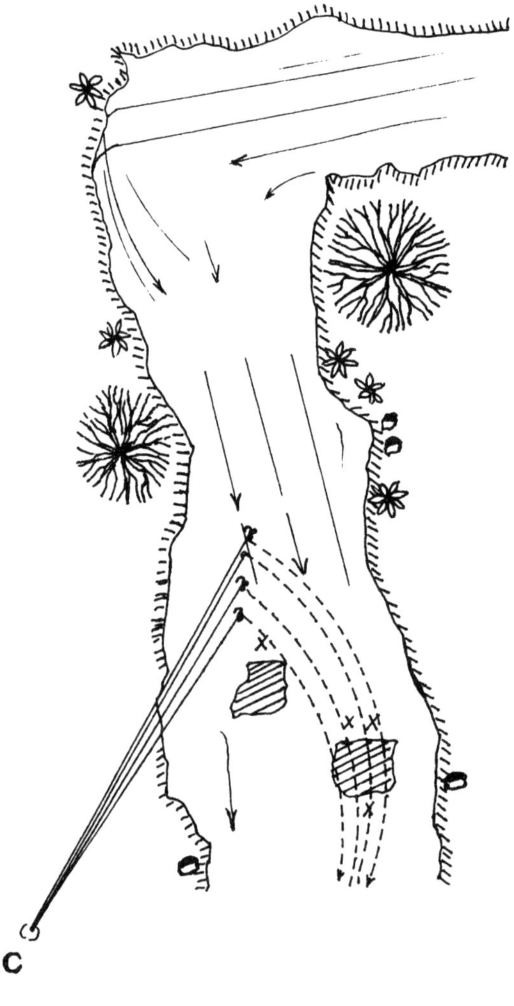

If the Caster "C" is correctly positioned, it is possible to track the fly close to the salmon (x) lying in the pool. Complete coverage of the fishable water is possible; see dotted lines in the illustration. If the correct depth is fished it is also possible with this technique to present a side view of the fly to the salmon. This is often necessary to induce a "take." The line is lengthened with each subsequent cast, and then shortened for the return series of casts.

I tyed on a Green Waters while Wilson commented about a flight of Canada Geese arrowing high above. It was quiet and cool in that leafy enclave. I heard the nasal ''beep'' of a Woodcock, seldom seen, in the forested growth. A Spotted Sandpiper ran along the water's edge. Rainwater dripped from scented foliage.

I began by false casting over the extreme left hand side of the pool. The left side could be traversed without too much difficulty if a salmon, once hooked, decided to run upstream from the pool toward the band of the river. But the pool had to be fished from below.

I wanted to fly fish that pool from one side, with casts extending across and upstream to the head of the pool. But the proliferation of tree branches would not allow for freedom of the backcast. My reasoning embraced the technique of placing each (successive) cast about one foot downstream so that the fly would swing over both boulders with a precise series of concentric current swings. Such was the position of the two boulders. Because this kind of extended current swing was not possible, I had to cast from almost directly below the pool.

The twelve foot leader turned over satisfactorily. Salmon fishing, in my experience, requires patience. It also calls for discipline, and I concentrated upon achieving as quiet an entry of the fly as possible. On about the thirtieth cast I watched, fascinated, as the line cut sharply upstream through the current. ''Salmon'' I called to Wilson, and set the hook. The fish ran right through the head of the pool and into a long smooth glide. The Hardy St. George released all of the fly line and about forty yards of backing. The salmon broke water and cartwheeled in a brilliant shower of spray as I lowered the rod tip. Moving quickly up the left side of the pool and reeling in backing, I had to stop running because the fish had turned and was racing towards me. Taking in backing quickly I was able to put strain on the fish again. As soon as the salmon felt pressure it turned and ran upstream. I followed the fish to the bend of the river and there we fought the remainder of the contest. It was punctuated by short runs and head-shaking soundings in ten to twelve feet of water. This is always the best time for me. The sense of accomplishment does not surface until the end is near. And it is enhanced by a view of this noble fish in all of its bright mint-coin-like shimmer.

Wilson netted the twelve pound salmon and, shortly afterwards, I released the salmon. It moved away with increasing vigour.

Those of us who flyfish know the magic of this moment. For it is in the act of giving that we assure for ourselves, and our progeny, a continuance of the rich heritage we enjoy today.

Tying Instructions

Hook Sizes:	No. 2 MUSTAD single #90240 No. 6 PARTRIDGE double regular
Tag:	medium gold tinsel
Tip:	black floss
Tail:	golden pheasant crests
Body:	green pure silk twist
Ribbing:	medium gold tinsel
Throat:	bluish-green feather (De Feo style)
Wing:	barred red pine squirrel tail
Head:	green No. 16 Veniard ''Cellire'' varnish

Best Usage

Conditions of medium light (cloudy bright) with good clarity of water.

Lake of Two Rivers, Algonquin Park.

CHAPTER 23

Those Incredible Bass on the Fly Rod

A superb setting in a conserved wilderness is readily accessible to the flyfisher.

When the history of our time is recorded for posterity this era will likely be entitled the "age of apathy." This indifferent or uncaring attitude manifests itself in tolerance for acid rain, polluted lakes and rivers, and the lack of effective criteria (and laws) for the disposal of toxic wastes. We are no longer certain about whether urban water for drinking poses a health problem. But we are aware of the toxic gases and hydrocarbons, among other substances, in the air we breathe.

It was therefore no small pleasure and satisfaction this year, to experience the relatively pristine environment of Algonquin Park. The Park provides an opportunity for unexcelled outdoor activity. Situated between Georgian Bay and the Ottawa River, Algonquin Park is within easy access from New York State, Quebec, Vermont, and the Province of Ontario. It is, for example, 410 miles from Detroit, Michigan, 265 miles from Buffalo, New York, and 450 miles from Cleveland, Ohio. The Park is open from May until September and, during Autumn, is a cavalcade of color in a Vermont-like setting. If you long for "the feel

---

The author, after forty years of sport fishing with the fly rod, has experienced three game fish whose fighting qualities, regardless of individual uniqueness, are the equal of the small mouthed black bass. Those three game fish are the salmon, the permit, and the brown trout.

That wily small mouth (Micropterus dolomieu) will be found in lakes near the Parkway (Algonquin Park) corridor. It is also widely distributed in the Haliburton Region. The small mouth has a fighting style that acknowledges no constraint. And when taken on the fly rod, especially in flowing water, every move, every nuance of motion and resistance results in a whole new experience with this magnificent game fish.

of wilderness,'' the joy of canoeing, and superb fly fishing for bass you will revel in this beautiful preserve. The bonus is the Haliburton Highlands with all of this area's surrounding beauty which includes its lakes. The Haliburton region is situated a few miles South of Algonquin Park.

BRIDLE LAKE

The breeze made it necessary to use an eight weight fly rod and matching line. But the wind moved the canoe along the shoreline at just the right speed. I watched a loon submerge as the canoe drifted close to its path, and continued to watch and tried to estimate the location at which the loon would resurface. I had previously placed a sixty-five foot cast in order to drop the fly near the rocky shoreline. Experience has confirmed, with monotonous regularity, that they always hit you when your attention has been diverted. And so it happened once more. The rod was almost pulled from my hands as my eyes searched for the reappearance of the loon. I contemplated the possibility that the loon had taken the streamer fly. But that wild guess was quickly dispelled when the bass broke water. The fish jumped only once but it was sufficient for me to note the size. (It subsequently weighed three pounds fourteen ounces.) And now began a steady long run by this black bass. The eight weight fly rod flexed sharply. I picked up the canoe paddle in my left hand and turned the canoe so that it was broadside with the wind. I wanted maximum drift downwind in the opposite direction to the path the bass was taking. Slack line with this fish could mean losing the battle. The Hardy Perfect reel purred like a miniature outboard motor. All of the fly line was in the water, and the dacron backing line was being taken at an alarming speed. Would the joint at fly line to backing hold I wondered? Would the 4X leader tippet hold this fish? I quickly eased drag off the reel spool. The bass continued its long run. I looked around the lake. Where did that loon go? The bass stopped its long run. I tightened up firmly but not too firm. Keeping the rod tip up I let this fish fight the power and spring in the rod—not the strength of the leader. Slowly I began to reclaim line from the fish. I had retrieved all of the dacron backing and some of the fly line when the bass broke water. I noted the line rising in the water, and then the series of spectacular vibrating leaps that this species is so capable of performing. I began to worry about the 4X tippet again. But the equipment held and now the bass appeared to be tiring. Resistance consisted of short rushes two or three feet below the surface of the water. As I reached under the seat of the canoe to check the position of the handle of the net, the bass made three quick jumps and began another run which—again—stripped all of the fly line from the reel. That run culminated in a beautiful display of acrobatics. The use of the fly rod is the only way to appreciate this kind of action sport. The bass, this time, was close to shore and sought a depth of water near the shoreline. It is a favorite trick of the dolomieu. They will try to break you off among rocks, boulders, or an assortment of logs or other deadfalls on, or near, the bottom. Bass attempt many tricks, and the larger they are the more tricks they seem to know. I had to put strain on the fish to move it away from the shallow water near the shoreline. The bass moved towards the canoe and shortly thereafter, I netted the fish, removed the barbless hook, weighed it quickly, and holding it firmly by the lower jaw (bass will not struggle if held by the lower jaw—thumb on the inside of the lower lip) admired its color, splendid condition, and shape. Gently I placed the fish in the water by the side of the canoe and released her. The bass moved away slowly, then with quickening acceleration she sought depth and disappeared.

After watching the bass disappear in the green and misty depth of the lake I looked up to see the loon reappear about two hundred feet off the starboard stern of the canoe. I watched this graceful water bird swim swiftly to a small island, leave the water, and move inland. Once more the loon disappeared from view. Most fly fishermen are naturally curious. It is fascinating, for example, to note how quickly the fly fisher develops an exploratory interest in entomology. I am convinced that most fly fishers have enquiring minds. Fifty plus years at the game has, time after time, reinforced this belief. Now I had become curious about this loon. Slowly and quietly I paddled the canoe to the shoreline of the island. Six feet from waters' edge, plainly visible because of the path the parent loons had made through the long grass, the mother loon was seated on the nest. Loons produce two eggs and, therefore, I had to believe that the mother loon was nesting the second egg. The first-born was resting at the back of the mother, at that age appearing like a ball of fluff with a beak. Long ago I made the decision to always carry a camera when fly fishing stream or lake. The mother loon did not appear disturbed as I photographed the scene. Perhaps the waning light in combination with my quiet, slow movement, dispelled her anxiety. But she continued to watch me as I slowly paddled away in the canoe.

Great experiences deserve to be shared. One experience which is richly remembered is the glory of a superb sunset in the midst of complete

Loon with First-born at rear.
Photo taken in Algonquin Park, Ontario by author.

silence as one paddles a canoe, homeward bound, through the closing phase of twilight. This area is a region of evergreens, the speckled alder, and the gorgeous Golden-winged Warbler. And at day's end the maples, aspens, and tamaracks reflect their soft and unique glow before darkness settles upon the land.

EVENTIDE–SIGHTS AND SOUNDS

At eight o'clock in the evening the Lake Of Two Rivers is a mirror which reflects the serenity of the surround. It is cool and the bonfire at the tip of a peninsula gives off the barely discernible aroma of woodsmoke. A whippoorwill has commenced its nocturnal song. The forest is as dark and still as the illustrations for fairyland. There is a special peace, a renaissance stillness at the edge of the lake, almost gothic in quality. The canoe glides smoothly toward the rocky point. Rocks and weeds are a favorite haunt for the black bass. The bass is the permit of fresh water. The small mouth, like the permit in salt water, does now know how to abandon the fight. I subscribe to the accuracy of Dr. James Henshall's description about the qualities of the small mouthed bass.

"He is plucky, game, brave, unyielding to the last. He has the arrowy rush and vigor of a trout, the untiring strength and bold leap of the salmon, while he has a system of fighting tactics peculiarly his own. I consider him, inch for inch and pound for pound, the gamest fish that swims."

Seventy feet from shore every tree is clearly reflected in the water with mirror-like precision. The "break" in the pattern of reflections is an area of weed extending into the lake. It is perhaps fifty or sixty feet wide and extends forty feet out from the shoreline. Its shape is almost a perfect rectangle; as though it had been manicured to a prescribed pattern. I had to look a second time to reassure myself that I had, in fact, detected movement. But now movement was undeniable. The bass broke water with a splash, evidently missed its food target and rocketed along the surface. The water was so clear that regardless of my forty-five foot vantage point, I could identify individual boulders and stones on the bottom of the lake. I also caught sight of what I estimated to be a two pound small mouth. It was possible that the bass was chasing a perch minnow. Crayfish, however, constitute a large percentage of the diet for bass in many of these lakes. And so I tyed an imitation of this freshwater crustacean to the 5X tippet at the end of the leader. I had dressed this crayfish on a size 6 3X long hook. A fairly heavy hook in combination with tying materials which readily absorb water, and a fly design which ensures quick entry to the water will allow the artificial to sink quickly. I do not apply any floatant (dressing) to the crayfish. The reason for this is that when crayfish are swimming above the rocky bottom, and are approached by a predator, they generally try to disappear among the rocks. It is therefore effective to fish the crayfish near the bottom close to submerged boulders, rocks, or sunken logs. Such was my objective and the equipment included a short fine leader. If the cast is made high and the line braked abruptly, the fly will fall vertical to the surface of the water. The fine diameter tippet will then allow the fly to sink quickly to the desired depth of water.

Following one cast and a reasonable amount of time for the lure to sink I began raising the rod tip six or eight inches each time I retrieved line onto the reel. I had not raised the tip of the fly rod more than two or three times when I felt the savage take that the small mouth exercises. The bass jumped clear of the water with the speed of a skyrocket, and I watched the crayfish travelling through air in the opposite direction to the path followed by the game fish. After reeling in I changed to a streamer fly, and while false casting to release line in the air, I noted the bass swirling under the surface of the water near a patch of water-lily pads. The streamer fly was taken almost as soon as the fly alighted on the water. This time I set the hook immediately, and when the small mouth jumped clear I could confirm it would weigh close to two pounds. I did not gamble with this fish. The chef at the resort had offered to cook a fresh catch for breakfast. Two more bass took the streamer fly that evening. I released the first one, an eleven inch fish that would live to spawn and fight another day. The second bass would go about one and three-quarter pounds. It was a great climax to a wonderful evening on the water.

SMALL MOUTHED BLACK BASS

Lake Opeongo and Smoke Lake in Algonquin Park offer good summer months fly fishing. Imitation crayfish are prime deceivers in the warmer upper water, especially along rocky shorelines.

TACKLE AND TACTICS

It can be truly sporting to capture the larger bass on balanced five weight fly tackle. But the predilection for light weight equipment is often frustrated by the force of the wind. Very often, therefore, during daytime I found myself using a seven or eight weight rod with weight forward (WF) floating line. The mornings and evenings, especially at dusk, are the periods when bass frequently rise to the floating offering. And it is usually at these periods—early morning and approximately two hours before sunset—that one experiences almost no wind and, therefore, the use of lighter tackle is practical. The bass in most of the lakes I have fished in Algonquin Park ranged from ten to fourteen inches. There are, of course, larger bass and, not infrequently, one is "jolted" by the smash of a two to three pound fish. I like to practice conservation (as do most fly fishers) and I released virtually all bass—unharmed. This procedure requires a barbless hook and equipment which is not too light in weight. Leaders which are strong enough to bring fish to net without having to play the fish for too long a period of time enable one to release the game fish before it is exhausted. This procedure ensures the survival of the game fish. The practice of catch-and-release includes an important bonus. The bass will live to spawn and, therefore, propogate the species. The fish may also be caught again and provide for another challenge—next time a larger game fish.

Most bass were taken on streamer flies fished two to three feet below the surface. Prime areas were sand bars, rock shoals, and submerged logs. Booth Lake, Lake Opeongo, and Bridle Lake were excellent producers of bass. Productive patterns at these lakes were the Mickey Finn, Royal Coachman, Harlequin streamer fly, and imitation crayfish. An imitation of the Golden Shiner minnow was productive.[1]

THE STRESSING FACTOR

Those of us who cherish and support conservation, who value our wildlife, and maintain a love affair with the outdoors are faced with a dilemma. Is it possible that a park which is governed by tenets which constitute conservation can remain a kind of genetic island? An island, that is, which preserves the natural legacy of evolution . . . protected from

---

[1]See Davis, E. G., *The Golden Shiner,* American Fly Tyer, 1987., Spring Issue.

human acts? The answer unfortunately to these questions may be, at this time, a qualified NO. That is not to say that Algonquin Park will not remain, with constant care, a mecca for backpacking, camping, canoe routes, and Beaver ecology. Its natural beauty, excellent resorts, and fascinating history[2] almost ensure its longevity. But what about the sport fishing? What about the growth and maintenance of fish life? The low nutrient levels in the lakes of Algonquin Park severely limit fish growth.[3] But now there is a more serious consequence for park lakes. The problem originates (often hundreds of kilometers from Algonquin) when we burn coal or smelt ores. Fish are often safe from acid rain because many areas have waters containing dissolved minerals which are sufficiently concentrated that acid rain entering the water is quickly neutralized. Algonquin Park is not one of these areas. The process of acidification in Algonquin is not presently destroying fish life. But some lakes (including Lake Louise) are "close to the brink."[4] Most experts believe that many park lakes will start to go in the next five or ten years.[5] The extinction of game fish in acid-stressed lakes is a problem which must be solved. Thousands of lakes in Scandinavia, the Adirondacs, and other areas have become fishless vats of mild acid. Acid in which the small fry cannot survive. In such cases catch-and-release angling is, at best, a temporary solution. The heritage that future generations will experience is inescapably linked to the preventive measures we undertake today.

THE HALIBURTON REGION

Just south of Algonquin Park is the Domain of the Pileated Woodpecker (Detucopus pileatus) and the Cedar Waxwing. But it is also the home of the wood duck and the black bass. The lakes of the Haliburton Region are, in fact, a mecca for bass; very often the large mouth.

I arrived at the Domain of Killien on Sunday evening. The major reason for the visit was to act in an advisory capacity for the stocking of a fish-depleted lake in the region, with a particular hybrid of the rainbow trout. This work was subsequently accomplished with excellent co-

---

[2]See Tozer, R. and Strickland, D., *A Pictorial History of Algonquin Provincial Park,* 1980 Printing, Ministry of Natural Resources, Province of Ontario, Canada.

[3]See Strickland, D., et al., *Fishing In Algonquin Park,* (1980) reprint by the Ministry of Natural Resources, Province of Ontario, Canada.

[4]ibid.

[5]ibid.

operation from the Ministry of Natural Resources of the Province of Ontario.

A bright fire was burning in the hearth of the main lodge. Chef Dante Larcade was opening oysters from New Brunswick, and the dinner entrees include a duckling Montmorency. We shared a bottle of Chassagne—Montrachet, Raoul Chergot '81 from the sumptuous Liste des Vins.

I had arrived too early for the late September wine tasting weekend, but not too late for the bass fishing in Ritchie Lake. It is a short drive from the lodge, followed by a ten minute hike on an old logging road to the lake. The trails in the Domain are color coded in red, yellow, and green. The neophyte hiker, if not color blind, cannot possibly become lost. It was a bright Autumn day; the forests inundated with the beguiling aroma of pine and resin. The proprietors of the Domain of Killien have always appreciated and practiced the conservation of magnificent forests. From the 13th century their ancient family lineage have managed and protected the lands and forests of the Seigneurie of Quillien in Brittany.

The present day resort on Drag Lake is a charming combination of main lodge and cottages. Now completely renovated, it was built in the nineteen twenties as a hunting and fishing camp by the beloved local character, Dr. L. Carroll.

The bass fishing in Ritchie Lake is superb. The lake is restricted to fly fishing. It is shaped like an egg-timer, the lower bulb being somewhat elongated. The lake is characterized by those features which support bass, that is, rock, sand, deadfalls, weed, and crystal clear water. Once again the streamer fly proved its worth and, after taking just sufficient bass for the one table, many bass were released. The bass had illustrated, once more, that it is a worthy opponent, and a game fish to be treasured.

Our stay was highlighted by a magnificent dinner at the Lodge. After dinner, in the superbly decorated and rustic lounge, and in front of a hardwood fire, we were joined by Count Edouard de Moustier, his charming wife, and two sons. It was a time of good discussion, reminiscence about casts of the past, future plans, and a splendid climax to the superb fishing offered by the Haliburton region of Ontario.

When not teaching Bud Hoffman is experimenting with new fly patterns.

CHAPTER 24

The Gathering of the Family Chironomidae

In Nature's infinite book of secrecy
A little I can read
—William Shakespeare

At 7:30 a.m. the sun was barely over the south-east range of mountains, casting orange light and purple shadows against the grassy bank. In the available light, which filtered through a willow tree on the river bank, I watched the incredible sipping riseforms. The family Chironomidae had gathered and there was disorder among the Diptera. At the time I was not certain about the kind of protein diet the two brown trout were ingesting. Each of the two trout were occupying a different line of drift; the larger of the two fish nine or ten feet upstream of the smaller trout. But the food form had to be small because repeated seining assured me that no large or medium sized terrestrial or aquatic insects were on, or in, the stream flow.

As I watched the large stillwater habitat, protected by an abrupt curvature of the bank, the greedy feeding stopped. At almost the precise moment I made the decision to seine the large backwater pool, with its glass smooth surface approximately thirty feet upstream, I noted one small insect floating in the film. Quickly reaching for the seining net I retrieved this specimen. It proved to be a tiny wasp.

There was no such imitation in my fly boxes; naturally. Has this not always been the case? There was, however, a small Welshman's Button. This fly, which I had dressed on a size twenty-two hook the previ-

---

The author is indebted to the staff of the Royal Ontario Museum's Department of Entomology, who graciously identified the samples of insects collected from the stream.

My thanks, also, to the Drew-Brook family for permission to fish their magnificent estate water.

ous Winter, is likely an imitation of a small beetle. The dressing features a somewhat bulky darkish body, no tails, and forty-five degree angled wings, which are a medium yellowish-brown. I removed all of the underside hackle and knotted the fly to the 7X leader tippet. I now had an offering which roughly imitated the retrieved insect. And it was attached to a .004" point with a breaking strength of 1.70 pounds. This kind of leader material, in my experience, will hold a large trout barring, of course, the fish disappearing into a maze of weed or a log jam.

In my hand was a Tonkin cane, seven and one-half foot impregnated fly rod. The rod is powerful yet capable of responding to the most delicate nuance. It possesses an action or frequency (the number of fundamental oscillations per second) which likely approximates that of the majority of carbon fibre rods. When this sensitive split cane rod is teamed with a light weight reel capable of velvet smooth tension adjustments, it is possible to protect the end of a delicate leader.

Two more trout were now rising and I made my cast high and firm to the closest fish. Across and upstream went the case, overshooting the nearest riseform. As I braked the line and momentarily pulled back on the rod tip, the cast recoiled and the tippet snaked on the water. The tiny fly settled in the required line of drift—floating freely. I watched, fascinated, as a tiny dimple appeared on the surface of the water. I began to tremble in anticipation of what was about to ensue. The suspense was relieved as I lowered the rod tip and drew the hook towards me from directly behind the trout. If I could set that tiny hook into a corner of the jaw there would be a chance of capture. I felt the bite of the hook and then the trout, startled by this curious resistance, cartwheeled out of the water as I lowered the rod tip close to the surface of the water. The reel purred as line issued forth and the heavy brown ran for the cover of a fallen tree and its myriad branches. The dive into deadfall maneuver is not uncommon. Somehow I turned the fish by moving quickly up the left bank and applying as much pressure as I dared. We then fought a long battle upstream and downstream. The brown made several runs and jumped twice, until it finally tired and I netted the fish. Before releasing the trout I removed several sample midges from its mouth and placed them in a small vial of alcohol labelled number one.

All this commotion had put down the other fish and, therefore, I walked up the opposite bank and seined the water with the long-handled net. The resulting collection of tiny terrestrial and aquatic insects went into a second vial of preserving liquid. It later proved to contain three tiny wasps, two-wing aphids, and midges of the family Chironomidae. The balance of the collection consisted of tiny terrestrial insects.

The insect Order Diptera derives its scientific name from the adults because of two (Di-) wings (ptera), in contrast to the four wings of the majority of most other winged insects. The family Chironomidae (the midges), however, have a large number of aquatic species. Trout rising in calm back water eddies often signify an intent to feed on midge pupae. The Chironomidae which interested the brown trout on this water were characterized by a single pair of membranous wings (for the adult) and large eyes. The thorax was well developed and the abdomen did not have tails. Note the thoracic legs on the sample dressing in the photo. The family Chironomidae is of the tribe Tanytarsini and the male has the furry antennae. I kept some of these features in mind when dressing an appropriate imitation for subsequent fishing on the river. What

Authors dressing for minute chironomidae.

I have tried to accomplish with this dressing is to create, in the geometry of the piscine world, an imitation acceptable to the trout. That is, from the point of view of insect motion, size, profile, and color.

One of the fascinating features about this experience was the contents of sample vial number one. This vial contained samples from the trout's mouth. Every midge was exactly the same. At least one of these trout (I cannot speak for the other fish) was feeding selectively. And on a midge which can be dressed on a size twenty-four hook. This, in my view, is not only a reiteration of selective feeding but an attestment to the vision of the brown trout.

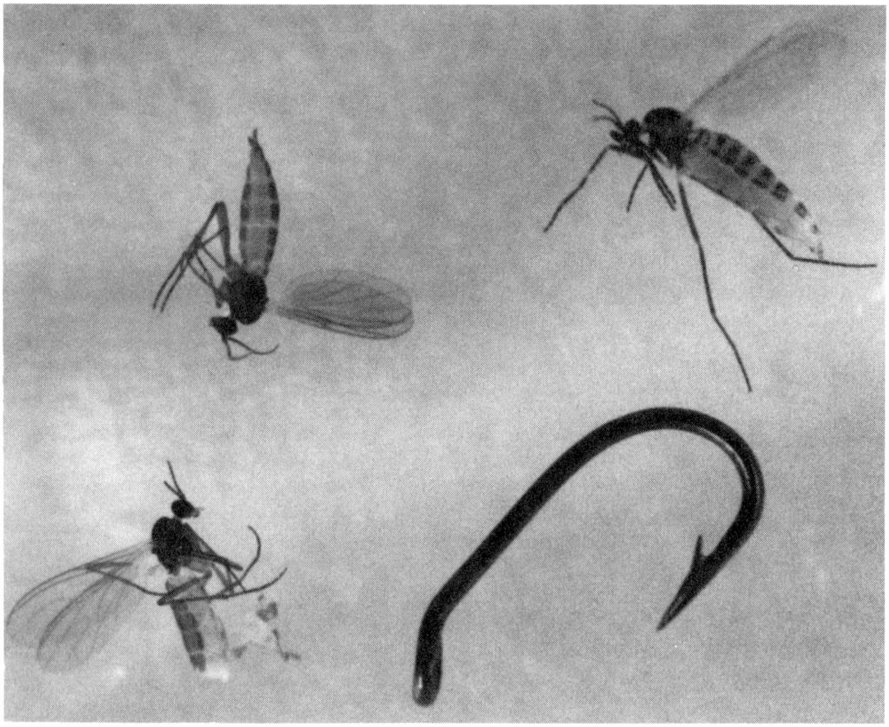

The size 24 K1A Marinaro midge hood is not too small for dressing the artificial Chironomidae.

The hook I use to dress this fly is the Vince Marinaro Midge Hook, size twenty-four. The Code K1A hook, manufactured by Partridge of Redditch, is very strong for its size and has excellent hooking capacity. My favorite pattern for the adult is simple to dress. I have placed a size twenty-four midge hook in the microphotograph of the midge samples in order to illustrate that there is adequate space on this hook shank to dress the pattern.

Hook:	PARTRIDGE K1A size 24 midge
Tails:	none
Abdomen:	one barb from the long side of a Condor feather—wound on edge (substitute: goose biots)
Antennae:	tips of two barbs from an owl feather (or fine tan ostrich herl)
Thorax:	three turns of yellowish olive hackle 4–5 mm long; trimmed top and bottom except for 6–7 barbs
Head:	predominant; brownish-black

This is surely one of the most demanding kinds of flyfishing. It required monomaniacal confidence, delicate equipment, and the touch of an artist. It necessitates limp leader material in order to allow the fly to float freely—without drag. The tackle must be handled with delicacy and each move made precisely and deliberately. It is a most thought-provoking and absorbing kind of fly fishing.

Seining to determine late-season food forms in the river.

Chapter 25

Seasons End

PREAMBLE

One of the intriguing aspects of fly fishing is the satisfaction which results from a diagnosis of the trout's current diet. And then, if you will, remains the interesting challenge of developing and presenting a likeness of the natural.

I parked the car in a clearing beside the gravel road, and took a short walk along a trail to the river. The last day of September had arrived, closing day for trout in the region, but grasshoppers and crickets were prolific. Distant scenes gave the impression of being enveloped in haze, and there was a softness about the available light.

Standing on the bank of the stream I looked for hatches, then waded into the water to look for potential trout food. The aqua stems of marine Dichelyma undulated gracefully in the currents. Their roots were attached to submerged branches and stones. The light revealed the chocolate color near the roots and the yellowish of their leafy tips. Moving slowly upstream for position to cast to a rise about forty feet away, I could see mayflies ten to fifteen feet above the water. The sun reflected a brilliant orange off the cut-leaf maples. Along the shore, above the left bank, staghorn sumacs had turned a brilliant fiery red. I stood in water mid-way up my thighs beside an over-hanging elm tree. Leaves floated past and I was able to note current speeds and feeding channels on a stretch of water I did not know as well as other parts of this stream. A trout rose regularly thirty feet upstream. I concentrated on snugging up a barrel knot.

The main hatch consisted of a very light, almost white mayfly. These flies varied slightly in size but, at first sight, appeared to be size twenty to twenty-two. It seemed likely that one of the Pseudocloeon's was on the water. I could not determine whether the rises were to subimago's or imago's. Finally one dun came to closer attention, plucked off the surface film by a small net. It had one pair of gray wings and a body of olive cast. The catch, of course, was that it looked about size 28, and nothing like it was in my fly box. Nothing, that is, resembling the size and form of a minute Cloëon, Neocloëon, or Pseudocloëon. Because this adult had two wings and my magnifying glass revealed two tails, not three, I was reasonably certain that this species was not Baetis but Pseudocloëon.

I reeled in, checked the leader for wind knots, and tyed on a new tippet. The Wheatley dry fly box contained three compartments for small dry flies of a style tyed to suggest a silhouette of the mayfly thorax. By this description I mean that the wings and hackle were positioned near the middle of the hook shank. Body material is dressed fore and aft of the hackle in order to stimulate the shape of the thorax and abdomen. The fly floats on the body and hackle. This fly is tyed on a shorter shank hook (at least by the writer), and the twin tails are curved upward to imitate the setae of the naturals. This style of dressing has been used for many years on selective trout of the Letort in Pennsylvania. It has been observed that this fly, when properly dressed, offers the suggestion of a light pattern consisting of abdomen, thorax, and legs in the surface film. I selected the palest color size eighteen offering. Stripping line from the Hardy LRH Multiplier reel, and easing slowly from behind a tree to face upstream, I was startled by a weighty splash approximately seven feet away and up against the bank. A beaver with a mouthful of deciduous-leaf-salad gave me an unconcerned look and swam upstream. Not a trout rose within sight. Moving to a position behind the tree I hung the Farlow cane rod across two branches and packed a pipe. Five or six minutes passed and rings, some containing tiny bubbles recommenced as trout began to rise again. And because these rise forms were characteristic of some trout when they rise to spinners, I assumed the rises were to spent mayflies. But as no spinners could be detected on the surface film it was likely that one of two situations were occurring. The trout were taking duns, or they were feeding on a predun stage in the surface film.

Casting upstream to a position about three feet above a rise-form when the timing was appropriate, a trout was hooked, the barbless hook removed, and the trout returned to the water. There was no evidence of any food in the trout's mouth. Frustration was experienced while continuing to fish the dun upstream to a plethora of rises. Twenty minutes passed without one take and I began to entertain doubts about my ability to make a delicate enough presentation for these fish. Surely the 6X tippet could not be detected by the trout on the surface of this water shaded from sunlight.

And then I remembered the three size 24 ''Paratilts'' that I had recently dressed. This half nymph/half adult dressing was designed by Mike Monroe, and is described in the Late-Season, 1979 issue of Fly Fisherman magazine. This pattern is for the purpose of imitating the stillborn dun and the nymph/dun. Although Swisher-Richards have developed a popular imitation of the stillborn pattern, I decided to try the ''Paratilt'' dressing. As the name implies the ''Paratilt'' rides in the surface film. I had tyed Mike Monroe's pattern with a white quill, the tip of which quill starts a third of the way around the bend of the hook. The quill constitutes the abdomen; and there is no tail on this dressing. Fortunately I had used light olive dubbing for the thorax, and grizzly hackle. Not having any white deer-hair for the wing, I mixed a little natural polar bear hair with the gray deer-hair to provide for improved visibility.

Leaving the river I made my way through a jungle of brush and re-entered the water upstream. I proceeded to dead-drift the nearly submerged fly over a feeding station. The ensuing results were better than I had a right to expect. Seven trout were released during the following forty-five minutes. Two of these fish were taken while the fly was almost completely submerged. Another lesson in selective feeding, I reflected.

It is often difficult to conclude anything where trout are concerned. Had it not been for the ''Paratilt'' I am reasonably certain I would have caught very few trout. The ''Paratilt'' was the answer to those intriguing little splashy rises on smooth pools. This kind of riseform, in my experience, is similar to the rise to the imago on smooth flowing flats. But the sipping rise to the spinner, when it lies flush on the film, is not usually accompanied by ''splash.''

A steady drizzle had developed and raindrops dripped from the trees overhanging the stream. Virtually all of the rises had ended and, inevitably, so had the trout season.

*****

Since recording the foregoing experience during the Autumn of 1979, an interesting series of observations has occurred on another stretch of this Southern Ontario river. These observations may be of interest to the reader because similar conditions likely occur on other waters, including rivers in the United States, Britain and Canada. These experiences were also responsible for some of the most fascinating and rewarding fly fishing that I have experienced during almost five decades of fly rodding.

During subsequent seasons we made several early day visits to the Credit River. For some time we could not identify the hatch which was hovering above the stream between 7:00 a.m. and 9:00 a.m. These tiny flies, which appealed to the trout so strongly, would move—en masse—up and down in the vagaries of the air currents. We put the rods aside one dark overcast morning, collected samples, and later made a positive identification of the insect. They were mayflies, of the genus Caenis, female spinners; some in the process of dragging the nymphal shuck. And it is accurate to estimate their size in terms of what can be dressed on a size 22 to 24 hook. The Caenis simulans bodies we measured were 5/16 inches long.

There were so many of these naturals on the water during a subsequent visit to this stream (about 10:00 a.m. during August) that you had to wonder if one of the many rising trout would see your deceiver. It was only when the majority of these flies had been taken by the trout that I began to hook some exiting eleven to fourteen inch wild brook trout. These trout were perky fighters in very good condition, with small heads and deep beautifully spotted bodies.

The special thrust of the enjoyment derived from taking these fish on limp 6X tippets which were of a matte or dull finish, rather than the type of tippet material which is bright and, therefore, may flash in the sun. The dimple riseforms to these flies were almost imperceptible in the silken currents of the river.

I describe below my dressing to imitate the female spinner. The British sometimes refer to this fly as the White Curse. I like to dress the imitation on a particular British made hook. The Partridge CODE B fly hook looks like an adaptation of the old bait hook. That is, the bend is offset and it has an up-eye. This design results in easier setting of the hook because it opens up the hook point for easier penetration. These hooks are about 1X short and have a short/medium point. If you cannot locate this hook I strongly recommend the Partridge L3A in size 20. It is a dry fly-down eye hook. I hone the point of the hook before I dress the female of the species as follows:

(Caenis simulans)	
Hook:	size 22 MUSTAD, or (alternate) PARTRIDGE size 20 CODE B "wide gape"
Tails:	three fibres of straw colored cock hackle
Abdomen:	starting at the middle of the hook shank I wind one long natural Polar Bear hair to hook bend and back to mid-shank position
Thorax:	dark brown or black mink underfur dubbed very sparingly
Hackle:	three turns of a tiny straw coloured or light grizzly hackle. Cut a small "V" in the underside of the hackle.

During recent years I have also used the following dressing for the hair-wing Caenis spinner (female). This fly is shown in the color plates.

Hook:	size 20–24 fine wire (preferably up-eye)
Thread:	white and black silk
Tails:	three blue dun Microfibbets spread slightly and tyed-in to extend three times the length of the hook shank
Wings:	white calf body hair tinted light gray with Pantone marker No. 448M; tyed three-quarter spent
Abdomen:	white silk varnished
Thorax:	black silk varnished
Head:	black

Notes From Fly Fishing Vest Pockets

THE VALUE OF SAMPLES

Nearly everyone seems to neglect this part of fly fishing, but it is simple and consumes a small amount of time. There is really no substitute for having an actual sample with the colors preserved to work from at the fly tying bench. Excellent preserving solutions are available, as are small vials with rubber stoppers. Seventy-five percent ethanol and twenty-five percent water is a satisfactory working solution for mayflies and caddis. Make certain to fill the vial right to the top so as to cause a small overflow of preserving liquid when the stopper is inserted. In this manner nearly all air is excluded from the sample vial. Five or six of these prefilled 1/2 " x 3 " containers fit in a fly fishing jacket pocket. If the samples are stored in a pocket and, therefore, away from ambient light, most of the original colors of the specimen will be retained. In order to optimize the actual color of, for example, ephemerella, a slide photo is very useful. The slide photo of the specimen can easily be reviewed for color (and proportion) by using a small illuminated hand viewer at the fly tying bench. It requires only a minute to record the date, hatch, water temperature, and time of day. This process facilitates a useful record about the variety of trout food in water that one fishes regularly. And it sets a pre-determined timetable, give or take a few days, about the order in which flies need to be tyed for the coming season. Experience has revealed the wisdom of recording the section, or part of the stream, from which the samples originated. Very often certain mayfly hatches predominate on specific sections of a river.

FLY LINES, CARE OF

When I first hefted a fly rod there was one fly line, and it was manufactured from pure (animal) silk. As Art Flick once remarked to me, "You paid your money and had no choice."

But today we have a choice of fine quality fly lines. We also have a wealth of information about fly lines whether they be polyvinyl, or a variation employing a different kind of plastics technology. The information about controlled sink rate, variation in tapers, shooting tapers, and buoyancy has been repeated many times. The care of fly lines is another matter. Poor backcast timing (cracking the whip) is a common cause of line damage. Some vinyl finishes may be incompatible with sun tan lotions, fly repellants, certain line dressings, and fuels. Most streams and lakes contain tiny organisms that collect on fly lines and cause the floating line to sit too low in the water. The floating line then becomes more difficult to pick-up. Years ago I formed the habit of cleaning the line after every day's fishing—with the manufacturer's cleaner. Lines so treated cast better and last longer. The modern fly line will last even longer if it is not stored in a hot area, and not subjected to prolonged exposure to sunlight.

NYMPHS

Aside from the spinner falls of the larger mayflies, nymph fishing with nymphs tied on hook sizes 10 to 20 will virtually always take the larger trout. If trout are feeding they will seldom refuse a correctly presented nymph. I have been fishing the nymph for almost four decades and, because the larger part of the trout's diet consists of underwater food forms, I can attest to the effectiveness of the nymph. Very often the nymph must be weighted. Try to find an experienced flyfisher to work with you at nymph fishing; preferably a dedicated nymph fisher. Skill with the presentation of the nymph will enable the flyfisher to catch trout under nearly all conditions including discolored or high water, and stocked or native (stream-born) fish. Keep in mind that many of these food forms are small. But a considerable number of the trout will be large. An absence of surface activity does not mean that trout are not feeding. Pocket water, deep pools with some current, and underneath deep overhanging banks are choice locations for nymph fishing. Try to keep the length of cast under thirty feet. When the nymph has sunk to the bottom, raise the tip of the rod enough to retain a line of drift just above the bottom. The majority of nymphs are not fast swimmers and, generally speaking, move slowly to the surface. The retrieve can be controlled to imitate this kind of emergence. As the nymph drifts back on a taut line and leader, watch the point of line entry at the surface of the water. If you cannot see the fish and the line stops or tightens, strike immediately. You cannot wait because in the large majority of cases the trout will eject the nymph very quickly. The technique requires practice, and successful nymph anglers develop a sixth sense about when to tighten up quickly. A fly rod with a relatively stiff tip helps immeasurably in setting the hook quickly.

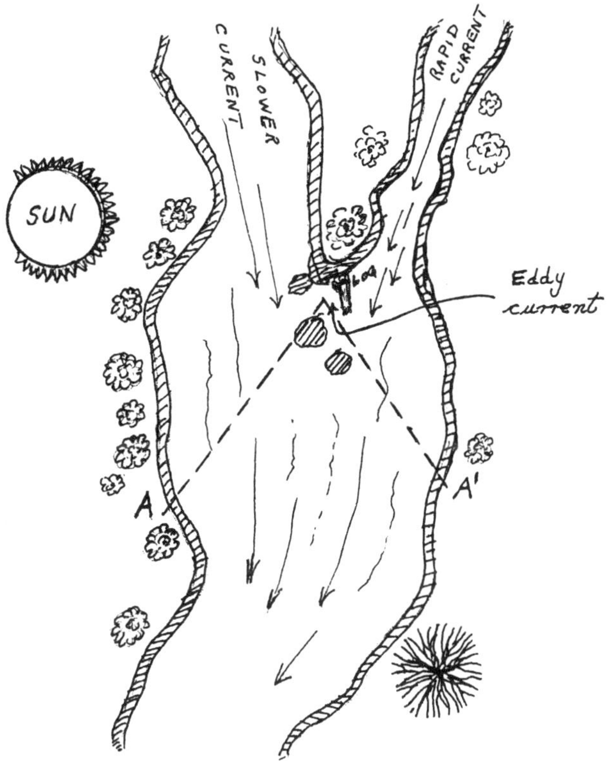

One major objective of stalking is to make the first cast effective. Angler "A" has several advantages compared with Anglers A'. Both can cast across and upstream (---), however, Angler "A" will experience less "belly" in the fly line because of a slower current speed. "A" is taking advantage of tree cover and has side-lighting for better vision; he has selected the right time of day with good sun position. "A" can also cover the current eddy and fish the line of drift between rapid current and slower water. There is less chance of "A" hanging-up on the log if there is wind. Such a procedure could be called the approach of the calm logician.

I think it is appropriate to mention one special fly tying material as it relates to nymph construction. The Condor flight feather is no longer available—if not illegal in most countries. But if you have one that you obtained twenty or twenty-five years ago, and there are some barbs remaining on the long side, there is, in my view, no finer material for representing the gill structure on nymphs. The barb should be tyed-in by the tip where the gills (on the natural) commence, and wound forward on one edge. The effect of this construction, as the nymph is moved through water, provides for an imitative form which is unexcelled by any other fly tying material for gill representation.

RELEASING TROUT AND SALMON

Volumes have been written about this subject and the various procedures, such as hand-tailing and netting. I am convinced that most trout and salmon are lost close to the net, or hand-tailing position, than at any other time since the hook was set.

Most salmon fishing guides are not enthusiastic about hand-tailing. I can understand this attitude because it can be a difficult procedure for anyone unless it is continuously practiced. Even then, experience bears witness to a considerable loss of fish during hand-tailing. This is particularly true of small and very large salmon. Why? you may ask. Just in front of the salmon's tail there is a peduncle which provides for a hand grip. The peduncle is less pronounced on small salmon (less than 10 lbs) making it more difficult to tail these fish. Larger fish (more than 20 lbs) present a problem due to the thickness at the peduncle (wrist) position. Integral to this situation, and to compound the problem, is the matter of depth of water. It is easier to hand-tail salmon in waist deep water. But it is not always possible to lead a salmon into hip or waist deep water even when the salmon is *almost* exhausted, and beginning to "show its silver." Then, of course, the question arises as to whether we wish to force a salmon to this condition, especially if it is to be released. If you must try hand-tailing wear a wool glove, and make your grip at the location where the salmon's tail joins the body. The thumb and forefinger should exert a pressure at that location. Do not attempt this technique with too long a rod. The rod should be of a length that, when arced, you can reach the salmon with one of your hands. I do not recommend hand-tailing salmon which are to be released. In my experience salmon for release should not be removed from the water.

Those of us who release trout should also consider not removing the fish from the water. Like the procedure with salmon, it is possible to remove the hook (very often barbless for trout) when the trout is in the net. The water should be at least knee deep and, like the net for salmon, free of rough or sharp edges, and wide enough at the top to provide for the entry of the larger fish. Many years ago I began to practice releasing trout in hip or thigh deep water while they were in the net. Very often played trout are fairly well spent, particularly if they are taken on a fine leader tippit. My procedure often includes one photograph of a trout in the net—a process simplified by the auto focus 35 mm. camera. The fish is still in the water and in the net when I reach in and quickly remove the barbless hook. The net is then lowered carefully to minimize contact with the trout, and the trout will swim out. If the trout is injured, for example, by a deep ingested nymph, I kill the fish im-

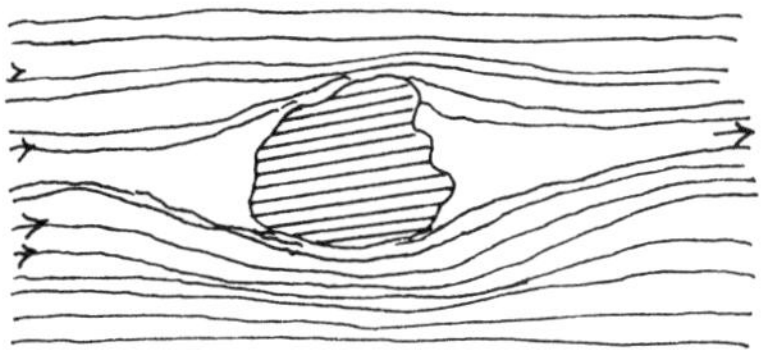

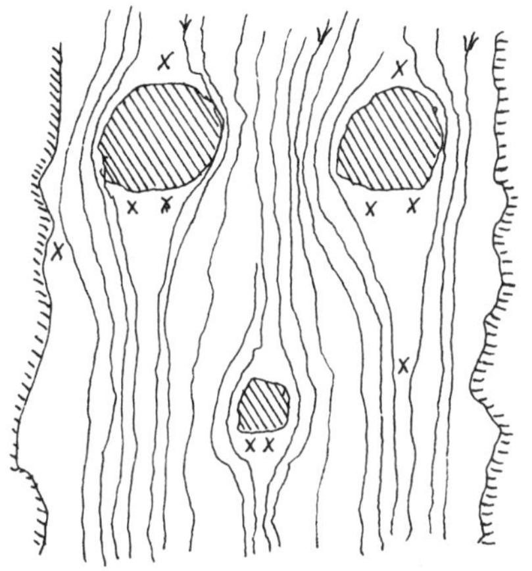

Top: Note flow of water passing a boulder. Away from the boulder the flow is normal. A trout will position itself at the "border" of the quiet water and the faster current. Very often this condition will prevail under overhanging banks or back-water eddies.

Bottom: Most likely locations for trout are indicated by "X." A fly presented right against the side of the boulder will often raise a trout. The "pockets" are just behind the boulders.

mediately with a persuader. While cleaning the fish (as soon as possible) I autopsy the stomach contents to see what food the trout has been feeding on recently. This knowledge can be useful as one continues to fly fish the stream. One last point. The net I use, a superb tool designed and built by the late John Palmer of Toronto (also a creative builder of bamboo rods) features a linen net. This linen net, made in Ireland, is considerably softer and less abrasive than most nets made of synthetic materials. This is an important property of a net made of linen, especially when it makes contact with the surface of a struggling and delicate gamefish—the trout.

FINDING THE TROUT

One of the major thrills of trout fishing is the exploration of an unfamiliar stream. It is skill at reading the stream bottom which, very often, results in fish-catching potential. Let's examine some of the important features we often find on a typical trout stream. Large rocks and boulders are not uncommon in a stream. Look for such obstructions which impede the flow of water, and realize that the pressure pattern creates an area of turbulence (loss of pressure) downstream of a boulder. But the area upstream of the boulder is quiet. Trout often lie in these two areas, near the bottom, because they expend less energy while waiting for food. And that food form may be your fly. These areas, upstream and downstream of the large boulder, are "collection agencies" for food. But there is another factor to be aware of about these pressure patterns. The pressure differential imposes itself vertically—not just horizontally. And it is this very narrow region, the regions of pressure differential, that is so important. It requires only a very small expenditure of energy by the trout to rise to the food path—or line of drift. Look for these areas that lie between different velocity flows of water. For here is where the trout obtains considerable of its food. The lesson that we as flyfishers must learn from these characteristics of water flow, is the need for accurate casting. Fine supple tippits also have their application for the purpose of fishing these narrow regions. This is because of the small eddies formed by frictional disturbance, and created by the interaction of the two currents. The small diameter flexible tippit material allows the fly to more readily "track," or move-in-step with the small eddies caused by the contact of these two currents. The most skilled flyfishers that I have observed cast to these areas from not more than thirty or thirty-five feet. Very few fly anglers can handle a longer line than this, and consistently achieve the accuracy, and delicate presentation required to place the fly in this narrow region of effectiveness. The moral here is ALWAYS OBSERVE AND STUDY THE STREAM BED. Remember that trout will nearly always be located at the boundary, on the slower current side and, therefore, it can be rewarding to evaluate relative current flow velocities.

In some cases you may be fishing a nymph in discolored or silty water, but remember that if you cannot observe features below the surface of the water, the just-submerged rocks will betray their presence when, at irregular intervals, a slight disturbance occurs on the surface of the water.

Just as many larger trout frequently occupy the head of a pool, or roam freely under a bridge during the evening, many of the smaller trout feed on immature nymphs and larvae in riffles. But there are exceptions, frequent exceptions, one of which consists of spinner falls at dusk and sometimes in the early evening. The Hendrickson (E. subvaria), Sulphur Dun, Grey Drake, and Mahogany Dun (Isonychia bicolor) indulge in spinner falls at riffles. These occur mainly at dusk, or during the hour before dusk. I have taken large fish on a size 18 Slate Wing Olive during the spinner fall at riffles in the first week of July. The size 14 White Dun (Ephoron leukon) offers excellent fishing on many trout streams in the U.S.A. and Canada, usually during August. This burrower type nymph's spinner fall can be blizzard-like near dusk, or at twilight on many Eastern and Midwestern rivers. My dressing for the spinner, on a size 14 hook, consists of white deer hair tips, tied three quarter spent and 16 mm. tails of natural Polar Bear hair, or pale blue dun hackle spread wide. White fur dubbing completes the body, and the head is formed from white tying silk. The gentle melody of the riffles will welcome any fly angler to the trout stream. And the rewards of fishing the riffles during the evening can be truly outstanding.

No discussion about finding trout and catching them consistently can ignore the importance of water temperature. A few years ago while fishing a tributary of the Snake, I observed a number of bright colored cutthroat holding on a deep ledge close to the head of a pool. The weighted nymph, cast across and upstream, drifted past their noses several times. They did not move; not a fin stirred.

The water temperature was 40 degrees F. These cutthroat were in a semi-dormant state. They simply were not feeding. The Brown Willow fly nymph, or Acroncuria pacifica, is indigenous to the water I was fishing. And it cannot be mistaken with its rich mottled brown thorax, wing cases, and orangish-brown legs and antennae. But matching the hatch was insufficient. The water was too cold for "trout action."

Hundreds of thermometer readings have convinced me that the best range of temperature to fly fishing is from 54 degrees F. to 67 degrees F. Unless the water in a particular trout stream is heavily oxygenated, the fishing, even for brown trout, will likely be less than satisfactory

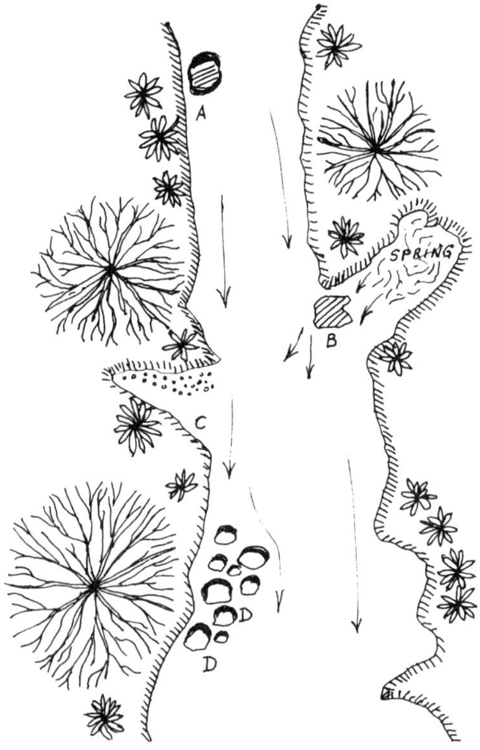

Memories of April on the Manistee in the Lower Peninsula of Michigan recall a section of the river described by the illustration. Large lake-run rainbows (steelhead) were holding cose to the bottom. A few fish were in the main currents, but the majority were found at the locations shown at "A," and at "B"—slightly downstream of the spring inlet. Two fish were lying on the bottom in the relative shallows at "C."

The eddying water below the rocks at "D" provided for extensive shade during early morning. The tail waters converge swiftly at the bottom of the run, and location "D" is best fished from the left side of the river by casting across and upstream. Sufficient weight and correct leader design is necessary to position the fly just above the river bottom.

if the water temperature is over 70 degrees F. Repeated temperature readings while astream will sometimes pin point springs with their attendant cold water. Because many trout often seek colder water, especially brook trout, these locations can usually offer better fishing, especially when the river water warms during July and August.

Having located the trout it becomes essential not to spook them or all may be lost. This does not mean that one cannot talk to a companion. Fish do not hear a sound made in the air, but their auditory organ will detect the vibrations made on the bank of a stream. Heavy foot falls, like noisy wading, are to be avoided.

It is also imperative, particularly on bright days and smooth-surfaced shallow water, to avoid detection by the trout. The vision of trout is such that a careful, deliberate stalking is required, taking advantage of the available natural cover. This procedure is not so important if water is rippled by wind, slightly discolored, or the day is heavily overcast. Fly fishers, however, achieve better results with a planned approach and a deliberately cautious stalk in order to present the fly on a shorter and, therefore, more accurate cast. Finding the trout is the important objective, but the objective is lost if the trout are spooked.

MATERIALS–NEW AND OLD, AND THEIR APPLICATION

There are many fly tying materials which find application for the purpose of imitating one stage or another in the life cycle of the fly. With the view of assisting the fly tyer I would like to list a few of what I consider to be materials which are outstanding and uncommon for certain applications. I will not discriminate on the basis of whether the materials are natural or synthetic.

MICROFIBBETS: superb for the tails on dry flies. They come in a variety of colors and are strong and resilient.

MARABOU: excellent action in the water when used as an integral part of streamer fly construction, e.g. wings.

UNDER FUR OF MINK: used as body dubbing it is one of the finest materials available for flotation.

BROWN HUNGARIAN PARTRIDGE: the legs of certain emerging nymphs, in particular the Pale Morning Dun.

KRYSTAL FLASH: the body structure of certain caddis pupae when used in conjunction with the appropriate colored dubbing. The dubbing is twisted with an appropriate number of Krystal Flash strands to yield the correct size of body.

LATEX: stone fly wing cases including the pronotum.

FLAT NYLON DYED IN A VARIETY OF COLORS: overwinding on stonefly nymphs, e.g. light brown for the Great Brown Stonefly Nymph (Acroneuria lycorts).

HARE'S MASK: the thorax of midge larva.

HOG BRISTLE: the long antennae on grass shrimp.

STYROFOAM: the wingcases of Ephemerella floating nymphs.

RINGNECK PHEASANT: a must . . . the large variety of feathers and colors have a myriad of applications including wing cases, tails for small nymphs, the legs on crickets, and the wings for dry flies.

ENGLISH GROUSE: superb for the brown mottled legs on certain nymphs.

TYVEK™: caddis wings and the wing cases of nymphs. It can be colored with a permanent marking pen and is virtually indestructible.

MONO QUILL: this thin, flat, strong synthetic material is superb for forming the bodies of caddis larva, and shrimp bodies for bonefish flies. There are a variety of colors available.

OWL FEATHER BARBS: unsurpassed for the medium brown, light speckled carapace and tail filaments of many fresh and salt water shrimp.

Also superb for nymph wing cases with the filmy barb ends tucked under to represent the legs of the nymph.

BRONZE MALLARD: veilings and toppings on salmon flies.

OSTRICH PLUMES: the short herl preferable for salmon flies.

HONEY COLORED GENETIC HACKLE: the point of the hackle for veiling over the posterior-joint of the JOCK SCOTT. The feather should be shiny.

GRAY GOOSE PRIMARY WING QUILLS: for the slip-wing these primaries offer excellent adhesion of fibers together with firmness. There is just the right amount of flex to the wing. The short side of the flight feather provides for a superb quill for dry or wet flies.

ETIQUETTE

The American Heritage Dictionary defines etiquette as "any special code of behavior or courtesy." We see these codes of behavior in golf, tennis, and many other sports. The codes of behavior are usually spelled out by means of rules in competitive sport. But the competition in fly fishing is the quarry. And, in my experience, that kind of competition is sufficient. Blowing one's cool usually results in a loss of credibility with the culprit. I clearly recall one fellow who cast a large piece of hardware across my fly line and into the same deep pool where I was working a nymph. By some miracle he did not snag my fly line or leader. When he looked me in the eye, I pointed to the sign on the tree beside him—"Fly Fishing Only; Catch and Release." Whether his surprised expression was feigned or real I do not know. However he left the scene with haste and, shortly afterwards I heard a car engine start and a vehicle move away. Good manners and good will cannot always be legislated. Experienced and capable flyfishers will rarely crowd you, or prove to be a nuisance. On two occasions I have reeled in when someone else's fly has become "my dropper fly" (but without the dropper loop). In both cases the flyfisher was a novice. You may not know the reason until you have explored the cause. I explained the etiquette of distance, and the need to move quietly to both of these chaps. One of them was experiencing casting problems and he asked my advice. It was too early for the hatch, so I gave him a casting lesson. My point in all of this is: avoid anger, seek out the reason for the breach of etiquette, and the result can be turned into an enjoyable interlude.

Good fly fishing etiquette means not entering a pool that is being fished by another angler, or entering the water at a position close upstream of the other angler. Good etiquette means slow, quiet, patient wading and resisting the urge to get ahead of another angler. If a fly fisher is resting a pool it is good manners for another fisherman to walk around that pool and give it a wide berth.

One of the traditions of fly fishing is that if you are invited to fish with someone, it is good conduct not to bring any other persons along with you. Fly fishing is not a competitive sport. The quarry, with its shyness and selectivity is sufficient competition. Many anglers cherish silence and solitude on the river. The person who invites you to fish with him is often making a special dispensation, and such a considerable offer carries with it the implicit understanding that you are the one person invited. This is especially the case when one is asked to fish a "new lake or stream," with amounts to a sacred trust between friends.

If there is one rule which constitutes good etiquette that should never be violated, that rule is to always request permission prior to entering private property. Landowners have the right to peaceful enjoyment of their property, and permission to fish a section of the river which flows through private land should include asking first. I have fished widely through the North American continent in such places as New York State, Vermont, Massachusetts, Idaho, Montana, Wyoming, Oregon, British Columbia, Ontario, New Brunswick, Newfoundland, Labrador, and Quebec, and have not once been refused access to private water when I have requested permission. My approach always includes the statement that I will return trout to the water unharmed from a barbless hook and, in the case of a dairy farm, will report any broken fences to the landowner.

Good etiquette is best defined as consideration for others, and an attitude that does not betray the honorable origins of fly fishing.

Bibliography

Atherton, John, "The Fly and the Fish," Freshet Press, New York, 1971

Baker, R. Palmer Jr., "The Sweet of The Year," William Morrow & Co., New York, 1965

Borger, A., "Nymphing: A Basic Book," Stackpole Books, Harrisburg, Penn., 1979

Brooks, Charles E., "Nymph Fishing for Larger Trout," Crown Publishers, New York, 1976

Clarke, Brian and Goddard, John, "The Trout and the Fly," Benn, London, 1980

Cutter, Ralph, "Sierra Trout Guide," Frank Amato Pub., Oregon, U.S.A.

Dunne, J. W., "Sunshine and the Dry Fly," A. & C. Black, London, 1924

Elder, Frank, "The Book of the Hackle," Scottish Academic Press, Edinburgh, 1979

Fedden, Romilly, "Golden Days," A. & C. Black, Soho Square, London W.1., 1949

Flick, Art, "Art Flick's Streamside Guide," Crown Publishers, New York, 1969

Frances, Francis, "A Book on Angling," Herbert Jenkins, London, 1920

Gingrich, Arnold, "The Well Tempered Angler," Knopf, New York, 1966

Gordon, Sid W., "How to Fish from Top to Bottom," The Stackpole Company, Harrisburg, P.A., 1955

Grove, Alvin R. Jr., "The Lure and Lore of Trout Fishing," Freshnet Press, Rockville Centre, N.Y., 1971

Haig-Brown, Roderick L., "Fisherman's Winter," Crown Publishers Inc., New York, 1975

Haig-Brown, Roderick, L., "Return To The River," Crown Publishers Inc., New York, 1974

Hewitt, Edward R., "A Trout and Salmon Fisherman for Seventy Five Years," Scribner's, New York, 1950

Hills, John Waller, "River Keeper," Bles, London, 1934

Hills, John Waller, "A Summer On The Test," Nick Lyons Books, Winchester Press, 2nd Edition, N.J., U.S.A.

Jennings, Preston, "A Book of Trout Flies," Crown Publishers, New York, 1970

Jorgensen, Poul, "Modern Trout Flies and How to Tie Them," Nick Lyons Books, New York, 1979

Lamb, Dana S., "Where the Pools are Bright and Deep," Winchester Press, 460 Park Avenue, N.Y., 1973

Lively, Chauncey, "Chauncey Lively's Flybox: A Portfolio of Modern Trout Flies," Stackpole Books, Harrisburg, 1980

Lyons, Nick, "The Seasonable Angler," Funk and Wagnalls, New York, N.Y., 1970

Lyons, Nick, "Bright Rivers," J. B. Lippincott Company, Philadelphia and New York, 1977

McClane, A. J., "Fishing with McClane," Edited by George Reiger, Prentice-Hall Inc., Englewood Cliffs, New Jersey, 1975

McDonald, John, "Quill Gordon," Knopf, New York, 1972

McDonald, John, "The Complete Fly Fisherman," The Notes and Letters of Theodore Gordon, Charles Scribner's Sons, New York, 1947

Marinaro, Vincent C., "In the Ring of the Rise," Crown Publishers, New York, 1976

Marinaro, Vincent C., "A Modern Dry Fly Code," Crown Publishers, New York, 1970

Mosely, Martin E., F.E.S., "The Dry Fly Fisherman's Entomology," George Routledge and Sons Limited, London, 1921
Parsons, John, "A Fisherman's Year," Collins, Auckland, N.Z., 1974
Plunket-Greene, H., "Where The Bright Waters Meet," Andre Deutsch, London WC1, 1983
Raymond, Steve, "Kamloops," Frank Amato, Portland, Oregon, 1980
Ritz, Charles, "A Fly Fisher's Life," Winchester Press, New York, 1969
Sawyer, Frank, "Nymphs and the Trout," A. & C. Black, London, 1981
Schaldach, William J., "The Wind on Your Cheek," Freshnet Press, Rockville Centre, N.Y., 1972
Schwiebert, Ernest G., "Matching the Hatch," Macmillan, New York, 1955
Schwiebert, Ernest, "Nymphs," Winchester, 1973
Schwiebert, Ernest, "Trout," Deutsch, London, 1979
Shepard, Odell, "Thy Rod And Thy Creel," Dodd, Mead & Company, New York, 1930
Skues, G.E.M., "Side-Lines, Side-Lights & Reflections," Seeley Service, London, 1932
Sparse Grey Hackle, (Miller, Alfred W.), "Fishless Days, Angling Nights," Crown Publishers Inc., New York, 1971 A. & C. Black, London, 1972
Swisher, Doug, and Richards, Carl, "Selective Trout," Crown Publishers, New York, 1971
Taverner, Eric, "Trout Fishing from All Angles," Seeley Service, London 1950
Taverner, Eric, "Salmon Fishing," The Lonsdale Library of Sports, Games and Pastimes, Volume X, Seeley Service and Co., London
Traver, Robert, "Trout Majic," Crown Publishers Inc., New York 1974
Turrell, W. J., "Ancient Angling Authors," Lond, Gurney & Jackson, 1910
Veniard, John, "Fly Dressers' Guide" A & C Black, London 1972
Walden, Howard T. 2nd, "The Last Pool," Crown Publishers Inc., New York, 1972
Walton, I., "The Complete Angler," London, England, (1653)
Weddell, Mike, "Ten of the Best New Zealand Trout Flies," McIndoe, Dunedin, 1987
Whitlock, Dave, "Guide to Acquatic Trout Foods," Nick Lyons Books, New York, 1982
Wright, Leonard M., Jr., "Fishing the Dry Fly as a Living Insect," Dutton, New York, 1972
Younger, J., "On River Angling For Salmon And Trout," Edinburgh, 1840